A DOCUMENTARY HISTORY OF BRAZIL

Borzoi Books on LATIN AMERICA

General Editor

LEWIS HANKE

COLUMBIA UNIVERSITY

A
Documentary
History
OF

BRAZIL

EDITED
WITH AN INTRODUCTION BY

E. Bradford Burns

University of California at Los Angeles

19   66

NEW YORK: Alfred A. Knopf

L. C. catalog card number: 65–17482

THIS IS A BORZOI BOOK,
PUBLISHED BY ALFRED A. KNOPF, INC.

FIRST EDITION

Dedicated
with deepest gratitude
to

Charles Gibson
William J. Griffith
Frank Tannenbaum
Lewis Hanke

*

ACKNOWLEDGMENTS

My thanks are due foremost to Dr. Lewis Hanke whose good advice was indispensable and whose constant encouragement was appreciated. I thank the following scholars for their suggestions and comments: in Brazil, David Carneiro, Francisco Iglésias, Caio Prado Júnior, José Honório Rodrigues, Luiz Viana Filho, and Hélio Vianna; in Great Britain, C. R. Boxer; in the United States, Dauril Alden, Harry Bernstein, Troy S. Floyd, Richard Graham, John J. Johnson, Charles J. Kolinski, Joseph Love, Rollie E. Poppino, Engel Sluiter, Donald Warren Jr., John D. Wirth, and Donald E. Worcester. Nicholas Polites read the introductions to the documents and made valuable suggestions. Stanley L. Rose translated very ably the *carta de doação* and *floral* of Duarte Coelho. I translated those other documents which appear in English for the first time. A grant from the Newberry Library and the assistance of its excellent staff, particularly Frederick Holden Hall, permitted me to complete a good portion of this book during the summer of 1964. I was pleased to have had the opportunity to become well acquainted with the Greenlee Collection of Braziliana. It merits the attention of scholars and students of Luso-Brazilian studies.

E. BRADFORD BURNS

Los Angeles
November, 1965

Contents

. II .
IMPERIAL PERIOD

. III .
REPUBLICAN PERIOD

A DOCUMENTARY HISTORY OF BRAZIL

Introduction

"It seems a fitting and necessary thing that our own people should have . . . information [about Brazil]." So wrote the Portuguese chronicler Pero de Magalhães de Gândavo in 1587 in presenting the first history of Brazil, *História da Província de Santa Cruz*. His sixteenth-century motivation seems equally valid in the twentieth-century United States, where for the past four or five decades there has been a growing interest in Latin America in general but a dearth of information about the largest nation in that area, Brazil.

President John F. Kennedy pointed out that the importance of Brazil is immediately obvious to anyone glancing at a map. Fifth largest nation of the world and the eighth most populous, it borders on all but two of the nine other South American countries, dominates the South Atlantic, and pushes a strategic finger at Africa. A nation of rich resources and great potential, a nation closely linked with the United States in history and sentiments, it deserves more attention and understanding in this country.

The average history book on Latin America circulating in the United States devotes less than a seventh of its text to Brazil regardless of the fact that that giant republic accounts for well over a third of the territory and population of the area. Brazilian history is customarily handled as a vague afterthought to a full discussion of Spanish-American history. This collection of documents, then, will serve as a dual supplement to those general histories. First, obviously, it treats

Brazil more fully and provides those details usually omitted. Secondly, it gives the Brazilian example illustrative of problems besetting all of Latin America: monoculture, latifundia, Indian-European relations, centralization, militarism, etc. In this way, it offers a different perspective of old Latin American problems to an inquisitive audience in this country.

In addition to being useful to students and the general public desirous of a more complete picture of Latin America, this work is intended to facilitate the study of those seeking an understanding of Brazil in particular. For the interested public, there still remain a number of formidable obstacles to gaining access to a knowledge of Brazil. Only a dozen or so major libraries have sufficient collections of documentary sources to permit their readers to study Brazil in depth. Even in those few libraries, the documents are widely scattered throughout numerous, diverse volumes. Only a handful of those documents, of course, have been rendered into English, and even if we make the unrealistic assumption that the curious reader has a knowledge of Portuguese, he is still faced with the challenge of translating the difficult idiom of the sixteenth and seventeenth centuries. This anthology overcomes some of those obstacles. It makes available to the non-Portuguese-reading public a few of the important documents in Brazilian history. Taken from a great variety of sources, these documents cannot be found in any single library in this country.

This particular collection aims to create an understanding of Brazil through pertinent documents. The word document is used here in its broadest sense to mean any written source of historical information. Louis Gottschalk in *Understanding History* defines document as "synonymous with source, whether written or not, official or not, primary or not." Such a generous definition permits the compiler latitude in the choice of material for this volume, with the result that the types of documents selected vary considerably. Some are official state papers; others are selections from novels. Regardless of source, all these documents have in common an ability to explain or to help to explain the broader currents of Brazilian development. They are meant to serve as the basis for an analytical or interpretive discussion of Brazil's past in order that its present can be better understood.

A few words should be said about the reasoning which prompted the choice of these particular eighty-four documents. It was not an easy choice. Obviously in a history so long, rich, and varied as Brazil's a single volume of documents cannot be complete and must be highly selective and that selection must be arbitrary. Surprisingly enough there is neither guide nor precedent to follow. A documentary history of Brazil covering the sweep of its development, similar to numerous such volumes for United States or European histories, does not exist even in Portuguese. In compiling this first one, I at once ruled out any effort to prove a thesis. My guiding principle was to pick those documents which illustrate as fully as possible three major themes in Brazil's history and the historical precedents for three contemporary national problems.

Historians by no means concur on the major themes prevailing through nearly five-hundred years of Brazilian development. A discussion of those themes could serve as the basis for a fascinating book on historiography. Certainly there are more than three themes which seem to give pattern and meaning to Brazilian history. Of the possibilities, I have used the three most commonly accepted and obvious ones: territorial expansion, political evolution, and cultural fusion. As is evident, these broad themes draw heavily upon three sister disciplines of history: geography, political science, and sociology.

One of the most dramatic themes in Brazil's history is expansion and conquest. The eminent Brazilian historian, João Capistrano de Abreu, singled this theme out as the principal one of the colonial period, but certainly it extends into the early twentieth century as well. The Treaty of Tordesilhas (selection 1) gave Portugal legal entry into South America. The first tiny settlements hanging nervously to the coast grasped desperately at the sea lifeline connecting them to Lisbon. As the colonists grew in number and strength, they gradually closed the distance between São Vicente in the south and Recife in the north, but they clung "crablike"

to the beaches. Then they expanded along the coast northward to conquer the mouth of the Amazon. With the coast
conquered by 1616, the Luso-Brazilians, in disregard of the
Tordesilhas line, began to penetrate the interior with increasing boldness in search of slaves and gold. They carried the
banner of Portugal to the Andes in the West and to the Prata
River in the south. Too late Spain realized what had happened, and in the Treaty of Madrid (selection 17) the Cas-
tilian crown was forced to recognize its rival's conquest of
the heartland of South America. But expansion did not stop
in 1750. As late as the end of the nineteenth century, Brazil's modern conquerors, the rubber gatherers, were occupy-
ing Bolivia's neglected province of Acre, which became a part
of Brazil. The legal recognition of four-hundred years of
Luso-Brazilian expansion and conquest was achieved through
the skillful diplomacy of the Baron of Rio-Branco, who from
the Missions settlement of 1895 (selection 56) to the treaty
with Peru in 1909 definitively and advantageously established the national frontiers. He thereby concluded one of
the most important chapters in Brazilian history, territorial
expansion.

A second historical theme is political evolution from colony to viceroyalty to kingdom to empire to republic. This
theme receives the most attention from national historians
and until recently was almost the only subject covered in
histories of Brazil. Undeniably the gradual and pacific evolution of the country is an appealing topic, particularly so for
one making a comparative study of the histories of Latin
American nations. In its peaceful political evolution, Brazil
remains unique among its neighbors.

Unable to hold its New World territories through the customary trading posts, the Portuguese crown decided in 1530
to colonize for the first time. King João III divided his South
American possession into fifteen captaincies and granted
them to twelve courtiers. The captaincy system with its
feudal underpinnings proved to be inefficient as well as irreconcilable with the emergence of the modern, capitalistic
European state. The king dispatched a governor-general to

centralize the government of the colony. When the economic and political importance of the colony increased, the crown sent out a viceroy to govern it. Then an unexpected event occurred. The victorious Napoleonic armies chased the Braganzas from their imperial capital on the Tagus to the New World. Pleased by his new tropical environment, the monarch elevated Brazil to a kingdom and thus to equality with Portugal. With its declaration of independence a few years later, the new nation decreed itself an empire out of respect for its own continental size. The empire progressed under the rule of the two Pedros, father and son, the first dashing and impulsive, the second scholarly and deliberate. The salutary reign of Pedro II prepared Brazil for the advent of the republic. The three principal constitutions, 1824, 1891, and 1946 (selections 32, 54, and 64), illustrate the national search for suitable political institutions.

An important aspect of that search, a subtheme which deserves greater attention, has been the struggle between the forces representing federalism and those advocating centralism. The unwieldy size and diverse geography of the colony encouraged regionalism. Through the semi-feudal captaincies, decentralization was at first permitted, a decentralization never completely overcome until the Marquis of Pombal (selection 19) imposed a vigorous, unitary government in the third quarter of the eighteenth century. The reaction to the overcentralization characteristic of the kingdom under João VI and of the First Empire was the adoption of federalism during the regency, the centrifugal consequence of which was nearly the collapse of unity as revolts rocked every corner of the country. Once more the pendulum swung back to centralism. After the proclamation of his majority, Pedro II showed throughout his forty-nine-year reign that all roads led to Rio de Janeiro. The newly proclaimed republic reinstituted federalism, and in turn the Vargas government abolished it in all but name. Truly remarkable has been the unity of the nation in the face of a potent and appealing regionalism. That Brazil has not yet found a solution to the problem of the proper relationship between the central government and the states is illustrated by the constitutions, which on the one hand call for federalism, while on the other grant the federal government wide powers to intervene in the states.

This aspect as well as other details of political evolution has not yet been solved. Politically, then, Brazil has not yet found itself. The evolutionary search for an answer to the problem of how it should govern itself constitutes one of the most fascinating themes in its history. Illustrative are the many readings ranging from the "Royal Letter Granting Powers in Brazil to Martim Afonso de Sousa" (selection 3) to "The Inaugural Speech of President Humberto Castello Branco" (selection 69).

The third historical theme, which formed the basis for the selection of these documents, concerns the fusion of representatives of the three races, European, African, and Indian, into a homogeneous society, or to use a popular contemporary expression, the Brazilian family. The Portuguese in 1500 were already well acquainted with the African, but as the letter of Pero Vaz de Caminha (selection 2) attests, the Indian proved to be a novelty to the otherwise cosmopolitan Lusitanians. The proper treatment to be accorded the indigenous American perplexed the European, as can be seen in the selections from the Jesuit Letters (selection 7) and Padre Antônio Vieira's sermon (selection 11). At the insistence of the religious, the Portuguese kings outlawed Indian slavery in 1570, 1605, and 1609, but the colonists, always short of labor, found innumerable ways to circumvent the laws. The speech of José Bonifácio in 1823 (selection 30) reveals that Brazil inherited the unsolved Indian problem from its mother country. The Negro posed problems as well. During the colonial period, the white population lived in fear their slaves might revolt, which they did on numerous occasions. One of the greatest concerns in nineteenth-century Brazil was the extinction of slavery and the absorption of the Negro into Brazilian society. The classic statement about the way in which the three races have been fused into one Brazilian society or civilization is contained in Gilberto Freyre's *The Masters and the Slaves*. Some brief excerpts from Freyre are included in the readings, but since *The Masters and the*

Slaves[1] is now available in a handsome pocketbook edition, a full reading of that masterpiece is recommended.

Attention to those three major themes prompted the selection of part of the documents, and most of the remainder were picked because they reveal the historical precedent for three major, contemporary national problems: land reform, economic instability, and militarism.

Land monopoly has its origins in the *cartas de doação* to the donees and in the generous *sesmarias* to the settlers of the colonial period. In an amazingly short time, the prime coastal lands, on which the majority of the population lived and still lives, were distributed among relatively few owners. The presence of a dominant latifundia class shaped the society which Herbert Smith described in "The Social Classes in Rio de Janeiro during the Last Decade of the Empire" (selection 48). The maldistribution of the land provoked one Brazilian to lament as early as the year of independence, "Our lands are already almost all divided and there are few left to distribute." That lament is echoed in the reading "The Problem of Large Landholdings in Pernambuco in the Mid-Nineteenth Century" (selection 39). The failure to remedy this historical problem gave rise in our own day to the Peasant Leagues of Francisco Julião and their demands for a just solution to the unequal distribution of the land. The present concern with a more equitable distribution finds expression in nearly all the contemporary political pronouncements. Furthermore, the historical inequity of landholding contributes in some measure to the general economic instability of the country.

Brazil is no stranger to economic chaos. The entire economic history of the country has been an unhappy one. As some of these documents reveal, Brazilians have evidenced a depressing inability to solve their economic problems. Portugal must bear some of the blame for this, for the royal government applied the mercantilist policy to its overseas pos-

....

[1] Gilberto Freyre, *The Masters and the Slaves: A Study in the Development of Brazilian Civilization,* trans. Samuel Putnam, rev. (New York: Knopf, 1964).

sessions from the start. Mercantilism meant that the colony in America had to furnish raw materials and agricultural products at the lowest possible price and to purchase the manufactured goods of the mother country. The result was monoculture, the dependence on one raw product for sale abroad. First it was brazilwood, then sugar, then gold, and now coffee. With no control and little influence over the price its principal product receives in international ports, Brazil remains at the mercy of the world market, and it must pay out its hard-earned foreign exchange for expensive manufactured goods. Mercantilism of a more modern but nonetheless deadly variety still enervates the economy.

The lack of economic planning and efficiency which haunts present developmental planners is but a carryover from the colonial period. The reading "Observations on Life in Minas Gerais during the Gold Mining Era" (selection 21) decries the general ineptitude and lack of coordination in the principal economic center of the eighteenth century. As selection 24, "Economic Complaints," demonstrates, the Brazilians were cursing bungling bureaucracy and monolithic monopolies nearly two centuries ago. Most distressing is the report "The Standard of Living of the Worker in the Northeast in the Mid-Nineteenth Century" (selection 38). It could just as easily have been written today. Little has changed for the masses in the past century. Equally disturbing is the discussion of the economic and financial conditions of the Old Republic, 1889–1930 (selection 61). Obviously inflation, unbacked paper money, mounting debts, and fiscal irresponsibility are not characteristics new to the Brazilian economy. Parts of "The Economic and Financial Conditions of the Old Republic" (selection 61) read almost like a contemporary cabinet memorandum or newspaper report. As these documents show, the roots of today's economic problems lie deep in the past.

Military intervention under the guise of the *poder moderador*, the extra-constitutional moderating power, is a relatively new phenomenon. The military's first major role was in the War of the Triple Alliance. Thereafter the army began to take an increasing interest in politics. Interest changed to action in 1889 when the military overthrew the monarchy to establish the republic. Rui Barbosa foresaw the danger militarism posed and he denounced it vehemently in the presidential campaign of 1910 (selection 60). His warning went unheeded. As the contemporary documents show, military intervention in 1930, 1945, 1954, 1961, and 1964 has done much to alter the course of Brazilian history. The military has proven itself to be the court of final appeal in national politics. Today the military is more powerful than at any time in the past. As the comments of Juracy Magalhães (selection 70) indicate, the nation accepts the military's relegation to itself of the imperial *poder moderador*.

There exists, then, an historical continuity which explains to some degree contemporary Brazilian problems. These documentary readings are designed to suggest some of the antecedents of these problems as well as to place them in their historical perspective.

In the treatment of these precedents and themes, I have tried as much as possible to give equal attention to the three major divisions of Brazilian history: colony, empire, and republic. However, because the colonial period lasted twice as long as a combination of the imperial and republican periods, I have tended to be slightly more generous with that period. Except for a few instances when it seemed that a topical grouping would be more appropriate, the order of the selections is chronological. I have made no effort to standardize Portuguese spelling which has varied erratically over the past five centuries. I used the spelling which I found in the document consulted for proper names. Since physical limitations meant that many desirable and essential documents had to be omitted, I hope that the selections included will stimulate the curiosity of the reader to investigate more intensely those subjects which he finds particularly interesting. The bibliography in Appendix II is intended to suggest additional readings available in English.

❖ I ❖
COLONIAL
PERIOD

1. The Treaty of Tordesilhas*

Throughout the fifteenth century, the Portuguese mariners slowly extended their discoveries down the coast of Africa, until finally, in 1488, Bartolomeu Diaz rounded the Cape of Good Hope. Four years later Christopher Columbus, sailing westward for the monarchs of Castile, discovered America, then generally conceded to be a part of coveted Asia. Both Iberian nations jealously guarded their new sea lanes, considered to be the roads to wealth, and feared the incursion of the other. In an effort to avoid war between the two, the pope intervened by designating a line 100 leagues west of the Cape Verde Islands to separate Spanish and Portuguese discoveries. Finding the demarcation unsatisfactory, the Portuguese king, João II, sent three emissaries to negotiate with Ferdinand and Isabel for a more equal distribution of the world. The result of their negotiations was a treaty, signed on June 7, 1494, at Tordesilhas, which established a new dividing line running pole to pole, 370 leagues west of the Cape Verde Islands. Portuguese dominion would hold sway for 180 degrees east of the imaginary line and Spanish for the 180 degrees west of it. Six years later, the Portuguese discovered that this division entitled them to ownership of the eastern edge of South America.

....
* From N. Andrew N. Cleven, *Readings in Hispanic American History* (Boston: Ginn and Co., 1927), pp. 73-76.

. . .

Thereupon it was declared by the above-mentioned representatives of the aforesaid King and Queen of Castile, Leon, Aragon, Sicily, Granada, etc., and of the aforesaid King of Portugal and the Algarves, etc.:

[1.] That, whereas a certain controversy exists between the said lords, their constituents, as to what lands, of all those discovered in the ocean sea up to the present day, the date of this treaty, pertain to each one of the said parts respectively; therefore, for the sake of peace and concord, and for the preservation of the relationship and love of the said King of Portugal for the said King and Queen of Castile, Aragon, etc., it being the pleasure of their Highnesses, they, their said representatives, acting in their name and by virtue of their powers herein described, covenanted and agreed that a boundary or straight line be determined and drawn north and south, from pole to pole, on the said ocean sea, from the Arctic to the Antarctic pole. This boundary or line shall be drawn straight, as aforesaid, at a distance of three hundred and seventy leagues west of the Cape Verde Islands, being calculated by degrees, or by any other manner as may be considered the best and readiest, provided the distance shall be no greater than abovesaid. And all lands, both islands and mainlands, found and discovered already, or to be found and discovered hereafter, by the said King of Portugal and by his vessels on this side of the said line and bound determined as above, toward the east, in either north or south latitude, on the eastern side of the said bound, provided the said bound is not crossed, shall belong to, and remain in the possession of, and pertain forever to, the said King of Portugal and his successors. And all other lands, both islands and mainlands, found or to be found hereafter, discovered or to be discovered hereafter, which have been discovered or shall be discovered by the said King and Queen of Castile, Aragon, etc., and by their vessels, on the western side of the said bound, determined as above, after having passed the said bound toward the west, in either its north or south latitude, shall belong to, and remain in the possession of, and pertain forever to, the said King and Queen of Castile, Leon, etc., and to their successors.

[2.] Item, the said representatives promise and affirm by virtue of the powers aforesaid, that from this date no ships shall be despatched—namely as follows: the said King and Queen of Castile, Leon, Aragon, etc., for this part of the bound, and its eastern side, on this side the said bound, which pertains to the said King of Portugal and the Algarves, etc.; nor the said King of Portugal to the other part of the said bound which pertains to the said King and Queen of Castile, Aragon, etc.—for the purpose of discovering and seeking any mainlands or islands, or for the purpose of trade, barter, or conquest of any kind. But should it come to pass that the said ships of the said King and Queen of Castile, Leon, Aragon, etc., on sailing thus on this side of the said bound, should discover any mainlands or islands in the region pertaining, as abovesaid, to the said King of Portugal, such mainlands or islands shall pertain to and belong forever to the said King of Portugal and his heirs, and their Highnesses shall order them to be surrendered to him immediately. And if the said ships of the said King of Portugal discover any islands and mainlands in the regions of the said King and Queen of Castile, Leon, Aragon, etc., all such lands shall belong to and remain forever in the possession of the said King and Queen of Castile, Leon, Aragon, etc., and their heirs, and the said King of Portugal shall cause such lands to be surrendered immediately.

[3.] Item, in order that the said line or bound of the said division may be made straight and as nearly as possible the said distance of three hundred and seventy leagues west of the Cape Verde Islands, as hereinbefore stated, the said representatives of both the said parties agree and assent that within the ten months immediately following the date of this treaty their said constituent lords shall despatch two or four caravels, namely, one or two by each one of them, a greater or less number, as they may mutually consider necessary. These vessels shall meet at the Grand Canary Island during this time, and each one of the said parties shall send certain persons in them, to wit, pilots, astrologers, sailors, and any others they may deem desirable. But there must be as many on one side as on the other, and certain of the said pilots, astrologers, sailors, and others of those sent by the said King and Queen of Castile, Aragon, etc., and who are experienced, shall embark in the ships of the said King of Portugal and the Algarves; in like manner certain of the said persons sent by the said King of Portugal shall embark in the ship or ships of the said King and Queen of Castile, Aragon, etc.; a like number in each case, so that they may jointly study and examine to better advantage the sea, courses, winds, and the degrees of the sun or of north latitude, and lay out the leagues aforesaid, in order that, in determining the line and boundary, all sent and empowered by both the said parties in the said vessels, shall jointly concur. These said vessels shall continue their course together to the said Cape Verde Islands, from whence they shall lay a direct course to the west, to the distance of the said three hundred and seventy degrees, measured as the said persons shall agree, and measured without prejudice to the said parties. When this point is reached, such point will constitute the place and mark for measuring degrees of the sun or of north latitude either by daily runs measured in leagues, or in any other manner that shall mutually be deemed better. This said line shall be drawn north and south as aforesaid, from the said Arctic pole to the said Antarctic pole. And when this line has been determined as abovesaid, those sent by each of the aforesaid parties, to whom each one of the said parties must delegate his own authority and power, to determine the said mark and bound, shall draw up a writing concerning it and affix thereto their signatures. And when determined by the mutual consent of all of them, this line shall be considered as a perpetual mark and bound, in such wise that the said parties, or either of them, or their future successors, shall be unable to deny it, or erase or remove it, at any time or in any manner whatsoever. And should, perchance, the said line and bound from pole to pole, as aforesaid, intersect any island or mainland, at the first point of such intersection of such island or mainland by the said line, some kind of mark or tower shall be erected, and a succession of similar marks shall be erected in a straight line from such mark or tower, in a line identical with the above-mentioned bound. These marks shall separate those portions of such land belonging to each one of the said parties; and the subjects of the said parties shall not dare, on either side, to enter the territory of the other, by crossing the said mark or bound in such island or mainland.

[4.] Item, inasmuch as the said ships of the said King and Queen of Castile, Leon, Aragon, etc., sailing as before declared, from their kingdoms and seigniories to their said possessions on the other side of the said line, must cross the seas on this side of the line, pertaining to the said King of Portugal, it is therefore concerted and agreed that the said ships of the said King and Queen of Castile, Leon, Aragon, etc., shall, at any time and without any hindrance, sail in either direction, freely, securely, and peacefully, over the said seas of the said King of Portugal, and within the said line. And whenever their Highnesses and their successors wish to do so, and deem it expedient, their said ships may take their courses and routes direct from their kingdoms to any region within their line and bound to which they desire to despatch expeditions of discovery, conquest, and trade. They shall take their courses direct to the desired region and for any purpose desired therein, and shall not leave their course, unless compelled to do so by contrary weather. They shall do this provided that, before crossing the said line, they shall not seize or take possession of anything discovered in his said region by the said King of Portugal; and should their said ships find anything before crossing the said line, as aforesaid, it shall belong to the said King of Portugal, and their Highnesses shall order it surrendered immediately. . . .

❀

2. The Letter of Pero Vaz de Caminha*

King Manoel I decided to follow up Vasco da Gama's discovery in 1498 of an all-water route to India with a larger expedition. Under the command of Pedro Álvares Cabral, a fleet of thirteen vessels sailed from the Tagus River on March 8, 1500. Veering westward from their course for some, as yet, unexplained reason, the Portuguese sighted land at 17° latitude south on April 22. Cabral at once claimed the land for his sovereign and spent about a week reconnoitering the coast. Aboard the fleet was an educated government official named Pero Vaz de Caminha, who wrote the king a glowing report of a beautiful land and innocent natives. Dated May 1, 1500, this letter is the first chronicle of the newly-found land of Brazil, a name derived from its first important export, brazilwood.

· · ·

This same day, at the hour of vespers we sighted land, that is to say, first a very high rounded mountain, then other lower ranges of hills to the south of it, and a plain covered with large trees. The admiral named the mountain Easter Mount and the country the Land of the True Cross.

He ordered them to drop the plumb-line, and they measured twenty-five fathoms. At sunset, about six leagues from the shore, we dropped anchor in nineteen fathoms, and it was a good clean anchorage. There we lay all that night. On Thursday morning we set sail and made straight for land,

....

* From the book *Portuguese Voyages 1498-1663* edited by Charles David Ley. Everyman's Library No. 986 (New York: Dutton & Co., 1947), pp. 42-45, 53-54, 56-59. Reprinted by permission of E. P. Dutton & Co., Inc.

with the smaller ships leading, the water being seventeen, sixteen, fifteen, fourteen, thirteen, twelve, ten and nine fathoms deep, until we were half a league from the shore. Here we all cast anchor opposite a river mouth. It must have been more or less ten o'clock when we reached this anchorage.

From there we caught sight of men walking on the beaches. The small ships which arrived first said that they had seen some seven or eight of them. We let down the longboats and the skiffs. The captains of the other ships came straight to this flagship, where they had speech with the admiral. He sent Nicolau Coelho on shore to examine the river. As soon as the latter began to approach it, men came out on to the beach in groups of twos and threes, so that, when the longboat reached the river mouth, there were eighteen or twenty waiting.

They were dark brown and naked, and had no covering for their private parts, and they carried bows and arrows in their hands. They all came determinedly towards the boat. Nicolau Coelho made a sign to them to put down their bows, and they put them down. But he could not speak to them or make himself understood in any other way because of the waves which were breaking on the shore. He merely threw them a red cap, and a linen bonnet he had on his head, and a black hat. And one of them threw him a hat of large feathers with a small crown of red and grey feathers, like a parrot's. Another gave him a large bough covered with little white beads which looked like seed-pearls.

. . .

Thus we sailed along the coast, and, ten leagues from the spot where we had weighed anchor, the aforesaid small ships found a ridge of rock which contained a very good, safe port with a very large entrance. So they went in and struck sails. The bigger ships came up behind them, and, a little while after sundown, they struck sails also, perhaps at a league from the rocks, and anchored in eleven fathoms.

Our pilot, Afonso Lopes, was in one of the small ships, and he received orders from the admiral to go in the skiff to take the soundings inside the port, for he was a lively and capable man for the work. He took up two of the men of the country from a canoe. They were young and well formed and one of them had a bow and six or seven arrows. There were many others on the shore with bows and arrows, but they did not use them. Later, in the evening, he took the two men to the flagship where they were received with great rejoicings and festivities.

They are of a dark brown, rather reddish colour. They have good well-made faces and noses. They go naked, with no sort of covering. They attach no more importance to covering up their private parts or leaving them uncovered than they do to showing their faces. They are very ingenuous in that matter. They both had holes in their lower lips and a bone in them as broad as the knuckles of a hand and as thick as a cotton spindle and sharp at one end like a bodkin. They put these bones in from inside the lip and the part which is placed between the lip and the teeth is made like a rook in chess. They fit them in in such a way that they do not hurt them nor hinder them talking or eating or drinking.

Their hair is straight. They shear their hair, but leave it a certain length, not cutting it to the roots, though they shave it above the ears. One of them had on a kind of wig covered with yellow feathers which ran round from behind the cavity of the skull, from temple to temple, and so to the back of the head; it must have been about a hand's breadth wide, was very close-set and thick, and covered his occiput and his ears. It was fastened, feather by feather, to his hair with a white paste like wax (but it was not wax), so that the wig was very round and full and regular, and did not need to be specially cleaned when the head was washed, only lifted up.

When they came, the admiral was seated on a chair, with a carpet at his feet instead of a dais. He was finely dressed, with a very big golden collar round his neck. Sancho de Toar, Simão de Miranda, Nicolau Coelho, Aires Correia, and the rest of us who were in the ship with him were seated on this carpet. Torches were lit. They entered. However, they made no gesture of courtesy or sign of a wish to speak to the admiral or any one else.

For all that, one of them gazed at the admiral's collar and

began to point towards the land and then at the collar as if he wished to tell us that there was gold in the country. And he also looked at a silver candlestick and pointed at the land in the same way, and at the candlestick, as if there was silver there, too. We showed them a grey parrot the admiral had brought with him. They took it in their hands at once and pointed to the land, as if there were others there. We showed them a ram, but they took no notice of it. We showed them a hen, and they were almost afraid of it and did not want to take it in their hands; finally they did, but as if alarmed by it. We gave them things to eat: bread, boiled fish, comfits, sweetmeats, cakes, honey, dried figs. They would hardly eat anything of all this, and, if they tasted it, they spat it out at once. We brought them wine in a cup; they merely sipped it, did not like it at all, and did not want any more of it. We brought them water in a pitcher, and they each took a mouthful, but did not drink it; they just put it in their mouths and spat it out.

One of them saw the white beads of a rosary. He made a sign to be given them and was very pleased with them, and put them round his neck. Then he took them off and put them round his arm, pointing to the land, and again at the beads and at the captain's collar, as if he meant they would give gold for them.

We took it in this sense, because we preferred to. If, however, he was trying to tell us that he would take the beads and the collar as well, we did not choose to understand him, because we were not going to give it to him. Then he returned the beads to the man who had given them to him. Finally they lay on their backs on the carpet to sleep. They did not try to cover up their private parts in any way; these were uncircumcised and had their hairs well shaved and arranged.

The admiral ordered one of his cushions to be put under either of their heads, and the one in the wig took care that this should not be spoiled. They had a cloak spread over them. They consented to this, pulled it over themselves, and slept.

· · ·

The admiral ordered the exile[1], Afonso Ribeiro, and the two other exiles to mix in amongst them. And he told Diogo Dias, of Sacavém, to do the same, since he was a merry fellow and knew how to amuse them. He told the exiles to stay there that night. So they all went in amongst those people.

As they afterwards related, they went a good league and a half to a hamlet of nine or ten houses. They said those houses were each as big as this flagship. They were made of wooden planks sideways on, had roofs of straw, and were fairly high. Each enclosed a single space with no partitions, but a number of posts. High up from post to post ran nets, in which they slept. Down below they lit fires to warm themselves. Each house had two little doors, one at one end and one at the other. Our men said that thirty or forty people were lodged in each house, and they saw them there. They gave our men such food as they had, consisting of plenty of *inhame*[2], and other seeds there are in the country which they eat. It was getting late, however, and they soon made all our men turn back, for they would not let any of them stay. They even wanted to come with them, our men said. Our men exchanged some varvels and other small things of little value which they had brought with them for some very large and beautiful red parrots and two small green ones, some caps of green feathers, and a cloth of many colours, also of feathers, a rather beautiful kind of material, as Your Majesty will see when you receive all these things, for the admiral says he is sending them to you. So our men came back, and we returned to our ships.

. . .

The admiral had said when we had left the boat, that it would be best if we went straight to the cross which was leaning against a tree near the river ready to be set up on the next day, Friday; we ought then all to kneel and kiss it so

....

[1] As a form of punishment, criminals were exiled to distant parts of the empire [ed.].
[2] A species of manioc [ed.].

that they could see the respect we had for it. We did so and signed to the ten or twelve who were there to do the same, and they at once all went and kissed it.

They seem to be such innocent people that, if we could understand their speech and they ours, they would immediately become Christians, seeing that, by all appearances, they do not understand about any faith. Therefore if the exiles who are to remain here learn their speech and understand them, I do not doubt but that they will follow that blessed path Your Majesty is desirous they should and become Christians and believe in our holy religion. May it please God to bring them to a knowledge of it, for truly these people are good and have a fine simplicity. Any stamp we wish may be easily printed on them, for the Lord has given them good bodies and good faces, like good men. I believe it was not without cause that He brought us here. Therefore Your Majesty who so greatly wishes to spread the Holy Catholic faith may look for their salvation. Pray God it may be accomplished with few difficulties.

They do not plough or breed cattle. There are no oxen here, nor goats, sheep, fowls, nor any other animal accustomed to live with man. They only eat this *inhame*, which is very plentiful here, and those seeds and fruits that the earth and the trees give of themselves. Nevertheless, they are of a finer, sturdier, and sleeker condition than we are for all the wheat and vegetables we eat.

While they were there that day they danced and footed it continuously with our people to the sound of one of our tambourines, as if they were more our friends than we theirs. If we signed to them asking them if they wanted to come to our ships they at once came forward ready to come. So that, if we had invited them all, they would all have come. We did not, however, take more than four or five with us that night. The admiral took two, Simão de Miranda one whom he took as a page, and Aires Gomes another, also as a page. One of those whom the admiral took was one of the guests who had been brought him when we first arrived here; on this day he came dressed in his shirt and his brother with him. That night they were very handsomely treated, not only in the way of food, but also to a bed with mattress and sheets, the better to tame them.

To-day, Friday, 1st May, in the morning, we went on shore with our banner. We made our way up the river and disembarked on the southern bank at a place where it seemed best to us to set up the cross so that it might be seen to the best advantage. There the admiral marked the place for a pit to be made to plant the cross in. Whilst they were digging this, he and all of us went for the cross, down the river to where it was. We brought it from there as in a procession, with the friars and priests singing in front of us. There were a quantity of people about, some seventy or eighty. When they saw us coming, some of them went to help us to support the cross. We passed over the river along by the beach. We then went to set up the cross where it was to be at some two bow-shots from the river. When we went to do this a good hundred and fifty of those people and more came up. The cross was then planted, with Your Majesty's arms and motto on it, which had before been fastened to it, and they set up an altar by its side. Friar Henrique said Mass there, and the singing and officiating was done by the others who have been already mentioned. About fifty or sixty of the people of the place were at the Mass all on their knees as we were. When the Gospel came and we all stood with uplifted hands, they arose with us, lifted their hands, and stayed like that till it was ended. After which they again sat, as we did. When God's Body was elevated and we knelt, they all knelt and lifted their hands as we did and were so silent that I assure Your Majesty it much increased our devotion.

They stayed with us thus until the Communion was over. After the Communion, the friars and priests communicated, as did the admiral and some of us. Since the sun was very strong some of them arose whilst we were communicating, but others stayed to the end. Amongst those who stayed was a man of fifty or fifty-five years old—or rather he came up amongst those already there and also called others to come. He went in amongst them and spoke to them pointing to the altar and afterwards at Heaven, as if he were speaking to a good purpose. We took it so.

When Mass was over, the priest removed his vestments, and mounted on a chair near the altar in his surplice. He preached to us on the Gospel and about the Apostles whose day it was. At the end of the sermon he referred to the aim of your most holy and virtuous quest, which caused much devoutness.

The men who stayed all through the sermon looked at him as we did. The one I have spoken of called others to come. Some came and some went. At the end of the sermon Nicolau Coelho brought a number of tin crucifixes which had remained over from his former journey. It was thought well that those people should each have one hung round their necks. Friar Henrique stood beside the cross for this purpose. There he hung a crucifix round each of their necks, first making him kiss it and raise his hands. Many came for this. All who came, some forty or fifty, had crucifixes hung round their necks.

At last, a good hour after midday, we went to the ships to eat. The admiral took with him the man who had pointed out the altar and Heaven to the others; he also took a brother of his. The admiral did him much honour and gave him a Moorish shirt and his brother a shirt like the others had had.

My opinion and every one's opinion is that these people lack nothing to become completely Christian except understanding us; for they accepted as we do all they saw us do, which makes us consider that they have no idolatry or worship. I believe that if Your Majesty could send someone who could stay awhile here with them, they would all be persuaded and converted as Your Majesty desires. Therefore, if any one is coming out here, let him not omit to bring a clergyman to baptize them. For, by that time, they will have knowledge of our religion through the two exiles who are remaining with them, who also communicated to-day.

Only one woman came with those who were with us to-day. She was young and stayed throughout the Mass. We gave her a cloth to cover herself with and put it around her. But she did not pull it down to cover herself when she sat down. Thus, Sire, the innocence of Adam himself was not greater than these people's, as concerns the shame of the body. Your Majesty will judge if people who live in such innocence could be converted or no if they were taught the things that belong to their salvation.

Our last action was to go and kiss the cross in their presence. We then took our leave and went to eat.

I think, Sire, that two cabin-boys will also stay with the exiles we are leaving here, for they escaped to land in the skiff to-night and have not returned again. We think, I say, that they will stay, because, if God be willing, we are taking our departure from here in the morning.

It appears to me, Sire, that the coast of this country must be a good twenty or twenty-five leagues in length from the most southerly point we saw to the most northerly point we can see from this port. In some parts there are great banks along by the shore, some of which are red and some white; inland it is all flat and very full of large woods. All the coastal country from one point to the other is very flat and very beautiful. As to the jungle, it seemed very large to us seen from the sea; for, look as we would, we could see nothing but land and woods, and the land seemed very extensive. Till now we have been unable to learn if there is gold or silver or any other kind of metal or iron there; we have seen none. However, the air of the country is very healthful, fresh, and as temperate as that of Entre Douro e Minho[3], we have found the two climates alike at this season. There is a great plenty, an infinitude of waters. The country is so well-favoured that if it were rightly cultivated it would yield everything, because of its waters.

For all that, the best fruit that could be gathered hence would be, it seems to me, the salvation of these people. That should be the chief seed for Your Majesty to scatter here. It would be enough reason, even if this was only a rest-house on the voyage to Calicut. How much more so will it be

....

[3] A northern province of Portugal [ed.].

if there is a will to accomplish and perform in this land what Your Majesty so greatly desires, which is the spreading of our holy religion.

. . .

❀

---

3. The Royal Letter Granting Powers in Brazil to Martim Afonso de Sousa*

Early Portuguese trading expeditions, mostly of a private nature with governmental authorization, were active in the wood trade along the Brazilian coast after 1501. Their reports of the presence of French merchant ships trading with the Indians caused João III to pay greater attention to the vast stretch of coast he claimed in America. In 1530, turning his attention from spice-laden Asia, he dispatched Martim Afonso de Sousa with a fleet of five small ships and 400 crewmen and colonists to Brazil. His instructions were to explore the coast, establish a colony, and drive away the French. To carry out those ambitious tasks, the king granted extensive powers to his first deputy in the New World.

To Whomever it may concern, I make known that I am sending Martim Afonso de Sousa of my council as Chief Captain of the Fleet, which I am sending to the land of

....

* Translated from Carlos Malheiro Dias (ed.), *História da Colonização Portuguesa do Brasil* (Porto, Portugal: Litografia Nacional, 1924), III, pp. 159-160. Printed by permission of the publisher.

Brazil, and also of all the territories that said Martim Afonso might find and discover in the said land. I order the captains of the said fleet, the nobles, gentlemen, squires, soldiers, pilots, masters of vessels, sailors, and any other persons who might go with the fleet as well as any persons of whatsoever capacity who might be in or remain in the said lands he will discover to acknowledge said Martim Afonso de Sousa as Chief Captain of the Fleet and Lands and to always obey him in everything that he commands them and to fulfill and carry out his orders exactly as if I myself ordered them under the penalty that he may make retribution for their crime by the bodies or estates of those who do not fulfill his orders. In addition to that, I give to him all power of jurisdiction in criminal as well as in civil cases over all persons of the said fleet and all others who live in, visit, or migrate to the said lands he might discover or who might go there for any reason whatsoever, and he will decide those criminal and civil cases and hand down sentences, including the death penalty, which appear just to him and are in conformity with the law and my orders. From his sentences there will be no recourse or appeal because I have given to him full powers and authority to hand out justice in the manner already mentioned. However, if some nobles who are in the said fleet or who might come to or live in the said land commit some crime for which they deserve to be imprisoned or tried, said Martim Afonso can order them arrested or held according to the gravity of their crime and sent to me with the accusations of their crimes so that they might be tried here and a sentence passed on them because he does not have said jurisdiction over such nobles in cases of crime. I give power to said Martim Afonso de Sousa to plant proper markings, the symbol of my power, in the lands conquered and explored and in all that he might find and discover and to take royal and legal possession of them and to take whatever legal action is required and necessary for which I give him special and extensive power. In order to further carry out his missions in the new land he carries with him whatsoever legal powers might be necessary to insure his success. Although those powers are not herein specified, they are granted when required and I do so order given to Martim Afonso this letter signed by me and sealed with my seal given in the town of Crasto Verde, the twentieth day of the month of November in the year of Our Lord Jesus Christ 1530. Be it further known, if the said Martim Afonso should leave the lands he there discovers, he may select the person best suited in his opinion to govern in his place. He may delegate to that person all or part of the powers enumerated above. I command that said person shall be obeyed exactly as said Martim Afonso and shall hand out justice when necessary. The nobles will be, as above stated, exempt from that justice, but should any nobleman commit a crime, he shall be arrested and sent here to receive my justice.

❧

4. The Founding of the First Settlements in Brazil*

Accompanying his brother as second-in-command, Pero Lopes de Sousa kept a diary of the trip, an account of the major adventures and undertakings of the expedition from Pernambuco, where they destroyed a French trading post, to the Rio da Prata, where they explored the estuary of that great river network. In that diary, he briefly described the founding in 1532 of the first two settlements in Portuguese America, São Vicente near the present-day Santos, and Piratininga from which São Paulo grew. Although terse, these diary entries are a rich source of information telling of the

....

* Translated from Paulo Prado (ed.), *Diário da Navegação de Pero Lopes de Sousa* (Rio de Janeiro: Typ. Leuzinder, 1927), I, pp. 334-346.

first land grants, the transference of Portuguese institutions to Brazil, the peaceful encounter between Portuguese and Spaniards, the consuming desire to find gold, etc. When Martim Afonso de Sousa returned to Portugal in 1533, he left behind the first permanent settlements, the modest beginning of Portuguese colonization of the New World.

Sunday, the 20th of said month [January, 1532]. In the morning four leagues from me I saw the entrance to the port of São Vicente. . . .

Monday, January 21. We set sail for a beach on Sun Island [Santo Amaro] to protect ourselves there from all the winds. At mid-day the galleon *São Vicente* approached us to say that because of the southeast wind no further sailing could be done for the day.

Tuesday morning. Taking a small boat, I went to the west of the bay where I found a very narrow river in which the ships could be harbored safe from all winds. In the afternoon, with the help of a south wind, we maneuvered the ships into the river. Once inside, Captain Martim de Sousa ordered a hut built on land for the sails and some supplies. Here in this port of São Vicente we beached one of the ships. To all of us this land seemed so good that Captain Martim de Sousa decided to settle it, and he granted to all the men land for farming. He ordered a village established on the island of São Vicente and another in the interior, nine leagues away, along a river called the Piratininga. He divided the people between these two villages and named officials for them. He put everything in good legal order, which pleased the people. In that way the men inhabiting those settlements enjoyed law and order, could enter into marriage, and live in a manner according to their customs, and be the owner each of his own land, and could right private injuries, and enjoy the benefits of a settled life.

On the 5th of February, there entered into the port of São Vicente the caravel *Santa Maria do Cabo*, which Captain

Martim de Sousa had ordered to the port of Patos in search of survivors of a small ship lost there. They encountered survivors of another wreck, fifteen Spaniards who had spent considerable time in that port. Those Spaniards informed Captain Martim de Sousa of many things including the gold and silver to be found in the interior. They showed him samples to illustrate their words and affirmed that the metals were very far from there. Captain Martim de Sousa called together the ship masters and pilots as well as others to confer about what was to be done. After two months in port the ships were deteriorating and becoming worm-eaten so they could not make the journey to Portugal. The sailors were earning their pay without doing any work and had eaten all the supplies. They agreed that Captain Martim de Sousa ought to send the ships and sailors back to Portugal. He would remain with the others in the two villages he had founded waiting for word from the expedition he had sent into the interior. I was ordered to return to Portugal with the two ships in order to inform the King of what we had done.

❀

5. The Royal Letters Granting Pernambuco to Duarte Coelho*

Extensive overseas expansion in Africa and Asia and then in America overtaxed the abilities, financial and administrative, of the Portuguese monarchs. To hold Brazil, it would be necessary to colonize it. With no extra funds for that pur-

....

* Translated from Carlos Malheiro Dias (ed.), *História da Colonização Portuguesa do Brasil* (Porto, Portugal: Litografia Nacional, 1924), III, pp. 309-313. Printed by permission of the publisher.

pose, the crown found it expedient to resort to the captaincy system already successfully tried in the Atlantic islands of Madeira, the Azores, and Cabo Verde. Between 1534 and 1536 the king granted fifteen captaincies to twelve different donees, who, in return, promised to colonize and to hold the land in his majesty's name. The average captaincy measured fifty leagues along the coast and extended inland to the imaginary line of Tordesilhas. In general, the land grants were set forth in a carta de doação and the obligations of the donee to the monarch in an accompanying foral. The captaincy system shared undeniable characteristics with feudalism, then nearly extinct on the Iberian peninsula: the grants were transmitted by inheritance to the oldest son, a hierarchy of landowners was interposed between subject and king, and the grantees enjoyed certain attributes of government. Other arguments have been posed by historians who see the grants as more capitalistic than feudalistic in nature. Few of the donees took advantage of their large domains; only two of the captaincies prospered: São Vicente in the south and Pernambuco in the north. Duarte Coelho received Pernambuco in 1534 and energetically exploited it. Producing cotton, tobacco, and especially sugar, he was able to balance his books by 1550; and twenty-five years later his son was the richest man in Brazil, exporting more than fifty shiploads of sugar a year to the mother country.

*

LETTER OF THE GRANT OF
THE CAPTAINCY OF PERNAMBUCO
TO DUARTE COELHO

Dom João, etc. To whomever may see this letter of mine I make it known that, considering how much it serves God and is to my advantage and to the good of my kingdoms and landholdings as well as to that of their natives and subjects, that my coastal area and land of Brazil be more settled than they have been up to now, in order to have the divine wor-

ship and services celebrated there, and to exalt our holy
Catholic faith by bringing to it and interesting in it the
natives of the aforesaid land who are infidels and idol wor-
shippers, as well as because of the great profit which would
accrue to my kingdoms and landholdings, and thus to the natives and subjects of them, if they settle and take advantage
of the aforesaid land by means of having them divided and
organized into captaincies of a prescribed size, I wish to bestow them on those persons who seem qualified to me.
Therefore, considering the many services that Duarte
Coelho, nobleman of my lineage, has done for the King, my
lord and father, may he rest in peace, and for me in these
kingdoms as well as in the parts of the Indies where he
served a long time and in my services where he always gave a
good account of himself, I hold that it is right to do this for
him because of the deeds he has done up to now and those
that I expect him to do for me in the future. For all these
reasons and for some others that move me to do this, and to
enjoy rewarding him of my own free will and sure knowledge, royal and absolute power, without his asking me for it,
nor anyone for him, I consider it fitting and it pleases me to
do as is done. By this present letter I irrevocably grant, *inter
vivos,* valid from this day on by law and inheritance for him
and all his children, grandchildren and inheriting successors
that might come after him, descendants as well as transversal
and collateral kinsmen, according to what will be declared
below:

Sixty leagues of land on the said coast of Brazil which
begin at the river of São Francisco, which is from the cape of
São Agostinho to the south, and end at the river that encir-
cles all the island of Tamaraca; which river I now name river
of Santa Cruz and order that it be so named and designated
from now on; and this with the declaration that the land on
the south bank of the said river where Cristóvão Jaques established the first of my trading posts belong to the said
Duarte Coelho; and fifty steps from the said trading post up
the river along the beach a marker with my coat of arms will
be placed. And from the said marker will be drawn a line
cutting to the west into the mainland and from the said line

to the south will belong to Duarte Coelho as well as from the said marker down the river to the bar and sea; likewise half of the said river of Santa Cruz to the south bank will belong to the said Duarte Coelho. And thus all of the said river São Francisco and half of the river Santa Cruz will enter into the said land and demarcation of it by the abovementioned boundary. He will give the neighboring people access along these rivers from one part to the other; and, since there are some islands on the border of the said boundary, I think they should belong to Duarte Coelho and be annexed to his captaincy, the said islands being up to ten leagues into the sea from the boundary of the said demarcation along the western line, that is, the line from the center of the bar of the said river of Santa Cruz cutting directly to the west; and the said sixty leagues of land will be understood to be mainly along the length of the coast and will enter in the same width into the backlands and mainland as far as it can go and as far as my conquest extends. I grant and reward him the land bounded by the aforementioned demarcation by law and inheritance forever, as I said, and I wish and it pleases me that the said Duarte Coelho and all of his heirs and successors who inherit and succeed to the land be called captains and governors of it; and likewise I make the grant and reward, by law and inheritance forever for him and his descendants and successors in the aforesaid manner, of the civil and criminal jurisdiction over the aforesaid land which the said Duarte Coelho and his heirs and successors will use in the following form and manner, *viz.*, by himself or through his magistrate he can enlist the judges and officials and set and check schedules and write letters of confirmation to the said judges and officials who will be called by the captain and governor; and he will place a magistrate who will be able to know of new lawsuits within ten leagues from wherever he is and he will know about appellations and grievances in all of the said captaincy and territory; and the said judges will appeal to his aforesaid magistrate for the sums set forth in my ordinances and for that which his said magistrate might judge for original lawsuit as well as for appellation and appeal; in civil cases there will not be complaint or appeal up to the sum of one hundred *mil-réis* and from there on up appeal will be given secretly. And in the criminal cases I think it a good idea that the said captain and governor and his magistrate have jurisdiction and have power to sentence natural death including over slaves and heathen and likewise over Christian footsoldiers, freemen, in all cases, whether to absolve or to condemn, without appeal or complaint; and the higher class people will have a sentence of ten years' exile and up to one hundred *cruzados* fine without complaint or appeal in the following four cases: *viz.*, heresy, when the heretic is handed over by the ecclesiastical power; treason; sodomy; and counterfeiting money. The governor and magistrate will have jurisdiction over all people whatever their social rank to condemn the guilty to death and to give sentence and execution without complaint or appeal. However, in the said four cases, in order to absolve of death, in case they wished to give a punishment less than death, they will give the right of complaint and appeal and they will resort to the law court.

And likewise I would like the magistrate to be familiar with complaints and appeals that might come to him from any village or place in the said captaincy in which he might be placed, even though he is far from this place, provided that it is in his own captaincy. And the said captain and governor could provide a bailiff for the magistrate and scribes and whatever other offices are necessary and customary in these kingdoms for the running of the office of the magistrate as well as for all the villages and places of the said captaincy and territory; and the said captain or governor and his successors will be obligated, when the population of the said land has increased to the point that it is necessary to provide another magistrate, to place him wherever it be ordered by me or my successors.

Likewise it pleases me that the said captain and governor and all his successors establish, on their own initiative, villages and whatever settlements that might seem in order to them; which settlements shall be called villages and will have a boundary, legal rights, liberties and insignia of villages as is the law and custom of my kingdoms; and this, however, is understood: that they can establish all the villages they wish out of the settlements that might be along the coast of the said land and along the navigable rivers, but inland they cannot make them less than six leagues apart so that there might be at least three leagues of boundary land to each one of the said villages; and at the time that they establish such villages or each one of them, they will limit them and give them boundaries immediately, and afterwards they may not make any other village from the land already given as boundary without my permission.

Likewise it pleases me that the said captain and governor and all his successors that might come to this captaincy can newly create and provide by their letters of contract public and judicial scribes that seem necessary to them in the villages and settlements of the said land now and in future times; and they will give them their contracts signed and sealed with their seal and the scribes will swear to do their jobs well and honestly and the said scribes will serve for the said contracts without extracting others from my chancery; and when the said offices are vacated by death or renunciation or by errors, for if it is thus they can and will set regulations like the ones in my chancery for how the work is to be carried out; and I think it is a good idea that the captain and governor call them into service and pay them their wages as set forth in the charter that I just had drawn up for the said land; thus I grant and reward him the setting of the wages by law and inheritance forever.

Likewise I grant and reward him by law and inheritance forever the positions of chief bailiff of all the said villages and settlements of all the said land with all the rents and taxes and levies and duties that belong to them as written and declared in the charter. And the said captain and governor and his successors will have and collect the revenues in the manner set forth in the said charter; and the said captain and governor who hands out the positions of chief bailiff will receive homage from the recipients of the positions as set down in my ordinances.

Likewise it pleases me to reward the said Duarte Coelho and all of his successors who might come to this captaincy and territory by law and inheritance that they have all the water or salt mills or whatever other kind of machine that there might be made in the said captaincy and I think it a good idea that the said water mills or machines be made only by the said captain and governor or by those to whom he gives permission, whereby they will pay him that rent or tax agreed upon.

Likewise I grant and reward him by law and inheritance forever ten leagues of land along the coast of the said captaincy and territory which will go back inland as far as possible and as far as my conquest extends; this land will be his free and clear without having to pay rent, tribute or duty at all, only the tithe ordered by Our Lord Jesus Christ; and within twenty years of the day that the said captain and governor takes possession of the said land, in whatever part he might wish, however, not taking the parts together but divided in four or five parts not being less than two leagues from one to the other, the said captain and governor and his successors may lease or rent small portions to persons or however they wish, and for the rent or income they might wish; and when the unleased lands are leased the rent will go to whomever may succeed to the said captaincy or territory in the manner set forth in this grant; and in case of unforeseen difficulties that God might visit upon the said lands: neither the said captain or governor or the people who suffer the difficulty have to pay me any rent or duty at all, just the holy tithe that is generally paid in the other lands of the said captaincy as will be stated below.

Item: neither the said captain and governor nor those who come after him may take any allotted land in the said captaincy for himself nor for his wife nor for his first-born son; rather they will give and divide the said allotted lands to any people of whatever quality or condition they may be, as it may seem best to them, freely, without tax or duty at all except the holy tithe which they will be obligated to pay on all that there might be in the said lands according as I have declared in the charter; and in the same way they can give and divide the lands to his non-inheriting sons and also to his relatives. However, he may not give these sons and relatives any more land than he would give or have given to any other person, and all the said lands that he gives in this way to anyone must be given according to the ordinances governing the allotment of land; neither the said captain and governor nor his successors can ever take these lands for themselves nor for their wives nor for their first-born, as I have said, nor can they award them to someone else to later get them themselves in any way whatever; they can only have the lands by title of valid purchase from the people who wish to sell them after eight years and after the lands have been used, and in no other way.

Likewise I grant and reward him by law and inheritance, half of the tenth of the fishing of the said captaincy that belongs to me because the other half is to be collected for me, as I have said in the charter; half of the tenth is to be understood from all of the fish caught in all of the said captaincy except for the ten leagues belonging to the said captain and governor—these ten leagues are his free and clear as I have stated before.

Likewise I grant and reward him by law and inheritance forever the one-hundredth of all the rents and duties of the said captaincy that rightly belong to the said order and to me, viz., all the revenue that is due me and the said order, the tithes as well as any other rents or duties of whatever kind—a tenth of this tenth goes to the said captain and governor.

Likewise it pleases me, concerning the care that the said captain and governor and his successors take to guard and preserve the brazilwood that might be in the said land, to grant and reward him by law and inheritance forever a twentieth part of what the wood that is brought to this kingdom yields in liquid profits for me outside of all costs; and the account of the profit will be made in the House of Mines in the city of Lisbon where the said brazilwood is to come; and in the said House, as soon as the wood is sold and the money collected, a twentieth of the money from it will be paid him and handed over in cash by the administrator and officials of the House; all of the brazilwood that there might be in the said land will always be mine and my successors', and neither the said captain and governor nor anyone else can deal with it or sell it outside of the country; with the exception that the said captain and also the inhabitants of the said captaincy can use the wood there in the land as they need it according as I have stated in the charter; and in dealing with it or selling it outside the country they will risk the penalties contained in the said charter.

Likewise it pleases me to grant and reward the said captain and governor and his successors by law and inheritance forever that, of the slaves that they recover and that there are in the said land of Brazil, they may send to this kingdom twenty-four allotments each year to do with as they see fit; these slaves will come to the port of the city of Lisbon and not to any other port; and he will send with them a voucher of the officials of the said land certifying that they are his; by the voucher the said slaves will be sent free without their having to pay any duties, not even five percent; and beyond these twenty-four allotments that he may send out each year, I approve of his using all the slaves he may wish and that are necessary for sailors and seamen on his ships.

Likewise it pleases me to grant and favor the said captain and governor and his successors and also the neighbors and inhabitants of the said captaincy that in it there may not at any time be rights to tax or levies on soapmaking or duty on salt or tax of any kind whatever except those which are now ordered by the will of this grant and of the charter.

Item: I consider it right and it pleases me that this captaincy and territory and the revenues and properties of it be inherited and passed on by law and inheritance forever by the said captain and governor and his descendants, legitimate sons and daughters, with the declaration that as long as there is a male child of the same degree of kinship, no female child may inherit, even though she might be older than the son; and, if there is no male, or if there is but not in as close a kin relationship to the last possessor of the captaincy as the female, then the female inherits; and as long as there are legitimate descendants in the said captaincy no bastard offspring may inherit; but if there are no legitimate male or female heirs then the illegitimate males and females may inherit, not, however, being the result of a condemned union; and they will succeed in the same order as the legitimate heirs, first the males and then the females of the same degree of kinship, with the condition that if the possessor of the said captaincy wishes to leave it to a transversal kinsman rather than to a bastard offspring in the absence of a legitimate heir, he may do so; and if there are no male or female descendants, legitimate or illegitimate, in the manner stated, in such a case the male and female descendants, first the males and in their absence the females succeed; and if there are no descendants or lineal relatives, the transversal kinsmen will inherit in the abovesaid way, always first the males who are in the same degree of kinship and afterwards the females; and in the case of the bastards, the possessor if he wishes may leave the said captaincy to a legitimate transversal kinsman and take it from the bastard descendants provided they are descendants and of a much closer level of kinship; and this I consider right, without the restriction of the mental law which says that females, bastards and transversal kinsmen may not inherit; but in spite of everything, I consider it a good idea that in this captaincy females, bastards not being the result of a condemned union, transversal kinsmen and ascendant relatives may inherit in the way already declared.

Likewise I wish and it pleases me that at no time may the said captaincy and territory and all of the things I give to Duarte Coelho by this grant be divided or exchanged or split up or in any way transferred, either in marriage to son or daughter or given to any other person, not to ransom father or child or any other person from captivity or any other thing, even though it might be more righteous, because my intent and will is that the said captaincy and territory and things given to the said captain and governor in this grant always be held together and not be split up or transferred at any time; and he who divides it or transfers it or gives it in marriage or for something else whereby it is split up even though it might be for a righteous cause, for this deed he will lose the said captaincy and territory and it will go directly to the next in line of the abovesaid succession as if the one who did not comply were dead.

Likewise it is my will that in no case whatsoever may the said captain and governor commit aggression, for, according to justice and the laws of this kingdom he deserves to lose the said captaincy, territory, jurisdiction and revenues of it; his successor might not lose it if he is not a traitor to the crown; and in all the other cases in which he commits aggression he will be punished as befitting the crime. However, for this his successor will not lose the captaincy, territory, jurisdiction, revenues and properties of it as I have said.

Item: also it pleases me that the said Duarte Coelho and all his successors who might come to this captaincy and territory use entirely the jurisdiction, power and control contained in this grant and in the manner it is stated; and, because of the confidence that I have that they will observe in this all that complies with service to God and to me and to the good of the people and to common justice, I consider it good and it pleases me that at no time may a magistrate or circuit court or any other courts enter in any way in the lands of the said captaincy to assume jurisdiction in it; nor will the said captain be suspended from said captaincy and territory and control of it. However, whenever the said captain falls into some error or does something that he deserves to be and ought to be punished for, I or my successors will have him come to us to be heard with his defense and he will be given that penalty or punishment that the case might call for.

Item: this favor I bestow as King and Lord of these kingdoms and also as governor and perpetual administrator of the order of knighthood of the mastership of our Lord Jesus Christ, and by this present letter I give power and authority to the said Duarte Coelho that he by himself and by whomever he might approve might take royal and actual possession of the lands of the said captaincy and territory and of the revenues and properties of it and of all the other things contained in this grant and use them entirely as the grant sets forth; I desire and command that he comply and keep all of the clauses, conditions and declarations contained in it and declared without lack of clarity or weakness at all; and for all that I have said I derogate the mental law and whatever other laws, ordinances, censures and customs which might in any

way be contrary to this, if they are such that it be necessary
that they be expressed and declared here word by word without restriction of the ordinance of the second book, title
forty-nine[1] which says that when such laws are derogated
express mention of them is made; and therefore I promise
the said Duarte Coelho and all his successors not to go or
consent to go against this my grant in part or in full, and I
ask and charge all my successors that they comply with it and
uphold it; and also I command all my magistrates, judges of
the court of appeals, justices of the peace, judges, and justice
officials and people of my kingdoms and holdings that they
comply with, keep and make others comply with this my
letter of grant and all the things contained in it, without
placing doubt, restriction or contradiction on this at all because this is my wish; and for surety of everything, I had this
letter drawn up signed by me and sealed with my seal of
lead—Manuel da Costa made it in Évora the tenth of March
anno Domini 1534—I, Fernão de Álvares, chief treasurer of
our lord the King, scribe of his estate, copied it. This grant is
written on five folios along with the one with my sign; each
folio is signed on the bottom by doctor Cristóvão Esteves of
my council and court; the judge of the court of appeals in
my palace and judge of petitions, Manuel da Costa did it in
Évora March tenth, 1534—and although it says in the tenth
chapter of this letter that I grant and reward the said Duarte
Coelho by law and inheritance forever half of the tenth of
the duty on the fishing of the said captaincy, I wish that
reward to be null and void since it is obvious that he could
not have half of the tenth because it belongs to the order;
and to satisfy the order I am pleased by this present statement to grant and favor by law and inheritance forever another half of a tenth of the same duty on fishing that I ordered to be paid, beyond the entire tenth, as I have declared
in the charter of the said captaincy; the said captain and all
his heirs and successors who might come to the said captaincy will have and collect for themselves the said half of
the tenth of the duty on fishing in the way and manner con-

....

[1] The Manueline Ordinances, the governing laws of the realm [ed.].

tained in the said charter and according to its form; this rider
will go to the chancery and will be recorded at the bottom of
the record of this grant. Manuel da Costa executed it in
Évora.

September 25, 1534.

*

CHARTER OF DUARTE COELHO

Dom João, etc. To whom it may concern I make it known
that I now grant and reward Duarte Coelho, nobleman of
my lineage, for him and all his children, grandchildren, heirs
and successors, by law and inheritance, forever, the captaincy
and territory of sixty leagues of land along my coast of Brazil
which begin at the river São Francisco, which is from the
cape of São Agostinho toward the south, and end at the river
Santa Cruz, which is from the said cape to a line according
to a more explicit description in the grant which I have given
him for the said land; and because it is very necessary to have
here a charter stating the taxes, rents, duties and things that
are to be paid in the said land, the ones that belong to me
and the crown of these kingdoms as well as those which belong to the said captain by the authority of the said grant, I,
because I enjoy rewarding him, thought it best to draw up and
execute the said charter for said land, where he must now go
to dwell, populate and exploit. The sooner this is done the
better, for the service of God and myself and for the good of
the said captain and inhabitants of the said land.

Item: first of all, the captain of the said land and his successors will give and divide the allotted land to any persons
of any rank or status, so long as they are Christians, freely,
without rent or tax at all, except for the tenth that they will
be obliged to pay to the order of the mastership of our Lord
Jesus Christ from everything that there is in the land; they
will give these lands in the form and manner set forth in my
ordinances; they cannot take allotted lands for themselves
nor for their wives nor children; if they have any children
who are not heirs of the said captaincy they can give them

the land and likewise with their relatives as set forth in the grant; and if any of the children who are not heirs of the said captaincy or any other person who has any of this land who might come to inherit the captaincy, he will be obliged to give it up and to pass the land on to another person within a year after inheriting the captaincy; and if he does not pass the land on within the prescribed time he will lose the said land and be fined an additional sum equal to the price of the land; and to implement this I order my administrator or royal clerk who is in the captaincy on my behalf in such a case to take possession of the land for me and write it down in my courier's book and foreclose for the price of it; and if he does not do it in this way he will lose his job and will pay me the equivalent value of the said land.

Item: if there is any type of precious stones on the lands, coast, seas, rivers and bays of the said captaincy, such as pearls, seed pearls, gold, silver, coral, copper, tin, lead or any other type of metal whatsoever, a fifth of it will be paid to me; the captain will have his tenth from this fifth as set forth in the grant and it will be paid to him at the same time that my officials collect my fifth.

Item: brazilwood from the said captaincy and likewise any spice whatever or drug of any kind that might exist there will belong to me and will always be mine and my successors', without the said captain or any other person being permitted to deal in the said things, nor can they sell them there in the land, nor can they take them out for export to my kingdoms or holdings nor outside them under penalty of losing their property to the crown and being exiled to the island of São Tomé forever. Nevertheless, it is all right for the said captain and also the inhabitants of the said captaincy to use the wood as they find it necessary, except for burning, in which case the aforesaid penalties apply.

Item: of all the fish caught in the said captaincy, except that caught using a fishing pole, a tenth will be paid in the order of one fish out of ten; and beyond the said tenth I consider it good that also a half of a tenth be paid, that is one out of twenty fishes, which twentieth will go to the captain and will be collected by him according to how I rewarded him as set forth in his grant.

Item: when the said captain and inhabitants and settlers of the said captaincy bring or have brought for themselves or for someone else to my kingdoms any sort of goods that are found in the said land, except for slaves and the other things prohibited above, they may bring them and they will be accepted and received in any cities, villages or places of my kingdoms or estates into which they might come; and they will not be pressed to unload their goods or to sell in any of the said ports, cities or villages against their wishes if they wish to make their profits elsewhere; and when they sell in the said places of my kingdoms or estates they will not pay any duties except the tax on what they sell unless by the charters, rules or customs of such places they are obliged to pay other taxes or duties; and the aforesaid people may sell their goods to whomsoever they wish and may take them outside the kingdom if they wish without restrictions of the said charters, rules and customs that might be restrictive.

Item: all the ships that go with goods from my kingdoms and estates to the said land which have already paid the duties here in my customs houses and show a voucher for this to my officials there, do not pay any duty at all in the said land of Brazil; and if they carry goods there from outside the kingdom they will pay upon leaving a tenth to me from which the captain will have his tenth as set forth in the grant. However, bringing the goods to my kingdoms or estates they will not pay anything upon leaving, and those people who brought the said goods to my kingdoms or estates will be obliged to carry or send within one year to the said captaincy a voucher from the officials of my customs houses of the place where they unloaded, how they unloaded in my kingdoms, the quality of the goods that they unloaded and how much there was; and if they do not produce this voucher within the specified time they will pay a tenth of the value of the said goods or of that part of them that they did not unload in my kingdom or estates; and about the way that they are to pay the said tenth in the said captaincy: if they load for outside the kingdom and if the person is not going to return to the said captaincy, he will there give security in the amount of the said tenth that he will, within one year, send a voucher of how he unloaded in my kingdoms or estates; and if he does not produce the said voucher within the said time, the tenth will be collected from the said security.

Item: whatever foreigners who are not natives of my kingdoms or estates who take or have taken for them whatever goods, if they have taken them from various kingdoms or estates and have paid the tenth here, upon entering there will pay a tenth to me from the goods that they carry, and loading goods in the said captaincy from the land for outside the kingdoms, they will pay me also a tenth upon the exit of such goods from which the captain will have his tenth as set forth in his grant, and his tenth of the tenth will be handed over to him by my officials at the time they collect the said tenth for me.

Item: about provisions, arms, artillery, gunpowder, saltpeter, sulphur, lead and whatever other war provisions that the captain or inhabitants or whatever other people natives or foreigners, take or have taken to the said captaincy, I consider it a good idea that they pay no duties at all and that the aforesaid may sell all the said things freely in the said captaincy to the captain and to the inhabitants and settlers therein who are Christians and my subjects.

Item: all the people of my kingdoms and estates as well as those outside of them who go to the said captaincy may not deal with or buy from or sell anything to the heathen of the land; they will deal only with the captain and inhabitants of the land buying, selling and paying for all they have; and he who does to the contrary will lose double the amount of his goods and things he is dealing in with the heathen of which a third will go to my royal council, a third to the accuser and the other third to the spiritual establishment that might be in the said land; and if there is none, the money shall go toward building a church for one.

Item: any person who loads his ship in the said captaincy will be obliged before he begins to load and before he leaves the said captaincy to advise the captain to prove that he is not taking out prohibited goods; nor shall he leave the captaincy without permission from the captain; if he does not proceed thus or if he leaves without the said permission, he will lose double the value of his goods to me if they are not forbidden; this is to be understood if there is no administrator or official of mine; if there is, he should be notified as said above and it will fall to him to carry out the inspection and give the permission.

Item: the captain of the said captaincy and the inhabitants of it may freely deal, buy and sell their goods with the captains of the other captaincies that I have established on the said coast of Brazil and with the inhabitants of them, *i.e.*, from one captaincy to another; it will not be required to pay duties on any such goods bought and sold.

Item: all neighbors and inhabitants who live in the said captaincy who are administrators or who keep company with someone who lives outside of my kingdoms and estates may not deal with the indigenous natives even though they might be Christians; if they deal with them they will lose all their properties, a third of which will go to the accuser and two thirds toward building up the defenses of the captaincy

Item: the chief magistrates of the said captaincy and of the villages and settlements of it will have and collect for themselves all the duties and lands and levies which belong to them through my ordinances and which are conceded to chief magistrates.

Item: the captain will place boats on the rivers in the said captaincy in which it is necessary to put them for passage and will collect that levy or tax which has been determined by the royal council and confirmed by me.

Item: each one of the public and judicial scribes who lives in the villages and settlements of the said captaincy will be obligated to pay the said captain fifteen-hundred *reais* as an annuity.

Item: the inhabitants and settlers and people of the said captaincy will be obligated in time of war to serve in it with the captain if it be necessary. Thus I give notification to the present captain of the said captaincy and the one who will be in the future and to my administrator and clerk and officials, judges and justices of the said captaincy and all the other justices and officials of my kingdoms and estates, officials of justice as well as property, and I command that all in general and each one in particular comply with, preserve and make obeyed and preserved this my charter in the manner set forth by it without any doubt, restriction or contradiction whatsoever, for this is my will. For the sake of constancy I had this letter circulated, signed by me and sealed with my seal, in abeyance of which I order that it be recorded in the books of my administration of the said captaincy and also in my customs house in Lisbon; in the same way it will be recorded in the books of the councils and villages and settlements of the said captaincy so that all may know the contents of this charter and comply in every way. Manuel da Costa drew it up in Évora the 23rd of September in the year of our Lord Jesus Christ 1534.

❊

6. Foreign Interlopers in Brazil

Throughout the sixteenth century, French and English interlopers, and at times Dutch as well as others, harassed the Portuguese in America. The extensive and poorly patrolled Brazilian coast, with its unlimited supply of dye-woods for the textile industries of Europe, attracted English and French merchants. And it was these foreign threats that accelerated Portuguese conquest and colonization of the coast.

*

THE ENGLISH*

The English first visited Brazil in 1526. Their interest in trade with the Indians is revealed in the following account of the visit of the ship Barbara in 1540.

On Phelippe and Jacobbes day in the mornyng we fell with an ilande in the see, and there wente on lande with our boate and found nother man nor childe, but only fowle and bestes and cotten and peper there growyng. And there we dyd tary all day, and that nyght wente on borde withe our boate, and so ymmediatly departed and sayled from thens unto the lande of Brasell, and fell with the land in iiij dayes after ensueng. This don we ankered, and our pilot withe our specheman went on lande to here news, and ymmediatly came on borde agayne and toulde us. Here is no brasell to get, for we be fallen xl^{ty} leages to lye warde of that place where the brasell dothe growe, for the people sayde that they wolde not brynge it so farre unto us. Then, this saying, they sayde ther was no remedy but that we muste nedes go thither withe oure shyp. And as we were turnyng thothurwarde, we stake on the rockes with the shyppe, and like to have loste her clene, so that we had her of agayne, and she was sore leake, and the pilotte then sayde that it was not possible to turne thether with our shyppe, the way was so dangerous, wherfore our shyppe shall remain still here, and we will sende furthe oure great boate and barcke and put our wares in them, they do drawe but lytle water and be nymble and therfore they be necessarieste for to goe and come to fetche our ladyng hether. This doon they departed frome us and was

....

* From "Voyage of the *Barbara* to Brazil, Anno 1540," edited by R. G. Marsden in Sir John Knox Laughton (ed.), *The Naval Miscellany*, Vol. II, *Publications of the Navy Records Society* (London: Navy Records Society, 1912), XL, pp. 25-30. Reprinted by permission of The Council of the Navy Records Society, London.

frome us xij dayes yende they returned to us agayne, and were in greate jeopardy of losyng bothe boote and barcke. And the people of the countrey toulde us that it was not possible to have no brasell there, for because we were so farre shotte to lyewarde of it. And then oure pilotte dyd say, to tarry here and to spende our vyctuall it is but folly and have no proffet; for here is a place to lyewarde of us which is called Cally-balde, which I know very well, and it is C leages hense, and thethur I will, and there we shall have oure ladyng of cotten and beastes in a shorte space. And thethur we came and there ankoryed, and our pilotte with our specheman wente on shore, and dyd speak withe the people; and so doon they dyd come on borde us, and they sayde they wer glad of our comyng and promesed us to have of ther commodyties for our wares gladly, as our specheman tolde us. This doon our master commaunded us withe the captayne and pilotte to goe ashore and there to build an house; and at ther com-maundment we so dyd, and caryed wares on lande, and dyd bye and sell with them for cotten; and there we were for the space of xijth dayes, and bought certen cottens in them for our wares. And there came to us a Portyugale and a Frenche-man and certen of the same countrey with them by lande, and asked of us whence we were, and we sayd of Englande, and he demaunded us wherfore we dyd enterprise to come there. We answered we came for the trade of merchaundyse as they and other doe with us, etc. And then he com-maunded us in his kynges name for to avoyde the countrey, and not to tary therein upon payne of a further dyspleasure to us hereafter ensueing. Then we made hym answer that we wolde not departe for hym for thuttermoste that he could do in any weys to us. And upon the sayd answer he departed in a greate fury, and sayd he wolde make us repente the tyme that ever we dyd enterprise so boldeley and wolde not avoyde at his commaundemente, and so wente his wey. And we con-tynued in our trade with the people of the countrey still. So that the nexte nyght after foloweng, aboute xij of the clocke at nyght, the same Frencheman whiche was with the Portyu-gale before, and a man of the same countrey, whiche the Portyugale dyd sende with hym alongeste on the water to our

shyppe for thentente that they wolde have cut our cable that
our shyppe shulde have dreven on the rockes. And we beyng
on watche, parceavyng thentente of the sayde Frencheman
and thother, dyd take them and kepte them till the nexte
day in the mornyng, and our captayne dyd demaunde wherfore that they dyd come, and they sayd that they came to by
part of our wares; and then we tolde the Frencheman that
we wolde ponysshe hym onlesse that he wolde shewe us the
truythe wher fore he dyd come. And he sayd that in case he
wolde not dooe me no hurte, I wolde tell you the truthe of
oure purpose for comyng hether. Oure Captayne answeryed
and sayd he wolde not. And then he dyd confesse the
truythe as is before rehersyd, that it was to cut our cable,
etc. And then we kepte hym with us iiij dayes, and at the iiij
days ende we dyd cary hym on lande to helpe us to doe our
besynes. And in suche tyme as we wer moste besyeste aboute
our cheffe besynes he dyd scape away frome us. Then the
thrydde nyght after that he was thus goon oure spechemen
and xij[th] moe of the Frenchemen of our company which did
use to lye on shore in oure house to make our markettes
withe the people of that countrey dyd ron away in that sayd
nyght and caryed withe them all the wares whiche were on
lande in our bowthe withe them clene, and had withe them
an Englishe man, which was our cockswayne. And in the
mornyng our boate came on lande so sone as we coulde se;
and then ij of our company beyng Englysshe men whiche wer
smethes and lay on lande in a forge that they wroguth in
besydes our bowthe, dyd shewe us that oure Frenchemen wer
goon away in the nyght, and lefte nothing in ther bowthe.
And this we heryng John Podde and fyvetene other of our
company folowed them, and made greate spede after to
feche them agayne. And then when they wer lj leages above
in the wodds they besett our company with people of the
countrey, and so in conclusion set uppon them, and dyd slay
them all save one man by the councell of the Frencheman
and the Portyugale, and at that tyme we were at the water
side besye within our bowthe. And the same after none there
came above a m[ll] of the people and sette oure bowthe on
fyer, we beyng within; in so moche as then they burned all

our cotten that we had brought that we saved not a dell of it.
Then we fought with them iiij houres by the clocke, and in
conclusion we beate them of, but dyvers of our men were
hurte. And at the laste we gote oure boate and wente on
borde of oure owne shyppe, and rode there till the nexte day
in the mornyng. And then we sent our boate on shore and
caused a banner of truse to be set up to them, and withe it a
sworde and hatchett, and withe it a letter wherein was written to the Frenchmen, yf they had any of our men that wer a
lyfe, to sende them to us, and we wolde geve them ther owne
asking for them. This doon the people of the countrey returned agaynste us agayne, and a great nomber of them,
and dyd shote at us, and beate us of the lande, and wolde
not suffer us to lande ther no more. And at that tyme we
toke iij of them and brought them on borde with us, and
there we dyd ride that daye, and coulde not be suffered to
come on lande; in so moche that then oure captayne and our
other officers sayde, Masters ye se that we cannot be sufferyd
to doe our besynes as touchyng our purpose, wherfore it
shalbe moste meatiste for us to get us homewarde, for here
we doe but lose tyme, and our victualls are almost goon.

* * *

*

THE FRENCH *

*The initial French visit to Brazil took place in 1504, and at
once the French established a flourishing trade with the natives. In 1555 they founded Rio de Janeiro to take advantage
of one of the finest harbors in the world and to exploit the
easily accessible brazilwood. Known as Antarctic France, this
colony was the major French threat in the sixteenth century
to Portuguese domination of the coast. Not until 1567 were
the Portuguese, under the command of Mem da Sá, able to*

....

* Translated from Jean de Lery, *Viagem à Terra do Brasil* (São
Paulo: Livraria Martins, 1941), pp. 93-95. Printed by permission of the publishers.

dislodge the French and to establish their own colony at Rio de Janeiro. The selection below describes the first French settlement in Guanabara Bay.

This arm of the sea is the Guanabara River, thus named by the savages, but the Portuguese who claim to have discovered it on the first day of the year called it Rio de Janeiro. . . . It is one of the ports most frequented by the French.

．　．　．

Whoever comes in from the high sea is forced to sail along three small, deserted islands against which badly piloted ships run a great risk of striking and shattering because the mouth of the river is very treacherous. It becomes necessary at once to negotiate a strait which is not quite a quarter of a league in width, and it is bounded on the left side by a huge rock formation in the shape of a pyramid which not only is very high but even more marvellously from the distance appears to be artificial.[1] Because it is round like an immense tower, the French have hyperbolically called it *pot-au-beurre*. A little farther upstream there is a low, steep rock of a circumference of about 100 to 120 paces which we call *Ratier*. Upon arrival and after landing some goods and the artillery, Villegagnon[2] thought to fortify it but the tide forced him to abandon it.

A league farther in there is an island, deserted, as I have already observed, before Villegagnon arrived in the country, where we installed ourselves. With half a league in circumference and six times longer than it is wide, it is surrounded by rocks which impede the approach of ships closer than a distance of a cannon shot and thus is naturally defended. In effect no one can attack there, not even small boats. . . . In addition, on the extremes of this island there are two hills on which Villegagnon ordered two little huts constructed and he ordered built for himself a house on a rock formation fifty

....

[1] Apparently he is referring to Sugar Loaf Mountain [ed.].
[2] Nicolas Durand de Villegagnon, also spelled Villegaignon [ed.].

or sixty feet high where he lived. On both sides of that rock we flattened and prepared small spaces where there were constructed not only the hall where we met for praying and dining but various shelters which can accommodate about eighty persons, including the committee of Villegagnon. While the house is constructed of wood and some fortresses for the artillery of rough stonework the rest is nothing more than huts of rough logs and straw built in the fashion of the savages, who, in fact, built them. This is what, in a few words, composed the fort that Villegagnon gave the name Coligny in order to offer homage to M. Gaspar de Coligny, Admiral of France, without whose aid . . . it would have been neither possible to make the journey nor to construct any fort in Brazil.

7. The Jesuits and the Indians*

One of the most perplexing problems confronting the Portuguese was the treatment to be accorded the Indians. In a labor-scarce colony, the settlers looked upon them as a source of cheap manpower and began to enslave them. The crown and the religious regarded them as free souls to be saved by the Catholic Faith. The first to agitate for an enlightened policy toward the indigenous population were the Jesuits, who, under the able leadership of Manuel da Nóbrega and José de Anchieta, became the dedicated protectors of the Indians. Opposing their enslavement by the colonists, the Jesuits sought to incorporate them into the Portuguese empire by

....

* From E. Bradford Burns, "Introduction to the Brazilian Jesuit Letters," *Mid-America* (July, 1962), pp. 181-186. Reprinted by permission of the publisher.

Christianizing and civilizing them. To accomplish this task effectively, it was necessary to concentrate the scattered and wandering Indians into mission settlements, the aldeias, where they could more easily be indoctrinated in the beliefs of the Faith and taught useful trades and occupations as well as the customs of European life. The two letters below, the first written by Padre Antônio Pires from Bahia on July 19, 1558, and the second written anonymously from Bahia on September 12, 1558, describe the experiences of the Jesuits in establishing and administering these aldeias. They contain valuable information concerning initial Indian-Portuguese relations.

Pax Christi

Your Paternity already will have understood from the two communications written from here during this year of 1558 what Our Lord has done in this His indigent vineyard through the Fathers and Brothers of the Company of Jesus. Although it will not differ greatly from what was said in the past, I will write in this letter about the fruit which subsequently has been harvested with divine aid and favor. Father Ambrôsio Pires, who was with Governor Dom Duarte da Costa, will be able to give more details and clearer information.

First of all, Your Paternity must know that we always exert the greatest diligence possible to bring these Indians to a true knowledge of our Holy Faith. In order to do this we seek the simplest and most pleasant means possible since we hope for greater reward from our work than until now we have seen. Of course in proceeding with this work we never lose the propriety which it demands. The Governor, also, with the zeal and good will which Our Lord gave him does not leave undone one thing which he deems necessary to complete his work. Some means are sought so that larger number of Indians can be taught and indoctrinated with greater ease in the matters of the Faith. In order to proceed with this intention, it is necessary to get rid of some impediments which the Indians themselves have raised. The first step, which is already a great success, was to concentrate the Indians from four scattered villages into one large village. Whereas before many of us were needed to teach and indoctrinate them because they were scattered about, now that they are concentrated together fewer of us are needed. In this way it is also easier to correct their errors and sins which they committed before because they were so inconveniently located. We hope that with this good order and harmony, which Our Lord has given, we will have much success among them which will result in the honor and glory of His Holy Name and a clearer understanding of Him everywhere.

The impediments which we earnestly desired to get rid of were the continuous and very cruel wars which they carry on among themselves. Their restlessness was the principal impediment to a mutual understanding with them. From their constant wars many deaths resulted; and they would eat each other, something that was very difficult to prohibit although now they no longer do it. At least it is not known that they do it, because if it is known, they are severely punished for it in a manner merited by such a grave sin so foreign to the laws of nature. If this progress continues from now on, as it seems that it will with Divine Favor, we will be able to reap an even greater harvest in the future.

At the very beginning, when the Governor determined to put the land at peace and to forbid all those evil customs of war, murder, and the eating of human flesh, and when he issued a law forbidding all this, some Indians ridiculed it. Previously they were not punished much for doing it, and so they did not stop eating human flesh, rather they merely pretended that they did. As soon as the Governor learned of it, he ordered arrested the first one who ate flesh. Without consulting anyone except the Holy Spirit the Governor (we believed him to be learned in this business because he knew that the Devil would come with his denials which he never lacks), ordered the people and boats made ready. Then he ordered two chiefs, father and son, arrested. A great fear was felt by all the Indians, and much greater was the Devil's grief because he was prevented from keeping so many lost souls.

Then, in this conjunction, a similar event occurred in the

time of Governor Dom Duarte da Costa. Another Indian, the haughtiest of this land in whose village we intended to construct a building for indoctrination, lived in such liberty that he seemed to fear no one, and he did not want the building constructed there. Before, as well as now, judging the times by one set of standards, he disdained the laws, and he ate human flesh with his subjects at great feasts. For this the governor ordered him to appear before him; and in case he would not come, the governor said he would order the Indian arrested. The Indian upon hearing this came immediately believing that he would be put to death as the messenger, who came to inform him of the governor's orders, told him. Before leaving his people, he spoke to them advising that they work to become good and they stay where they now were because he would pay for them all. It happened that when the Indian came to the Governor's residence, he was badly received by him, and the Indian threw himself at the Governor's feet and kissed them and begged him pardon offering to receive the Fathers in his village where they would carry out all the Fathers' orders. He said all this with such signs of contrition that he merited pardon. Then another chief came to do the same thing. These are the fruits which the Lord is harvesting from this field that until now was sterile, and for the service of Our Lord it was decided to go immediately to that Indian's village to construct a building where the Indians could be indoctrinated.

At this time, a church was built one league from this city. There, four of the Indian villages, which were closest to this town and in which we had previously been indoctrinating, were joined together. It was the first Indian reduction that we made, and it has the name of São Paulo.[1] It certainly shows that Our Lord wants to open the door which has been closed for so long because, besides the Indians being subjugated and awed, they cease committing some of the sins which were frequently very common among them. In the

....

[1] Not to be confused with the present, well known, Brazilian city of the same name. The São Paulo mentioned here was an Indian reduction about one league from Bahia.

construction of the church and houses into which the Fathers, teachers of this new Christianity, gathered together the Indians, Our Lord manifested His pleasure, because, although they were built in the winter during which time it rains frequently in this land, the work was completed in four months. The first mass was said in that church on St. Peter and St. Paul's Day with the greatest solemnity possible. The Governor, accompanied by the most honorable men of the city, visited the church where a dinner was given for all. The solemnity began with the new catechumens. At the beginning of the mass, the Father, dressed in priestly robes, blessed the church and then began the solemn baptism during which he baptized eighty-four innocents. Of all these, the Governor was the godfather. In this ceremony, he demonstrated clearly the zeal and favor he has for such works because there he was next to the baptismal font touching his godchildren with much love as one must feel when he sees the salvation of a soul. Brother Antônio Rodrígues, their teacher and translator, was also their godfather.

Later, on the day of the Visitation, some thirty more were baptized. On the following Sunday, some twenty more were baptized to bring the total to 144. All of them are school children who have been indoctrinated. The older people are baptized more slowly. In former times the parents did not want to allow their children to be baptized; and, if they became ill, they hid them. Now, by the Lord's kindness, if they fall ill, they come offering the children for baptism; and after the first baptism was held in the new church, there were many who complained because we did not baptize their children on that day. They believed it would never be possible again to have their children baptized.

During this solemnity the Governor made one of the principal Indians the bailiff of the village, and he ordered him to be suitably dressed, and he handed to him his staff of office which caused considerable amazement among them because it was new. This good order affected many, not only those who live close to us but those who live ten leagues from here came to ask for the same laws and for us to teach them saying they will do all that is commanded of them. It would seem that they are adjusting to the Christian manner of living. Confident that the Lord will send from the homeland many laborers for these works of His service, we continue to expand our activities always asking the Lord for aid and help to be able to accomplish our tasks to the greater glory and honor of His Divine Majesty. We ask for His Holiest Grace so that aided by it we can work faithfully in His service as we are obliged. Amen.

. . .

Since the letter written on July 19, 1558, from Bahia, the Governor has continued zealously in his efforts and Our Lord has given him rewards for his efforts.

He continued to punish the wrongdoers with such prudence and temperance that he builds up the community and does not destroy it, and for that reason he has been able to subjugate all to the law and servitude whom he wanted.

Thus, from far away they [the Indians] send requests for priests to indoctrinate them because they want friendship with Christians and to change their habits for ours. In this way four large settlements are already constructed for them, but for the present only two of us reside among them in the newly constructed churches because there are only three of us in this Captaincy who can say mass and we are scattered in the following three areas: in the College of Bahia resides João Gonçalves with a few Brothers, Father Nóbrega is in São Paulo,[2] and Antônio Pires is in São João.[3] The other two settlements are awaiting aid.

Besides these, other settlements are being prepared in more remote parts where the Christians never imagined it possible to enter and subjugate, and we are taking care of this slowly until there are enough Fathers to reap the great harvest there. It is certain that if there were enough people

....

[2] São Paulo here again refers to the Indian reduction about one league from Bahia.
[3] São João was an Indian reduction about five leagues from Bahia.

to teach and to maintain them, we could easily establish twenty or thirty churches around which we could settle all the Indians from an area many leagues square.

All these are losing their habit of eating human flesh; and if we learn that some are about to eat flesh, we order them to send it to us. They send it, as they did several days ago, and they bring it to us from a long distance so that we can bury or burn it. In this way they all tremble with fear of the Governor, a fear which, although it may not last a lifetime, is enough so that we can teach them; it serves us so that we can tell them of Christ, and the kindness which Our Lord will show them will cause all human fear to flee so that they will remain a strong and stable people. This fear makes them more capable of being able to hear the word of God. Their children are instructed; the innocent ones about to die are all baptized; they are forgetting their habits and exchanging them for good ones. Proceeding in this way a noble Christianity will be inculcated at least among the youngsters.

With much diligence the children are being taught good habits, reading, and writing, and there are some very intelligent ones among them. From these we hope to have some good students, because, since they can no longer wander around and now remain among us, they will not be able to forget what they have learned. Those of São Paulo, the first settlement built, are all Christians, that is the children up to fourteen years of age, and every day more are baptized because those who are born again bring others for baptism and there are more than two hundred of these. We do not baptize the older ones who may already have committed some mortal sins unless they confess and live in a manner acceptable to Our Lord, and of these older ones many are living orderly lives so that already we have baptized and married a large number. This good order is encountered throughout the other Indian settlements we have created.

There are a great many things which I could tell your Paternity and all the Brothers which would please you very much, but I will concentrate only on two things. The first is that one of the boys whom we brought up some years ago and taught to weave is in São Paulo with his loom and is making cloth. The concern which before they all had for their feasts of human flesh and for their wars and ceremonies has been converted to the planting of cotton. They weave it and thus dress themselves. This now is their principal concern. All have begun to clothe themselves and many of them go around dressed now. The second is that in the settlement of São Paulo there is a young Indian girl who, for the love of virtue, determined to live a life of chastity and cleanliness. After the Fathers praised and commended her intention and told her various examples of Holy Virgins, she became even more set in her purpose. This is truly a novelty in this generation in which the flesh corrupts their lives so much that it frightens us; *sed manus Domini non est alligata.*

Not only is there an understanding with these Indians, who are here associated with us, but also with those around Bahia who are opposed to these [Indians] and have done harm to the Christians and have murdered many. These came once again to steal a boat from the Christians, and for this and other reasons war was declared against them because they refused to make the necessary satisfactions. Consequently the Governor commanded that they should be fought, and they [the Portuguese] entered the land of those Indians and killed all the men in one large village and took the women and children captive without losing one Christian. Such a feat amazed and frightened not only those Indians but those all along the coast because such a thing had never happened there before.

Then the Governor with many people set about to subjugate them and to make them understand the only path by which they can come to have an understanding of their Creator. Therefore, it is necessary that many laborers come to reap such a great harvest, and we hope in Our Lord that beside those of the Company of Jesus, His Highness will send people here who will be able to help to maintain the beginning which has been made and will finish subjugating this land which promises so much.

In this city many confessions are made now that celebrations are coming up. In this college many people, among those whom we are able to confess, confessed. They are

women and the poor who do not have the hindrance of own-
ing [Indian] slaves. Father João Gonçalves, who now resides
in this college with a few Brothers, is very industrious in
hearing confessions.

Now there is nothing else to write except to ask your bless-
ing for all these who are yours and your prayers for us to
Jesus Christ Our Lord.

❊

8. The Rediscovery of the Amazon*

*Portuguese energy in the sixteenth century was absorbed in
the conquest of the coast. Conflicts with truculent Indians
and with French, British, and Dutch interlopers increased
the difficulty of expansion, but slowly the Portuguese moved
northward from their base in Pernambuco. In 1585 the town
of Filipéia in Paraíba was founded; in 1599 Natal in Rio
Grande do Norte; in 1613 Ceará was pacified and incorporated into the colony; in 1615 the French were driven out of
Maranhão; in 1616 Belém was established. By the end of the
third decade of the seventeenth century, Lisbon held the
coast around the mouth of the Amazon River. That "river-
sea" was still largely unknown. Discovered by Francisco de
Orellana in 1539-1541 and revisited by the expedition of
Lope de Aguirre in 1559-1561, the river had been neglected
until 1636, when two Spanish Franciscans and six soldiers
descended the Amazon from Quito to Belém. Their arrival
spurred the Portuguese to take a greater interest in the river,*

....

* From Father Cristóval de Acuña, A New Discovery of the Great
River of the Amazons, in Clements R. Markham (ed.), Expeditions into the Valley of the Amazons (London: Hakluyt Society,
1859), pp. 60-61, 64-68, 74-77, 79-81, 83, 85-86, 133.

whose mouth they then controlled, and coincided with a new phase in Brazilian colonial history: the expansion into the interior of the continent. Accordingly, in 1637, the governor dispatched Pedro Teixeira to explore the river. With forty-one large canoes, seventy soldiers, some priests, and 1,200 Indians, he paddled up the Amazon, Solimões, and Napo to Quito. On his return in 1639, he founded Tabatinga, the most distant claim of Portugal in the heartland of South America, the place where today Peru, Colombia, and Brazil meet. Accompanying him on the return voyage was Father Cristóval de Acuña, a Spanish priest, who wrote the first thorough chronicle of the Amazon.

*

THE VOYAGE

On the 16th February 1639, they commenced their long voyage, which lasted for a space of ten months, when they entered the city of Pará, on the 12th of December of the same year. After they had crossed those lofty mountains on foot, which, with the liquor of their veins, feed and sustain that great river; they voyaged on the waves to where, spread out into eighty-four mouths, it pays its mighty tribute to the sea. They, with particular care, took notes of all that was worthy of remark, measured the heights, noted down all the tributary rivers by their names, became acquainted with the nations who dwell on their banks, beheld their fertility, enjoyed the resources of the great river, experienced its climate, and finally left nothing of which they could not say that they had been eye-witnesses. As such, as persons whom so many considerations oblige to be accurate, I pray to those who read this narrative that they will give me the credit that is just, for I am one of those, and in the name of both I took up my pen to write. I say this because other accounts may be brought to light, which will not be so truthful as this narrative. This will be a true account, and it is an account of things which, with face uncovered, not more than fifty Spaniards and Portuguese can testify to, namely, those who made the same voyage. I affirm that which is certain as certain, and that which is doubtful as such, that in an affair of so much importance, no one may believe more than is stated in this narrative.

The River of Amazons is the Largest in the World

The famous river of Amazons, which traverses the richest, most fertile, and most densely populated regions of Peru, may be, from this day forth, proclaimed as the largest and most celebrated river in the whole world. For if the Ganges irrigates all India, and, with the great volume of its waters, eclipses the sea itself, which loses its very name and is called the Gangetic Gulf (or sometimes the Bay of Bengal): if the Euphrates, the famed river of Syria and Persia, is the joy and delight of those countries: if the Nile irrigates and fertilizes a great part of Africa: the river of Amazons waters more extensive regions, fertilizes more plains, supports more people, and augments by its floods a mightier ocean: it only wants, in order to surpass them in felicity, that its source should be in Paradise; as is affirmed of those other rivers, by grave authors.

. . .

The narrowest part in which the river collects its waters, is little more than a quarter of a league wide. A place, doubtless, which has been provided by divine Providence, where the great sea of fresh water narrows itself, so that a fortress may be built to impede the passage of any hostile armament of what force soever; in case it should enter by the principal mouth of this mighty river.

The depth of the river is great, and there are parts where no bottom has yet been found. From the mouth to the Rio Negro, a distance of nearly six hundred leagues, there is never less than thirty or forty *brazas*[1] in the main channel; above the Rio Negro it varies more, from twenty to twelve or eight brazas, but up to very near its source there is sufficient depth for any vessel; and, though the current would impede

....

[1] Fathoms.

the ascent, yet there is not wanting usually, every day, three or four hours of a strong breeze, which would assist in overcoming it.

Islands, Their Fertility and Products

All this river is full of islands, some large, others small, and so numerous that it is impossible to count them, for they are met with at every turn. Some are four or five leagues, others ten, others twenty in circumference, and that which is inhabited by the Tupinambas (of whom I shall speak hereafter), is more than a hundred leagues round.

There are also many other very small ones, on which the Indians sow their seeds, having their habitations on the larger ones. These islands are flooded by the river every year, and are so fertilized by the mud which it leaves behind, that they can never be called sterile. The ordinary products, which are maize and yuca, or manioc, the commonest food of all, are in great abundance; and though it would seem that the Indians are exposed to great loss, on account of the powerful floods; yet nature, the common mother of us all, has provided these barbarians with an easy means of preserving their food. They collect the *yucas*, which are roots from which they make the *casava*, the ordinary substitute for bread in all parts of Brazil; and forming caves or deep holes in the earth, they bury them, and leave them well covered up during all the time of the floods. When the waters subside, they take them out, and use them for food, without their having lost any part of their virtue. If nature teaches the ant to store up grain in the bowels of the earth, to serve for food during a whole year: how much more will she suggest a contrivance to the Indian, how barbarous soever he may be, to protect him from harm, and to preserve his food: for is it not certain that Divine Providence will take more care of men than of dumb animals?

The Kinds of Liquor Which They Use

This [yuca?] is, as I have said, the daily bread which always accompanies their other food; and it not only serves for food, but also as a drink, to which all the natives are usually much inclined. For this purpose they make large thin cakes, which they place in an oven and bake, so that they will last for many months: these they keep in the highest part of their houses, to preserve them from the dampness of the earth. When they wish to use them, they melt them in water, and having boiled the liquor at a fire, they let it stand as long as is necessary; and, when cold, it is the usual wine which they drink. It is sometimes so strong that it might be taken for grape wine, and intoxicates the natives, making them lose their judgment.

With the help of this wine they celebrate their feasts, mourn their dead, receive their visitors, sow and reap their crops; indeed there is no occasion on which they meet, that this liquor is not the mercury which attracts them, and the riband which detains them. They also make, though they are not so common, other kinds of wine, of the wild fruits which abound on the trees; so fond are they of drunkenness. They put the juice into water, and produce a liquor which often exceeds beer in strength, that beverage which is so much used in foreign countries. These wines are kept in large earthen jars, like those used in Spain; also in small pipes made of one piece of the hollowed trunk of a tree; and in large vases woven from herbs, and so smeared with bitumen, that not one drop of the liquor which they contain is ever lost.

The Fruits Which They Have

The food with which they accompany their bread and wine is of various kinds—not only fruits, such as plantains, pine apples, and guavas, but very palatable chestnuts, which in Peru they call "almonds of the Sierra," for in truth they more resemble the latter than the former. They name them chestnuts, because they are enclosed in shells which resemble the prickly husk of the real chestnut. The Indians also have palms of different kinds, some of which produce cocoa nuts, others palatable dates which, though wild, are of a very pleasant taste. There are also many other different kinds of fruits, all proper to tropical climates. They have likewise nourishing roots such as the potatoe, the *yuca mansas*, which the Portuguese call *macachera, garas, criadillas de terra*, and others which, either roasted or boiled, are not only palatable, but also very nutritious.

. . .

Nature of the Land, and of Medicinal Drugs

From this mildness of the climate arises without doubt the freshness of all the banks of this river, which, crowned with various beautiful trees, appear to be continually delineating new countries, in which nature brightens, and art is taught. Although for the most part the land is low, it also has tolerably high rising grounds, small plains clear of trees and covered with flowers, valleys which always retain moisture, and, in more distant parts, hills which may properly receive the name of Cordilleras.

In the wild forests the natives have, for their sicknesses, the best dispensary of medicines; for they collect the largest cañafistula, or fruit of the purging cassia, that has even been found; the best sarsaparilla; healing gums and resins in great abundance: and honey of wild bees at every step, so abundant that there is scarcely a place where it is not found, and it is not only useful medicinally, but also very pleasant and palatable as food. The wax, though black, is good, and burns as well as any other.

In these forests too are the oil of *andirova*, trees of priceless value for curing wounds; here too is the *copaiba*, which has no equal as a balsam; here too are found a thousand kinds of herbs and trees of very peculiar qualities; and to find many others a second Dioscorides or a third Pliny should come out, to investigate their properties.

Timber and Materials for Ships

The woods of this river are innumerable, so tall that they reach to the clouds, so thick that it causes astonishment. I measured a cedar with my hands, which was thirty *palmas* in circumference. They are nearly all of such good wood that better could not be desired; there are cedars, cotton trees, iron wood trees, and many others now made known in those parts, and proved to be the best in the world for building vessels. In this river vessels may be built better and at less cost than in any other country, finished and launched, without the necessity of sending anything from Europe, except iron for the nails. Here, as I have said, is timber; here are cables made from the bark of a certain tree, which will hold a ship in the heaviest gale; here is excellent pitch and tar; here is oil, as well vegetable as from fish; here they can make excellent oakum which they call *embira*, for caulking the ships, and also there is nothing better for the string of an arquebuss; here is cotton for the sails; and here finally is a great multitude of people, so that there is nothing wanting, for building as many vessels as may be placed on the stocks.

Of Four Valuable Products Found on the Banks of This River

There are on the banks of the great river of the Amazons four products, which, if cultivated, would undoubtedly be sufficient to enrich not only one, but many kingdoms. The first of these is the timber; of which, besides there being so many curious kinds, of great value; there are such quantities fit for building that while as much may be cut as is wanted, there will be the certainty that the supply can never be exhausted.

The second kind is the *cocoa*, of which the banks of this river are so full that in some places the wood of it would suffice, if cut, for lodging a whole army. There is scarcely any difference between this tree, and that which yields this much valued fruit in New Spain; which, when cultivated, is of such value that the trees, growing a foot apart, are every year worth eight silver rials, after all expenses are paid. It is clear with what little labour these trees may be cultivated on this river, when, without any help from art, nature alone covers them with abundance of fruit.

The third kind is tobacco, of which great quantities are found, in all the country near the banks of this river, and if it were cultivated with the care that this seed requires, it would be the best in the world. In the opinion of those who understand the subject, the soil and climate are all that can be desired to produce prolific harvests.

The product which, in my view, ought to be most cultivated on this river is sugar, which is the fourth kind. It is the most noble, most productive, most certain, and most valuable to the royal crown; and many farms ought to be established, which in a short time would restore the losses on the Brazilian coast. For this purpose neither much time nor much labour would be necessary, nor, what now-a-days is more dreaded, much outlay, for the land for sugar cane is the most productive in all Brazil, as we can testify who have visited those parts; and the floods, which never last more than a few days, leave it so fertile that it might be thought to be too rich. Nor will it be a new thing to raise sugar cane on the banks of this river; for along its whole vast length, from its first sources, we were always meeting with it: so that it seemed from that time to give signs of its future increase, when mills should be established to work it. These would not be expensive, because all necessary timber is at hand, with water in abundance. Copper is alone wanting, which with great ease might be supplied from Spain, in anticipation of the rich return which would be afterwards received.

Of Other Valuable Products

Not only may these four products be promised, from this newly discovered land, to supply the whole world; but there are also many others, which, though in less quantities, would not fail to enrich the royal crown. Such, among others, is the cotton which is picked in abundance; the *uruca*,[2] which gives the best dye, and is much valued by foreigners; the fruit of the cassia; the sarsaparilla; the oils which rival the best balsams in curing wounds; the gums and sweet resins; the agave,[3] whence the best cord is obtained, which is plentiful, and many others; which necessity, or the desire of riches, are bringing to light every day.

. . .

*

THE INDIANS

All this new world, if we may call it so, is inhabited by barbarians, in distinct provinces and nations. . . .

They exceed one hundred and fifty, all with different languages. These nations are so near each other, that from the last villages of one they hear the people of the other at work. But this proximity does not lead to peace; on the contrary, they are engaged in constant wars, in which they kill and take prisoners great numbers of souls every day. This is the drain provided for so great a multitude, without which the whole land would not be large enough to hold them.

But though, among themselves, they are so warlike, none of them shewed courage to face Spaniards, as I observed throughout the voyage, in which the Indians never dared to use any defence against us, except that of flight. They navigate in vessels so light that, landing, they carry them on their shoulders, and, conveying them to one of the numerous lakes near the river, laugh at any enemy who, with heavier vessels, is unable to follow the same example.

. . .

All those who live on the shores of this great river are collected in large villages, and, like the Venetians and Mexi-

....

[2] *Achiote*, heart-leaved *bixa* or *anotta*.
[3] The American aloe.

cans, their means of communication are by water, in small vessels which they call canoes. They are usually of cedar wood, which the providence of God abundantly supplies, without the labour of cutting it or carrying it from the forest; sending it down with the current of the river, which, to supply their wants, tears the trees from the most distant Cordilleras of Peru, and places them at the doors of their habitations, where each Indian may choose the piece of wood which suits him best.

. . .

The rites of all these infidels are almost the same. They worship idols which they make with their own hands; attributing power over the waters to some, and, therefore, place a fish in their hands for distinction; others they choose as lords of the harvests; and others as gods of their battles. They say that these gods came down from Heaven to be their companions, and to do them good. They do not use any ceremony in worshipping them, and often leave them forgotten in a corner, until the time when they become necessary; thus when they are going to war, they carry an idol in the bows of their canoes, in which they place their hopes of victory; and when they go out fishing, they take the idol which is charged with dominion over the waters; but they do not trust in the one or the other so much as not to recognize another mightier God.

I gathered this from what happened with one of these Indians, who having heard something of the power of our God, and seen with his own eyes that our expedition went up the river, and, passing through the midst of so many warlike nations, returned without receiving any damage; judged that it was through the force and power of the God who guided us. He, therefore, came with much anxiety to beseech the captain and ourselves, that, in return for the hospitality he had shown us, we would leave him one of our gods, who would protect him and his people in peace and safety, and assist them to procure all necessary provisions. There were not wanting those who wished to console him by leaving in his village the standard of the cross, a thing which the Portuguese were accustomed to do among the infidels, not with so good a motive as would appear from the action itself. The sacred wood of the cross served to give color to the greatest injustice, such as the continual slavery of the poor Indians, whom, like meek lambs, they carried in flocks to their houses, to sell some, and treat the others with cruelty. These Portuguese raise the cross, and in payment of the kind treatment of the natives when they visit their villages, they fix it in the most conspicuous place, charging the Indians always to keep it intact. By some accident, or through the lapse of time, or purposely because these infidels do not care for it, the cross falls. Presently the Portuguese pass sentence, and condemn all the inhabitants of the village to perpetual slavery, not only for their lives, but for the lives of all their descendants.

For this reason I did not consent that they should plant the holy cross; and also that it might not give the Indian, who had asked us for a god, occasion for idolatry, by attributing to the wood the power of the Diety who redeemed us.

. . .

It is worthy of notice that they all hold their sorcerers in very great estimation, not so much on account of the love they bear them, as for the dread in which they always live of the harm they are able to do them. These sorcerers usually have a house, where they practice their superstitious rites, and speak to the demon; and where, with a certain kind of veneration, the Indians keep all the bones of dead sorcerers, as if they were relics of saints. They suspend these bones in the same hammocks in which the sorcerers had slept when alive.

These men are their teachers, their preachers, their councilors, and their guides. They assist them in their doubts, and the Indians report to them in their wars, that they may receive poisonous herbs with which to take vengeance on their enemies.

. . .

After having bathed with its waters a distance of thirteen hundred and fifty-six leagues of longitude, after sustaining on its banks an infinite number of barbarous tribes, after fertilizing vast territories, and after having passed through the centre of Peru, and, like a principal channel, collected the largest and richest of all its affluents, it [the Amazon] renders its tribute to the ocean.

Such is the sum of the new discovery of this great river, which excludes no one from its vast treasures, but rewards all who wish to take advantage of them. To the poor it offers sustenance, to the labourer a reward for his work, to the merchant employment, to the soldier opportunities to display his valour, to the rich an increase to his wealth, to the noble honours, to the powerful estates, and to the king himself a new empire.

9. An Eyewitness Account of the First Battle of Guararapes*

The Dutch emerged as the major challenge to Portuguese control of Brazil. They had cast covetous eyes in that direction in the sixteenth century; but as they rose to the rank of a first-rate sea power in the early seventeenth century, their designs became more overt and ambitious. After the formation of the Dutch West India Company in 1621, incorporated to encourage colonization and commerce through con-

....

* Translated from a manuscript written by Francisco Barreto found in the Library of Évora, Portugal, and printed in *Documentos dos Arquivos Portugueses que Importam ao Brasil*, No. 2 (Lisbon: Oficina Gráfica, Secretariado Nacional da Informação de Portugal, 1944-45), pp. 1-3. Printed by permission of the publisher.

*quest, they turned full attention to the east coast of South
America. In 1624, they captured Bahia, the colonial capital,
and held it for nearly a year. Returning in 1627, they twice
attacked the city but failed to carry it. Turning their attention from the political to the commercial capital of the colony, they seized Recife in 1630. By 1641, the Dutch had
expanded their conquest until they controlled nearly a thousand miles of the coast, from the mouth of the Amazon to
the São Francisco River, and were at the height of their
power in Brazil. The disgruntled Luso-Brazilians began to
revolt in earnest three years later, and within a short time
they reduced effective Dutch control to Recife and the area
immediately surrounding it. The majority of the troops fighting the foreigners were Brazilian-born whites, mulattoes, Negroes, and Indians from every part of the colony. Their
small, heterogeneous army met and defeated a superior enemy force at Guararapes on April 19, 1648. It was a surprising victory for Brazil and foretold the end of Holland's occupation. The Luso-Brazilians repeated their triumph at the
second battle of Guararapes on February 19, 1649. The de-
moralized Dutch finally withdrew from Pernambuco in
1654, marking the end of the last significant foreign threat.
The Brazilians and the Portuguese could then turn their full
attention to the development and expansion of the colony.*

After being in Recife for a period of nine months, I fled the
close guard which the enemy had put on me, and I arrived in
the countryside of Pernambuco on January 23rd of this year.[1]
Although I had no command, I aided by giving necessary
advice which the commanders used to good advantage. In
this way everything started to go better both in the fighting
and in the handling of the campaign. The defensive war
went well and it also appeared possible to take the offensive.
The enemy's fleet arrived on March 17. They disembarked in
Recife. They prepared all their infantry until on the 18th of
April they marched into the countryside with an army con-

....
[1] 1648 [ed.].

sisting of 5,500 soldiers, 500 sailors, and 300 Tapuya Indians.[2] They carried in all their battalions 60 flags and one large standard with the coats of arms of the United Provinces and the Estates General, five pieces of bronze artillery, many supplies, munitions, and much money. General Segismundo Escop[3] commanded this army aided by six coronels, Urs, Vanelote, Plutim, Pedro Enverque, Vandebrande, and Brinque.[4] They marched along the south shore and on the same day, April 18, they beheaded 40 of the 100 men who were stationed along the shore to defend it. I heard news of how they quartered themselves at that place. Only two days had passed since I received an order from the Count-General in Bahia to govern these captaincies, a command I did not refuse to accept in order to serve Your Majesty. Despite the miserable state of the land, the great power of the enemy and the limited power which I had to oppose them, I immediately called a council of the chief leaders, André Vidal de Negreiros, João Fernandes Vieira, and the infantry captains; and after informing them of the state of affairs, it was resolved in council that we should go out to meet the enemy even though our strength did not exceed more than 2,200 men, among whom was the unit of Negroes of Governor Henrique Dias and the Indians of militia Captain Camarão,[5] after leaving our base guarded with only 300 men. With that limited force, I marched to the hills of Guararapes and after passing them I halted in the foothills to form the infantry in the best manner and shape which the terrain permitted. At that place, I spent the night. On the following day, which was Low Sunday, April 19, the enemy broke camp and came marching toward us. The mounted scouts began the battle. As soon as the enemy was discovered invading Guararapes, I ordered our troops into battle. I had stationed in the vanguard Commander André Vidal de Negreiros and behind him Commander João Fernandes Vieira, while the flanks

....

[2] The total number more likely was 5000 [ed.].
[3] Von Schoppe [ed.].
[4] Haus; Von Elst; Hauthain; Keweer; van den Broude; Brinck [ed.].
[5] Felipe Camarão [ed.].

were guarded on one side by militia Captain Camarão and on the other by Governor Henrique Dias. After the first discharge of shots on both sides, we drew our swords and broke through the enemy lines. Because two of the enemy's reserve battalions which had not engaged in battle detoured around the main battle and attacked the flank guarded by Henrique Dias, I dispatched 500 men whom I had kept in reserve to come to the aid of Henrique Dias. They aided him in his stand against the attackers. But our captains, who in two exchanges of shot, halted the enemy, did not observe the still present danger and turned toward another part of the battle where they thought they could inflict greater injury on the enemy. As a result of this error, we did not completely destroy our adversaries who fell upon Henrique Dias; and since he was unable to bear their full weight, he retreated toward our main body. There were few of us and we already were exhausted and so we, too, were forced to fall back. I immediately swung into action everywhere in order to prevent the enemy from recovering his artillery, munitions, and money which we already had won from him, but I was not able to do it because with the defeat we had inflicted on our enemy our troops became more disorganized than the very enemy we had defeated. However, in a few minutes, I took a stand at a creek located on the battlefield where, encouraging some and striking others, I forced our infantry to halt and I began to reform them ordering Commander João Fernandes Vieira to do the same. I put Commander André Vidal de Negreiros in the vanguard. With few soldiers but with great energy, he began again to attack the troop detachments the enemy sent against him. Skirmishing with them, he began to defeat them by killing some of their captains and many of their soldiers. The battle began anew all across the field. The battle lasted for a period of four hours during which we performed wonderous acts of bravery in which the commanders and the other officers distinguished themselves. The enemy retired to occupy some high ground within our sight, and behind the hills they gathered their wounded who had fallen in that vicinity. Then I considered how tired our own soldiers were. They had not eaten in twenty-four hours and many of them were occupied in rescuing the wounded and recovering the dead. I ordered them to collect the flags we had won, which numbered thirty-three, including the large standard bearing the arms of the United Provinces to which I already have referred. I sent that standard along with 19 flags to the Count-General in Bahia. The other 13 flags were destroyed by our Negro and Indian soldiers who saw no other value in them except as bright material to tear up for ribbons and other ornaments. The camps were within sight of each other, and at nightfall I dispatched some troops to harass the enemy and to bring back to me information about their movements; and since they did not follow all the orders, although they did needle the enemy, our foes were able to escape in the night without word of it reaching me. When Monday, the day of Our Lady of Pleasures, dawned, I learned that the enemy had fled with great speed and havoc because he left on the field 900 dead men among whom were some wounded, a bronze artillery piece, a lot of munitions and arms, the flags which I have mentioned, various insignias, in addition to other booty such as clothes and money of which our soldiers took advantage.

Among the enemy's dead were many important figures, the principal ones of which were Coronel Urs and Coronel Vanelle, and Coronel Autim died after returning to Recife. Among those captured was Coronel Pedro Erveque. Therefore, of the six coronels in their army only two escaped from us, Vandebrade and Brinque. Also, I have reliable information from the prisoners we captured that the wounded whom the enemy took from this field were more than 500, among whom was General Segismundo with a wounded leg and that their dead (as I have said) which seemed to us to number 900, numbered in reality more than 1,000. On this occasion our dead were 80 men, counting in that number the 40 whom the enemy decapitated at the post along the shore. Our wounded numbered close to 400, but, thank heaven, none seriously so. On the same Monday, I marched to occupy our plantations around Recife because the enemy had withdrawn within the city, and when I found that a captain whom I left in charge of a battery in a fort that we had located near Recife had abandoned it for lack of any artillery, I ordered it reoccupied. I did the same thing with the town of Olinda, which we had abandoned with five small iron cannons because the speed with which it was necessary to go out to meet the enemy only allowed us to take what we could carry easily. Immediately I reoccupied the posts of this Arraial do Bom Jesus. I gave orders to march to the town of Olinda to Governor Henrique Dias with his unit of Negroes, some companies of mulattoes, and one of white soldiers. Their orders were to enter and seize the town from many sides which they did with so much valor that they put to flight the 600 Dutchmen who were there. They fled to Recife, a distance of one league. We killed in this struggle 150 or more who were left in the fields, some officers, and doubtless others must have died in the waters where they jumped to escape. We captured a Frenchman and we recovered our five iron cannons which we had left there. I ordered them transported to this base in case we abandon the town again because it is indefensible or requires too many troops to garrison it when we could use them to better advantage elsewhere or we could use them also to assault the enemy when he tries to come out for battle. We did not have more than six wounded, among whom was a captain, but all without danger of dying. From these happy victories with which God favors the arms of Your Majesty at a time when the well known superiority of the enemy warned us of total destruction without any hope of success I can take heart that there will be still greater victories with which our Lord will free this Christian State threatened by the Dutch tyrants.

FRANCISCO BARRETO

❀

10 . A Description of the Sugar Industry*

Sugar was the principal source of wealth of the colony. The climate and soil of coastal Pernambuco, Bahia, and Rio de Janeiro made those regions the primary centers for its cultivation. By 1627 there were some 230 engenhos (sugar mills) scattered throughout a majority of the captaincies and exporting approximately twelve thousand tons of sugar a year. Those exports increased annually and sold well throughout Europe. The English traveller Richard Flecknoe left the following succinct description of that profitable industry in the mid-seventeenth century.

I will return to speak of the Riches of the Country, chiefly consisting in their Sugar, which when I have named, I have named all; not that it wants others, but that it can want no others, having that, since that country which abounds with that commodity which all others have need of, can never want any commodity which others abound withall. . . . Now for their Sugar thus it grows, and thus 'tis made; Their Sugar canes are prun'd to the heighth of standing corn: nor need they other culture, but every second year to cut them close by the roots, as we do Osiers, when against the next year they never fail to spring up agen, the flaggs of which Canes are of a pleasant green, and shew a far off just like in a Field of Corn, which being ripe about the month of June, they joint them in pieces some foot long, and carry them to the Mill, turn'd by Oxen, or Water, consisting of two round Cylinders, about the bigness of Mil-posts, plated

....

* From Richard Flecknoe, *A Relation of Ten Years Travells in Europe, Asia, Affrique, and America* (London, 1654), pp. 79-80.

with Iron, which turning inwards, and joyning as close together as they can meet, so squeez the canes in passing
through them, as they come out on th'other side all bruzed,
and dry as keques, which were all liquid before; which Liquor is conveyed by Troughs to certain Caldrons, where 'tis
boyl'd, still retaining its amber colour, till pour'd out at last
into their forms or coolers, with a certain Lee 'tis rendered
white; And in these Mills (during the season of making
Sugar) they work both day and night, the work of immediately applying the canes into the Mill being so perillous as if
through drousinesse or heedlessnesse a fingers end be but
engag'd betwixt the posts, their whole body inevitably follows, to prevent which, the next Negro has always a Hatchet
readie to chop off his Arm, if any such Misfortune should
arrive.

❀

11. Vieira's Sermon Condemning Indian Slavery*

*The question of the relationship between the Indians and
the empire remained an ambiguous and explosive one. Lisbon said one thing; the colonist did quite another. The Indians, greatly reduced in number by the European diseases,
fled into the interior to escape enslavement. The colonists
sent expeditions to capture and bring them back. In the tradition of Nóbrega and Anchieta, the Jesuits continued to be
the most effective protectors of the natives. Doubtless the
most eloquent spokesman of Indian rights was the eminent*

* Translated from Afrânio Peixoto, (ed.), *Vieira Brasileiro* (Paris:
Ailland et Bertrant, 1921), I, pp. 203-221.

Brazilian-educated Jesuit and scholar, Father Antônio Vieira. His fiery sermon condemning Indian slavery, delivered the first Sunday of Lent, 1653, in Maranhão, was the voice of the Luso-Brazilian conscience.

At what a different price the devil today buys souls compared to what he offered for them previously! There is no market in the world where the devil can get them more cheaply than right here in our own land. In the Gospel, he offered all the kingdoms of the world for one soul; in Maranhão the devil does not need to offer one-tenth as much for all the souls. It is not necessary to offer worlds, nor kingdoms; it is not necessary to offer cities, nor towns, nor villages. All he has to do is offer a couple of Tapuya Indians and at once he is adored on both knees. What a cheap market! An Indian for a soul! That Indian will be your slave for the few days that he lives; and your soul will be a slave for eternity, as long as God is God. This is the contract that the devil makes with you. Not only do you accept it but you pay him money on top of it.

. . .

Christians, nobles, and people of Maranhão, do you know what God wants of you during this Lent? That you break the chains of injustice and let free those whom you have captive and oppressed. These are the sins of Maranhão; these are what God commanded me to denounce to you. Christians, God commanded me to clarify these matters to you and so I do it. All of you are in mortal sin; all of you live in a state of condemnation; and all of you are going directly to Hell. Indeed, many are there now and you will soon join them if you do not change your life.

Is it possible that an entire people live in sin, that an entire people will go to hell? Who questions thus does not understand the evil of unjust captivity. The sons of Israel went down into Egypt, and after the death of Joseph, the Pharaoh seized them and made slaves of them. God wanted to liberate those miserable people, and He sent Moses there with no other escort than a rod. God knew that in order to free the captives a rod was sufficient, even though He was dealing with a ruler as tyrannical as Pharaoh and with a people as cruel as the Egyptians. When Pharaoh refused to free the captives, the plagues rained down upon him. The land was covered with frogs and the air clouded with mosquitos; the rivers flowed with blood; the clouds poured forth thunder and lightning. All Egypt was dumbfounded and threatened with death. Do you know what brought those plagues to the earth? Unjust captivity. Who brought to Maranhão the plague of the Dutch? Who brought the smallpox? Who brought hunger and drought? These captives. Moses insisted and pressed the Pharaoh to free the people, and what did Pharaoh respond? He said one thing and he did another. What he said was, I do not know God and I do not have to free the captives. However, it appears to me proper and I do declare them free. Do you know why you do not give freedom to your illicitly gotten slaves? Because you do not know God. Lack of Faith is the cause of everything. If you possessed true faith, if you believed that there was an eternal Hell, then you would not take so lightly the captivity of a single Tapuya. With what confidence can the devil today say to you: *Si cadens adoraveris me?* With all the confidence of having offered you the world. The devil made this speech: I offer to this man everything; if he is greedy and covetous, he must accept. If he accepts, then, he worships me because greed and covetousness are a form of idolatry. It is an idea expressed by St. Paul. Such was the greed of Pharaoh in wanting to keep and not to free the captive sons of Israel, confessing at the same time that he did not know God. This is what he said.

What he did was to take out after the fleeing Israelites with all the power of his kingdom in order to recapture them. And what happened? The Red Sea opened so that the captives could pass on dry land (because God knows how to make miracles in order to free captives). It did not matter that the Hebrews did not merit this. They were worse than the Tapuyas. A few days later they worshiped a golden calf and of all the six hundred thousand men only two entered into the promised land, but God is so favorable to the cause of liberty that he grants it even to those who do not deserve it. When the Hebrews had reached the other side, Pharaoh entered between the walls of water which were still open, and as he crossed, the waters fell over his army and drowned them all. What impresses me is the way Moses tells this: that the waters enveloped them and the sea drowned them and the earth swallowed them up. Now, if the sea drowned them how could the earth swallow them? Those men, like his, had both a body and a soul. The waters drowned the bodies because they were at the bottom of the sea; the earth swallowed the souls because they descended to Hell. All went to Hell, without a single exception, because where all pursue and all capture, all are condemned. This is an excellent example. Now, let us look at the reasoning.

Any man who deprives others of their freedom and being able to restore that freedom does not do so is condemned. All or nearly all are therefore condemned. You will say to me that even if this were true they did not think about it or know it and that their good faith will save them. I deny that. They did think about it and know it just as you think of it and know it. If they did not think of it nor know it, they ought to have thought of it and to have known it. Some are condemned by their knowledge, others by their doubt, and still others by their ignorance. . . . If only the graves would open and some who died in that unhappy state could appear before you, and in the fire of their misery you could clearly read this truth. Do you know why God does not permit them to appear before you? It is exactly as Abraham said to the rich miser when he asked him to send Lazarus to this world: *Habent Moysen et Prophetas* (Luc. 16.29). It is not necessary for one to appear on earth from Hell to tell you the truth because you already have Moses and the Law, you have the prophets and learned men. My brothers, if there are any among you who doubt this, here are the laws, here are the learned men, question them. There are in this State, three religious orders which have members of great virtue and learning. Ask them. Study the matter and inform yourselves. But it is not necessary to question the religious: go to Turkey, go to Hell, because there is no Turk so Turkish in Turkey nor no devil so devilish in Hell who will tell you that a free man can be a slave. Is there one among you with natural intelligence who can deny it? What do you doubt?

I know what you are going to tell me . . . our people, our country, our government cannot be sustained without Indians. Who will fetch a pail of water for us or carry a load of wood? Who will grind our manioc? Will our wives have to do it? Will our sons? In the first place, this is not the state into which I am placing you as you soon will see. But when necessity and conscience require such a thing, I answer yes and repeat again yes. You, your wives, your sons, all of us are able to sustain ourselves with our own labor. It is better to live from your own sweat than from the blood of others! . . .

You will tell me that your slaves are your very feet and hands. Also, you will say how much you love them because you raised them like children and took care of them as you would your very own. It may be so, but Christ said to this land: *Si oculus tuus scandalizat te, erue eum et si manus, vel pes tuus scandalizat te, amputa elum* (Math. 5.29; Marc. 9.42.44). Christ did not mean to say that we should pull out our eyes nor that we ought to cut off our hands and feet. What he meant was that if that which we loved as our eyes harmed us, or that which was as necessary as our hands and feet harmed us, we should cast away from us that source of harm even if it hurts us as if we had cut it off from us. Who amongst you does not love his arm or his hand but should it become gangrenous would not permit its amputation in order to save his life. . . . If, in order to quiet your conscience or save your soul, it is necessary to lose everything and remain as miserable as Job, lose everything.

But take heart, my friends, it is not necessary to arrive at such a state, far from it. I have studied the matter carefully and in accordance with the most lenient and favorable opinions and have come to a conclusion by which, with only minor worldly losses, all the inhabitants of this state can ease their consciences and build for a better future. Give me your attention.

All the Indians of this State are either those who serve as

slaves or those who live as free inhabitants in the King's villages, or those who live in the hinterlands in their natural or free condition. These latter are the ones you go upriver to buy or "to rescue" (as they say), giving the pious verb "to rescue" to a sale so involuntary and violent that at times it is made at pistol point. These are held, owned, and bequeathed in bad faith: therefore they will be doing no small task if they forgive you for their past treatment. However, if after you have set them free, they, particularly those domestics whom you raised in your house and treated as your children, spontaneously and voluntarily wish to continue to serve you and remain in your home, no one will or can separate them from your service. And what will happen to those who do not wish to remain in your service? These will be obliged to live in the King's villages where they also will serve you in the manner which I shall mention. Each year you will be able to make your expeditions into the interior during which time you can really rescue those who are prisoners ready to be eaten. Those justly saved from death will remain your slaves. Also, all those captured in just wars will be made slaves. Upon this matter the proper judges will be the Governor of the State, the Chief Justice of the State, the Vicars of Maranhão or of Pará, and the Prelates of the four orders: Carmelite, Franciscan, Mercedarian, and the Company of Jesus. All of these who after judgment are qualified to be true captives, will be returned to the inhabitants. And what will happen to those captured in a war not classified as just? All of them will be placed in new villages or divided among the villages which exist today. There, along with the other village Indians they will be hired out to the inhabitants of this State to work for them for six months of every year alternating two months of hired work with two months devoted to their own labors and families. Thus, in this manner, all the Indians of this State will serve the Portuguese either as legitimate slaves, that is those rescued from death or captured in a just war, or those former slaves who freely and voluntarily wish to serve their old masters, or those from the King's villages who will work half the year for the good and growth of the State. It only remains to set the wages of those village Indians for their labor and service. It is a subject which would make any other nation of the world laugh and only in this land is not appreciated. The money of this land is cloth and cotton, and the ordinary price for which the Indians work and will work each month is seven feet of this cloth which has a market value of about twenty cents. An Indian will work for less than a penny a day. It is an insignificant amount and it is unworthy of a man of reason and of Christian faith not to pay such a slight price to save his soul and to avoid Hell.

Could there be anything more moderate? Could there be anything more reasonable than this? Whoever is dissatisfied or discontent with this proposal either is not a Christian or has no understanding. To conclude this point, let us look at the advantages and disadvantages of this proposal.

The single disadvantage is that some of you will lose a few Indians. I promise you they will be very few. But to you who question this, I ask: Do not some of your Indians die or flee? Many do. Will death do what reason will not? Will chance do what a good conscience will not? If smallpox strikes and carries off your Indians, what will you do? You will have to show patience. Well, is it not better to lose the Indians to the service of God than to lose them by a punishment of God? The answer is obvious.

Let us look at the advantages of which there are four principal ones. The first is that you will have a clear conscience. You will no longer live in a state of mortal sin. You will live like Christians, you will be confessed as Christians, you will die like Christians, you will bequeath your goods as Christians. In short, you will go to Heaven and not to Hell, which would certainly be a tragic ending.

The second advantage is that you will remove this curse from your homes. There is no greater curse on a home or a family than to be unjustly supported by the sweat and blood of others. . . .

The third advantage is that in this way more Indians will be rescued from cannibal practices. . . . It is important to invade the forest to save Indians from being killed and eaten.

The fourth and last advantage is that henceforth your

proposals on the labor problem will be worthy of submission to His Majesty, and worthy of His Majesty's approval and confirmation. Whoever asks for the illegal and unjust deserves to have the legal and just denied him, and whoever petitions with justice, reason, and good conscience deserves the fulfillment of his request. You know the proposal which you made? It was a proposal which vassals could not make in good conscience, nor could ministers consult it in good conscience. And even if the King might have permitted it, what good would it have done you? If the King permits me to swear falsely, will it mean that the false oath is no sin? If the King permits me to steal, will the theft be any less a sin? The same thing applies to the Indians. The King can command the slaves to be free, but his jurisdiction does not extend to the power to order the free to become slaves. If such a request went to Lisbon, the stones of the street would have to rise up against the men of Maranhão. On the other hand, if you submit a just, legal, and Christian request, those very same stones would take your part. . . .

❀

12. The Discovery of Gold in Minas Gerais*

From the beginning, the Portuguese had hoped to discover gold and silver in their American colony. Spain succeeded in locating rich deposits of the precious metals in the sixteenth century. Encouraged by the good fortune of Castile, the Luso-Brazilians sent out increasing numbers of explorers to

....

* Translated from Affonso de E. Taunay, *André João Antonil e sua Obra* (São Paulo: Companhia Melhoramentos, 1922), pp. 207, 210, 213-214. Printed by permission of Sara de Souza Queiroz Taunay and Ana de Taunay Berrettini.

crisscross the colony and penetrate the hinterlands of the continent. The results continued to be disappointing. Then, as the seventeenth century closed—the date most frequently given is 1695—gold was discovered in the region known today as Minas Gerais. The exact circumstances surrounding the first discovery are not clearly known. The colonial chronicler André João Antonil gave one account in his Cultura e Opulência do Brasil, which is generally accepted as accurate. It is reprinted below. The long-desired discovery attracted adventurers from all over the empire, and within a few years Minas Gerais was one of the most populous areas of the colony. In recognition of the new status of the area, the crown created the Captaincy of São Paulo e Minas do Ouro in 1709. The rich deposits shifted attention from the coast and into the interior for the first time and moved the economic center from the sugar lands of the northeast to the gold fields of the southeast. In short, the discovery of gold opened a new era in colonial Brazil.

Just a few years back, when Artur de Sá was governor of Rio de Janeiro, they began to discover the general mines of Cataguas. They say that the first discoverer was a mulatto who had worked in the mines of Paranaguá and Curitiba. He accompanied some Paulistas into the interior to capture Indians and when they arrived at Tripuí he went down the bank with a wooden bowl to dip out some water from the creek now known as Ouro Preto. After scooping out some water in the bowl and throwing it on the bank, he noticed that the water contained some small grains the color of steel, and he didn't know what they were. He showed the grains to his companions who were unable to identify or to appreciate what had been discovered. They only observed that it was some kind of ill-formed and unknown metal. Arriving later at Taubaté, they asked about the kind of metal they had brought. Without any further examination, they sold some grains to Miguel de Souza, an eighth for 160 réis.[1] Neither

....

[1] An eighth was a unit of measurement equal to about 3.586 grams:

the sellers knew what they sold, nor the buyer what he bought until it was decided to send a few grains to the governor of Rio de Janeiro, Artur de Sá. He ordered them examined and found they were very fine gold.

. . .

Of all the general mines of Cataguas the best, that is those of greatest profit until now, are the mines of Ouro Preto Creek, of N.S. do Carmo Creek, and of Bento Rodrigues Creek where in little more than thirty feet it is possible to find five *arrobas*[2] of gold. Also the Velhas River is rich in gold along the banks and around the islands from which considerable gold is still taken.

The Paulistas call a creek profitable if each panning gives two eighths of gold. However, just as there are pannings of half an eighth or less so are there pannings which yield three, four, five, eight, ten, fifteen, twenty, and thirty eighths and more. Frequently this happens in the creeks of Ouro Preto and Bento Rodrigues and in the Velhas River.

Some of the large chunks which were taken out were one of ninety-five eighths, another of three pounds which was divided among three persons with a knife, another which exceeded one-hundred-and-fifty eighths, in the shape of an ox's tongue, was sent to the governor of the new colony, and another weighing more than six pounds.

. . .

The insatiable thirst for gold prompted so many to leave their homes and to take the rugged paths to the mines that it would be extremely difficult to count the number of persons who were actually there. Those who have been there for some time recently and have visited all the mines say that in total more than 30,000 people are busy at work there. Some pan in the creeks for gold; others supervise others in panning for gold; and others engage in the business of buying and

---

a *real* (plural *réis*), was valued at approximately $.0025 at that time [ed.].
[2] A dry weight equal to approximately 32 pounds [ed.].

selling not only what is necessary to sustain life but luxuries as well—more than are found in the port cities.

Each year the fleets bring a large number of Portuguese and foreigners who move on to the mines. From the towns, villages, seacoast, and the interior of Brazil, whites, browns, blacks, and many Indians, who serve the Paulistas, go to the mines. The mixture is of all conditions of man: male and female, young and old, rich and poor, nobles and peasants, laymen, clergy, and religious of diverse orders, many of which have neither convent nor house in Brazil.

Over all these people there is no effective temporal control or well-ordered government. They only honor some laws referring to deeds and divisions of land. There are neither officials nor judges who try, or attempt to try, to enforce the punishment for crimes, which are not few, particularly murders and thefts. As to the spiritual control, since up to the present there are doubts among the prelates about jurisdiction, those sent from one or another part either as priests or visitors find themselves in difficult, if not embarrassing, situations. This makes it hard for one and all who are never able to find out to which priest those new congregations belong. And once the questions are settled it does little good because the people are constantly on the move from one spot to another like the sons of Israel in the desert.

13. An Example of a Colonial Land Grant*

Soon after colonization got under way in the sixteenth century, the most fertile coastal lands had been distributed. The kings, governors, and captains-general continued

....

* Translated from Archivo do Estado de São Paulo, *Publicação*

throughout the colonial period to generously grant exten-
sive tracts. The most common method of acquiring land was
to petition for a vacant or unused piece. If the constituted
authority looked with favor on the request, he gave the land
to the petitioner. Those grants—known as sesmarias, *a term*
the kings of Portugal had used for centuries—are the basis
of the present land structure. The sesmaria which follows is
typical of most given out during the colonial period.

Land Grant Given to Balthazar Fernandes Leme by
D. Fernando Martins Mascarenhas de Lancastro,
April 12, 1706

D. Fernando Martins Mascarenhas, etc. Be it known to all
who see this land grant that in response to a petition, sent to
me by Balthazar Fernandes Leme—married inhabitant of
the town of Curitiba, who, for his sustenance and that of his
family, needs a share of land to farm and to raise livestock,
both of which will benefit His Majesty in the taxes to be
paid—for the land beginning at the holdings of Bazílio da
Silva Salgado and running in a direction from east to west
five leagues along the big river below on the left side and into
the hinterlands another five leagues from north to south, in
which he asked me in the end and at the conclusion to have
the kindness to give these above-mentioned lands as a grant
for the above-mentioned farm and livestock raising, since no
other person has already received or been given those lands
according to the Purveyor of the Royal Treasury and the
Attorney of the Crown, I do grant to Balthazar Fernandes
Leme in the name of His Majesty, may God guard him, the
land three leagues in length and one in width beginning at
the boundary of Bazílio da Silva Salgado and running in a
direction from east to west along the big river below on the
left side because these lands are vacant and do not involve
any third party. No one may make claim to these lands after

*Official de Documentos Interessantes para a História e Costumes
de S. Paulo,* LII (São Paulo: Casa Vanorden, 1930), 12-14.
Printed by permission of the Archivo do Estado de São Paulo.

this land grant becomes effective provided that within two years the grantee inhabits and cultivates these lands. Should the grantee fail to do this or sell them to someone who will cultivate them he is deprived of any claim to the land and the land will be judged vacant and available for anyone who can cultivate it and will be granted to the other according to the orders of His Majesty dated October 22, 1698. I command all the military and judicial officers of this captaincy and of his district to take note of the land grant which confers title of the above-mentioned lands on the said Balthazar Fernandes Leme in accordance with the above-mentioned declaration and to fulfill and carry out the provisions of this land grant. To achieve this, I order placed on this document my signature and my seal with my coat of arms accordingly as it is registered in the books of the secretariat of this government. Enacted in the city of S. Sebastian of Rio de Janeiro on the 12th day of the month of April of the year 1706.

Written by Secretary BERTHOLOMEU SIQUEIRA CORDOVIL.
Signed by D. FERNANDO MARTINS MASCARENHAS DE LANCASTRO.

❀
_____

14. Accounts of the Tietê River: Highway to the Interior

_____

One of the most dramatic chapters in Brazilian history relates the adventures of the bandeirantes, *the adventurous explorers of the interior. After expelling the foreign interlopers along the coast, the Luso-Brazilians turned their full atten-*

tion to the backlands. From Belém, Recife, Bahia, and particularly from the inland city of São Paulo, expeditions known as bandeiras left for the interior to hunt for slaves, to search for gold, or to explore the land. They found the slaves who helped work the coastal plantations; they discovered the gold that delighted Lisbon and filled, at least temporarily, the royal coffers; and they gathered the geographical information which soon appeared on the maps made in Europe. More importantly, they continually pushed the frontier westward toward the Andes. Because overland travel was difficult, rivers, when possible, became the most important routes of travel. The São Francisco connected the north and the south. The Tocantins, Uruguay, Paraná, Parnáiba, and numerous others played important roles in the penetration of the interior. One of the few rivers flowing directly east-west into the interior was the Tietê. Furthermore, it had its source near the bandeirante capital, São Paulo. It should not be surprising, then, that it became one of the principal highways into the interior. The excerpts given below were taken from the writings of three travelers on the Tietê. All three have one common theme: the hardship and danger of travel on the otherwise convenient Tietê.

*

I

One of the earliest accounts of a trip on the Tietê was a letter written by the Captain-General of Paraguay, Don Luis de Céspedes Xeria, to Phillip IV of Spain, dated 1628.*

By land and on foot, as that was the only route and there was no other way of traveling, I was harassed by much rain,

....
* Translated from a letter of Don Luis de Céspedes Xeria in Affonso de E. Taunay, História das Bandeiras Paulistas, III (São Paulo: Melhoramentos, n.d.), 109. Printed by permission of Sara de Souza Queiroz Taunay and Ana de Taunay Berrettini.

and we had to cross many rivers. I came to one where we stayed a month making boats out of enormous tree trunks. I ordered three made and the one I used was constructed from a trunk about sixteen feet in diameter. After it was hollowed out and made into a long boat, it measured about fifty feet long and four feet wide. Within it traveled fifty Indians, who rowed, myself, and my servants. The other two were half the size and carried our supplies and other Indians. For thirty-two days I traveled over that river with the greatest risks, thinking each time that I would be lost in the rapid currents and falls which are found in many places. Then I entered the Rio Grande de la Plata from that river and traveled for eight days.

*

I I

An account of the journey made by the Captain-General of São Paulo to Cuiabá in 1727 was included in a report by Gervásio Leite Rebelo:

On Tuesday, July 16, day of Our Lady of Mt. Carmel, His Excellency embarked in the port of Aratiguava for the down-stream voyage on the Tietê River. Among his crew for the boats and various other persons who wanted to accompany him, there were about ninety persons.

The journey proceeded down the Tietê for two days until they came to the Pirapora Rapids where they unloaded the boats and with great difficulty the loads were carried on the backs of the Negroes. During the two preceding days they already had passed some waterfalls and currents with great risk and strain, for each one of them was a continuous dan-

....

* Translated from a report by Gervásio Leite Rebelo in Affonso de E. Taunay, *História das Bandeiras Paulistas*, III (São Paulo: Melhoramentos, n.d.), 118-119. Printed by permission of Sara de Souza Queiroz Taunay and Ana de Taunay Berrettini.

ger, where even the pilots or experienced travelers blanch and lose their nerve because the waters rush with such force and violence that it is impossible to save anyone who falls in, even those who know how to swim are dashed on the rocks and disappear in an instant. On that day in this passage a white man, pilot of the scribe of the Reverend Vicar of Vera, drowned and later was found with his head broken. A mulatto saved himself miraculously.

On the 19th, Friday, dividing the boats into three groups they journeyed on in the morning. The first was under the command of His Excellency and the other two were commanded by two corporals, Bartholomeu Bueno and Gabriel Antunes de Campos, so that separated in that way there would be less confusion by giving more space to the others in the channels and narrow places, which was the correct thing to do.

From these rapids the journey down the Tietê was navigated with considerable work and risk and not a few scares because of the turbulence of the waters and because of the many rocks, currents, reefs, waterfalls, and drops. At times it was necessary to unload the boats and carry them by land, launching them later in the water, and the Negroes had to carry the cargoes on their backs, and since the proper vigilance was not taken much was lost or stolen. The trip continued. The pilots counted one unloading, and sixty rapids and reefs, and currents without number, each one of which was a threat to life itself, so much so that no journey had been made down this river which has been navigated for more than one hundred years without the loss of boats and the drowning of people. This year of the group that went to Cuiabá they lost the pilot, as I have already mentioned, and later at another rapids a woman from Portugal and in the rapids of Pau Santo three Negroes and a Negress of Alfêres Duarte Antônio de Barros Paiva, and later a boy who came with Luís Ribeiro de Faria.

This river is so torrential and impetuous that to undertake the difficult task of navigating it one can travel only by day because of the trees and rocks which are found in it—many of them hidden—which could easily tip the boats throwing the people into the water, and those who do not know how to swim run an even greater risk. Because of these rocks and trunks, which can also be found in the channels, one is obligated to navigate only during the daylight and after the fog has lifted to make it safer for the boats because even if the people are saved, the supplies are always lost and the powder gets wet, and without one or the other everything is exposed to danger because these hinterlands are far removed from any settlement, and there was only one farm which was cultivated a short time in Pitanduva. There are few fish in the water. When whites or Negroes arrive at a clearing or a field they are so exhausted that they hardly remember to eat. Besides being excessively hot on this river during the day and equally cold at night, the mosquitoes persecute everyone so that there is neither sleep nor rest.

All these risks, frights, and fears so disturbed me that I had no time to describe the countryside through which the group moved and much less to give the names of the rapids, reefs, waterfalls, and channels passed each day, which reminded us of the risk in which we constantly found ourselves and of our efforts to free ourselves. For that same reason, I did not mention the boats and people coming behind us. I have fallen into this river three times: first in the currents of Itapanema, second in the great waves, and third in the rapids, from all of which I was saved, thanks to Holy Mercy.

On Saturday, August 10, 1726, the group under the command of His Excellency floated out of the Tietê River and at three in the afternoon we set up camp at its bar where it meets the Grande River. We had navigated the river for twenty-six days covering 520 leagues. Taking into account the hours we traveled, the current of the river, and the speed of the boats, there are some who say the distance is more like 800 leagues. There are some groups which take up to two months to make the journey.

*

III

This report of Captain João Antônio Cabral Camelo tells of his journey to Cuiabá in 1727.*

Nearby the city of São Paulo flows a river called Tietê. According to its natural bed, this river passes three leagues, more or less, away from the town of Itú, a distance from São Paulo of two and one-half days journey. Three leagues away is the port of Aritaguaba which is the first principal one of the three from which those headed for the mines usually embark. From there, as is known, it is a journey of six days to the place where the Sorocaba flows into the Tietê. I will give no news of it because I never used it and only from information from some miners, who had been on it, I learned that it has various waterfalls, some of them dangerous, and among them is a waterfall called Abaremanduaba into which the venerable Father José de Anchieta fell and was found by the Indians beneath the water praying from his breviary.

Distant one day from Itú on the left bank is the port of Sorocaba. I will speak now of what I saw and experienced because it was here that I began my journey. After passing some rough currents, I arrived on the fourth day at a rapids known as Jurumirim, which in the language of the land means narrow gap and truly that is what it is because the river narrows and rushes through a very narrow channel which gives these rapids the look of a funnel. There are rocks and waterfalls for a distance of half a league. Here it is necessary to land the cargoes which are carried on the heads of Negroes, and the boats are towed part way and carried part

....

* Translated from a manuscript appearing in Affonso de E. Taunay, *História das Bandeiras Paulistas*, III (São Paulo: Melhoramentos, n.d.), 131-132. Printed by permission of Sara de Souza Queiroz Taunay and Ana de Taunay Berrettini.

way over innumerable rocks. Within sight of this is another rapids, although it is shorter, called Gequitaya, or "salt and pepper"; below it is a waterfall with the same name. At the rapids the boats are carried over the rocks and on down past the waterfall until they can be rowed again. Carrying cargoes and beaching the boats at Jurumirim and Gequitaya require three or four days and sometimes more depending on the disposition and diligence of the captains and pilots, and according to these matters the trip can be shortened or lengthened. Much depends on the navigational ability on the river and in passing the rough currents, reefs, and waterfalls. The skilled ones know how to bypass the greater part of them by rowing with full cargo aboard or at times with half cargo. Those who are less skilled tow the boats and at times unload them completely and thus it takes some longer to make the journey than it does others. Also, not all the boats have the same number of rowers nor the same strength. These are the reasons why I do not say exactly how many days it takes on each of the rivers on this trip but only make an approximation. From Gequitaya to the place where the Sorocaba makes a bar in the Tietê I spent five days traveling over some rough spots. All this river is surrounded by woods, but there are no settlements.

From the bar of the Sorocaba to the bar of the Piracicaba is a journey of two days. This river enters the Tietê on the right side; it has its port upstream, as I will describe in time, and it serves only on the return from Cuiabá and is easier when the river is at flood level. Below the Piracicaba River, a day and one-half's journey, are two settlers with their clearings which produce corn and beans, and they have pigs and chickens which they sell to the Cuiabanos. It is a journey of twelve or thirteen days from those farms to the Grande River. This part of the journey is made with considerable risk and danger because of the many rapids and waterfalls. The first of the three waterfalls one encounters is called Panhandabá [Avanhanhanava]. It is a high precipice where one beaches the boats on the right shore, and it is necessary to carry them and the cargo a distance of a quarter of a league or a little less. The second falls, called Araracanguaba, is less high and it is passed on the left-hand side for about the same distance. The third, which is near the bar where the Tietê enters the Grande River, is called Itapura, and it is the tallest of all. There you beach the boats on the right side. Between the falls are the rapids. Some are passed by towing, at others it is necessary to unload, but for the majority one can shoot them. To this last waterfall, they say, the Caiapó Indians frequently come on their rafts. These are the Indians who use the club or dart, and they are the most treacherous of all.

❀

15. A Bandeirante Epic: Overland from São Paulo to Belém*

Many of the bandeiras traveled remarkable distances in their search for gold and slaves. Not a few made it to the Andes, and several visited Quito. The following chronicle tells of an extraordinary journey through mountains, forests, and across arid plains from São Paulo in the south to Belém in the north, a distance of several thousand miles. The report of the trip, written in 1734 by one of the participants, José Peixoto da Silva, is valuable for its information about the countryside and description of the interior, as well as for the vivid portrayal of the hardships which had to be endured on those treks. Curiously enough, it helps to document the deepening feeling of enmity between the native Brazilian and the Portuguese immigrant, known disparagingly as the emboaba. This particular expedition took place several years after the War of the Embaobas in Minas Gerais, and apparently the

....
* Translated from a document printed in the *Revista do Instituto Histórico e Geográphico Brazileiro*, LXIX, Part I (1908), 219-233.

strong dislike of the native bandeirante for the emboaba was
carried into the interior.

On July 3, 1722, I left the city of São Paulo in the company
of Captain Bartholomeu Bueno da Silva, known by the nick-
name Fearless, who was in charge of a force consisting of
39 horses, two Benedictines, Brother Antônio da Conceição
and Brother Luiz de Sant'Anna, a Franciscan, Brother Cosme
de Santo André, and 152 soldiers along with twenty Indians
given by Rodrigo Cézar, then captain-general of São Paulo,
to Bartholomeu Bueno to carry burdens. Nearly all the whites
were from Portugal. One was from Bahia and five or six were
from São Paulo, with their Indians and Negroes.

Crossing the Tietê River, we stopped near the forest of
Jundiahy, four leagues away from the city of São Paulo. The
following morning we entered the forest and we spent four
days in it. Leaving the forest, we crossed the Mogig River,
which can be navigated by canoes, contains a variety of fish,
and shows some signs of gold but of little value. We spent
one day here and on the following, always headed northward, we came to another river also navigable by canoe, and
we spent the night there. The relatively flat land has clumps
of trees and good pasture and is well watered.

On the next day, we forded a stream whose water came up
to our chests, and we marched on for three or four leagues
and made camp in the middle of the fields. Traveling across
these fields is easy. The pastures are good, and there are
many animals to hunt. The streams contain many fish. We
continued on about four leagues and camped near another
stream which, like the others, flows into the Rio Grande.
From here we moved on to the banks of another stream
where we halted. The following morning we crossed it using
poles and holding stout vines in order to prevent the strong
force of the violent water from sweeping us away. We spent
a day there because the soldiers were demanding that Fearless divide up the shares as he had promised to do at Mogig
and as yet had failed to do. He excused himself with the
promise that he would do so as soon as Captain João Leite

da Silva Ortiz, his son-in-law, who was behind us with his own group, caught up, or, if he failed to arrive within a reasonable length of time, he would do it at Rio Grande.

With that hope, the troops marched again for seven or eight days through fields and thick woods, halting always at the banks of streams or rivers. There was game and fish. We came to the Rio Grande and in the morning crossed it in canoes made of the trunks of the kapok ceiba. We waited there for two days hoping he would make the promised division of shares, but as always Fearless failed to do so. We left that place somewhat discouraged and went another four leagues to camp by another stream which flowed into the Rio Grande. Here we began to feel a food shortage, and it was necessary to march five days living off of what our guns provided, birds and monkeys, as well as palm cabbage and some honey.

After five days we reached the Velhas River, which flows into the Rio Grande. It is torrential, full of fish, but without any signs of gold. We spent two days fishing and hunting in the nearby woods in order to get provisions for our trip. Here Fearless left us, going ahead with part of the group. The rest would follow him later. While he was gone, João Leite arrived with his men, and because of this, we delayed our departure one more day. On the following day, accompanied by João Leite, we followed Fearless and after a four-day march we found him in the forest with a camp already constructed. On the way we forded some streams which offered no difficulty because it is now the dry season.

After the men had had a talk with the chief, João Leite asked him to make the division of shares that he promised so many times to do, not only in São Paulo but in the backlands, because the way was far from certain. It was feared that the enterprise might fail despite the fact that both General Rodrigo Cézar and the sovereign himself had been assured of its success. He replied to them that he did not have to divide up the shares because the Emboabas, as those from Portugal are called, were not men who merited it. With that reply not only the Emboabas lost confidence but also the few Paulistas who accompanied us. They determined to return at once to São Paulo but João Leite hurried to entreat them with pleas, with promises, and, what is more important, with his natural charm, not to abandon the expedition. The chief decided to push on, out of dislike of the Emboabas whose hope he was. The group followed and we spent the night near a stream which contained some fish. Good pastures and woods were near at hand. Here we lost confidence in everything Fearless had told us, and we believed that he wanted to get rid of us in the middle of this hinterland. Some resolved to stay right there and to cultivate the land by planting some corn that they still had, for food. But Captain João Leite once again spoke with them, encouraging and persuading them to move on with the rest of the group.

For some days we trudged onward, crossing rivers and streams with a good deal of risk and work. The water was high and we were hungry. We made camp near Meia Ponte, where there is a dangerous river with plenty of fish and with good pastures and woods in the vicinity. We made it across the river in some small canoes of tree bark. We slept on the opposite bank, under the downpour of a raging thunderstorm which lasted until the following morning. There was so much rain that we were unable to build any shelters, and I made good use of a canvas I had with me. Two days' journey from Meia Ponte, Brother Antônio left us, along with ten Indians, his nephew, a mulatto, and another white Paulista, in order to start farming. The group missed the priest. Fearless sent word to him to rejoin the expedition again and to go along with the rest. As a response, Brother Antônio told him that his lies and false promises prohibited him from rejoining the group and that he was determined to plant corn and gather the natives around him in order to Christianize them.

Fearless set off again with the troops and judging that by going north, as he had done up to that point, that Goiás would lay off in another direction, he changed course and went to the northeast.[1]

We continued on for more than one-hundred leagues in that direction without anything more to eat than the forest

....

[1] The direction taken should have been west-northwest [ed.].

could give us, which was scanty. At that time eight Indians belonging to our leader fled, but first they warned everyone that we were headed in the wrong direction because we had bypassed Goiás, which lay in another direction. Of these Indians only three were brought back after some days. João Leite, with two Negroes and four whites, captured them after a search. He also brought with him Brother Antônio whose little settlement was about eighty leagues away. But even though Brother Antônio came he did not abandon his settlement, because he left his nephew there with almost all the Indians. We then came onto some extensive plains which were destitute of all necessities, without trees or any food, although there were streams in which there were fish, dorados, lungfish, and small freshwater fish, which were our only salvation. We also found some palm cabbage which they call *jaguaroba*, which we ate roasted, and, although it is bitter, it nourishes more than the other varieties.

Here everyone in our group began to weaken. Among the whites and Indians over forty persons died from starvation. I owe it to my horse that I remained alive. He carried me in my extremely weak state. I had to grab hold of the first grass we came across in order to feed and to sustain the horse.

When our leader saw this misery and began to fear the death of his followers and even more when he realized his error in taking the direction in which we were now headed, he called upon Heaven; and it was the first time that I witnessed his remembrance of God. He promised and said some novenas to St. Anthony so that we might come across some Indians who, once subdued, would be able to furnish us food to satisfy the hunger from which we were dying. After two weeks of considerable hardship, we found a rough path in those plains. We followed it for nine days, finding along it some huts made of poles and branches with some shoots of corn just beginning to grow. At the end of nine days, we arrived at some mountains whose watershed gave rise to streams flowing northward. Sending ahead four Indians to hunt out the natives, we followed behind three days later. We were only sixteen with our leader as we had left the rest of the expedition and equipment behind with the sick.

On the night of the third day, we caught sight of the huts and fires of the Indians. We hid in the woods in order to await dawn, but their dogs, of which they had many and excellent ones, sniffed us out so that when we approached they received us with their bows and arrows.

On the order of our captain, we did not fire a single shot. It turned out that nearly all of the Indians fled from us. One of them attacked the nephew of the leader with much courage. Grabbing the bridle of his horse with one hand, he tore his gun from him with the other hand and took from his belt his sword with which he struck him on the shoulder and on the left arm and then fled carrying the weapons with him. Embarrassed by the Tapuya, the Paulista chased him without any more results than retrieving the gun the Tapuya took from him and recovering his sword.

At that same moment, another Tapuya in one of the hut doors slightly wounded Francisco Carvalho de Lordelo in the chest with an arrow. Another rushed up and hit him on the head with a club and, as he fell, still another Tapuya struck him with a club, and they left him for dead.

It is amazing that throughout all this conflict not one person did anything except our leader, who rushed around shouting and ordering us to fire only into the air in order not to terrorize the Indians.

It was God's will to give us the huts under a rain of arrows and clubs.

Fleeing into the woods, the Tapuyas always kept us within their sight. So much so that when we made efforts to bury Carvalho, persuaded that he was dead, they attempted, in two attacks, to seize him in order to eat him, and seeing themselves beaten back, they asked us by signs, since their language was different from the general Indian tongue, to give them at least half of the body to eat. Attending to the body of Francisco de Carvalho we found his mouth, nose, and wounds full of bugs, but finding that his heart still beat and that he gave other signs of life we put him into a hut and tended his wounds with urine and smoke and we bled him with the point of a knife for lack of a better surgeon's lancet. He responded so well to the cure that by night Carvalho was himself again. He opened his eyes but he could not speak until the following day. We fed him as best we could on porridge and some potatoes we found in the huts.

During all this time, the Indians did not leave us. They harassed those whom we sent to get some potatoes from the twenty-five large and excellent potato fields. They killed one of them as well as a horse. When our captain learned of this, he made one of the huts into a fortress. He ordered all the corn that could be found to be collected and stored in a corn crib over which he put guards, as he also did over the seven Indians whom we captured. He ordered iron chains put on all of them except one lame Indian, also a captive, to whom he later gave freedom. From his hut, Fearless ordered an expedition to set out in search of the sick and the rest of the baggage.

By then the Indians had become more pacific, following us and serving us without their bows and arrows, and they greatly admired our weapons. They offered us their clubs. One of those days they brought us sixteen young Indian maidens, light of skin and well shaped, as a sign of friendship. Against the wishes of the soldiers, the captain refused to accept them, and it was I who did the most to try to persuade him to accept them. I pointed out to him that in consideration that we were few in number, weak, and starved and that the Indians were many, we ought not to offend them. We could use these maidens along with the Indians we had captured as a means of asking these tribes not only to have peace but to persuade them to give us some guide who could point out the right direction to Goiás. None of these arguments moved Fearless, who wanted to control all the Indians himself, the same motive which kept him from dividing up the shares. The Indians became suspicious and disappeared at once on the following day. We were afraid that these or other Indians would attack the huts containing the baggage and the sick in order to eat them up, and the Indians who were with us affirmed that that is just what they would do. Desperate at the absence of the Indians, the captain set the lame Indian free, giving him some knives, trinkets, and other gifts in order to persuade the others to return, but the lame one left and we never saw him again.

These Indians are known as the Quirixá. They live in villages; they use the bow, arrow, and war club. They are light skinned and well built; they go around completely naked, the men as well as the women. They have nineteen huts, completely round, quite high and covered with palm branches, with some openings near the ground instead of doors. In each of these twenty or thirty families live together. The beds are nets made of palm fiber which serves both as mattress and cover. They numbered about 600 souls. This entire village was situated next to a large stream that furnished many good fish. On the second day of our march in search of them, we came upon a large stream in which there were many fish. There was palm cabbage and the hunting was good, which was a great help to us. In the village we found corn, potatoes, macaws, and some parakeets which served both to feed and to amuse us. They also had a plentiful supply of gourds and pots and a tremendous number of dogs, which they killed when they fled, and they left everything behind so that they might not be heard by our forces, which went out to spy on them, as we discovered later in the bandeiras.

We stayed here three months, during which time the captain never once gave us any corn, reserving it all for himself and for his retinue and excusing his tyranny by telling us it was necessary to save it for the expeditions that had to be sent out, but even though two were ordered out he did not give them very much corn. However, his horses and his retinue never lacked this nor flour. I had the good luck of receiving seventeen ears of corn, and I got some more corn thanks to the effort and risk of harvesting it in the fields left behind by the fleeing Indians. The rest of them did the same thing including even the religious because if they wanted some they had to harvest it and carry it with their own hands, always escorted by others for fear of the Indians. Before we left, four of the Indians held by our leader fled and they were never seen again.

During our delay in this village, the men realized that the captain, by failing to make the division of the Indian shares so many times promised, bore the blame for the loss of the Indians, and they mutinied; two bastards and one Mameluco with some Paulistas wanted to take his life and to make his brother, Simão Bueno, the leader because he was considered better and more genial. I knew of their plans, and, although Fearless deserved no consideration, I did everything possible to dissuade them from their attempt by insinuating how much they owed to João Leite. Once the bastards and their followers had been dissuaded, we continued on our way by following the bank of the stream near the settlement or village until we came to a river which we also followed on the north bank in search of new Indians who could point out to us the way to Goiás. On this march we spent seventy-six days, two of them without finding any water so that when we did arrive at the bank of a river the joy among us was such that we took heart again and even the horses were so pleased to see water that we could not get them out of it no matter how many slaps we gave them. We stayed there twelve or fifteen days waiting for João Leite, who had remained behind in search of Indians, but he did not arrive.

At this place, having heard it said to the captain that we were near Maranhão, I decided to leave the expedition to move downstream in search of populated territory, in order not to perish from hunger and thirst in the middle of those forests. Three companions, José Alves, Francisco de Carvalho, his brother, Manoel de Oliveira, a Paulista, and João de Matta, a youngster from Bahia, accompanied me. José Alves, with a male and female Indian, his brother with one Indian, I with three and a mulatto were the only ones to escape from the expedition of Fearless. I had begun with six Indians and the mulatto, Alves with five, and his brother with three. The captain did not want the two brothers to leave with me without first paying a debt of forty-six *milreis*, which they owed to João Leite, who by this time had arrived with Brother Antônio. I paid for them because I saw no other solution. However, when João Leite saw that I was going to depart, he insisted, along with Brother Antônio (as much as he could), that we should not abandon them, but the insolence of Fearless, who publicly stated that he ought to hang all the Emboabas, forced me to go against the wishes of João Leite and Brother Antônio. It was certain that Fearless had given orders to one of his Tapuyas to kill Alves for some very insignificant reason and worse was the fact that when Fearless learned I was to leave him he took one of my Indians named Pascoal, a clever guide in the forest, and made him stay with him. When I noticed his absence, I returned to the captain, about half a league behind, and petitioned him to restore the Indian to me. He answered that the Indian was not in his power and that he knew nothing about him. I then went to Brother Antônio asking him that if he could get hold of the Indian to do so and to sell him and send the proceeds of the sale to my wife, Leonarda Peixoto, in the city of Braga. João Leite learned of this business, and being displeased with the action of his father-in-law, offered me, in place of my Indian, a boy named Estevão Mascaste Francez whom I immediately accepted because we needed more people to paddle the canoes. The captain spoke out saying that since we had gone and left him we would die in those rivers and forests and it would be better to kill us than to let us perish in those waters. I do not doubt that he wanted to inherit our Indians as he had done with those of our other companions.

We made two canoes, and I gave my horse to Brother Luiz, as his had died, so that he would say masses for me to Our Lady of Safe Journeys. We headed downstream where there was plenty of fish as well as good hunting. We spent a week's good journey and came upon the bar of another river which flowed in from the right hand, from Portuguese territory, every bit as large as the one on which we were paddling. We passed that bar and after four more days we caught sight of another bar of a smaller river that came from the right side also. Always seeking the north, which was the direction of our river, in another fifteen or twenty days we came upon a larger river that came from the left side in which we found many rafts made of vines, which was evidence that Indians were near. We pushed on, and after five or six days, we caught sight of some stone reefs and not a few rapids, which we passed near the right bank steering the canoes among the rocks but not with such caution that one did not avoid striking against a rock, and the canoe broke in two in the middle, and we lost two baskets with clothes, gold, silver, pans, guns, maps, hooks, cord, and other essential articles necessary for the back country. Among these, understandably, sank a package of lead weighing about sixty pounds, while another package of about the same weight was saved, as well as a small barrel of powder that came bobbing to the surface. We were able to rescue three of the eight guns we brought but all the rest was lost.

This danger past, we went in the other canoe to investigate the left bank below the rapids where the river made a backwash, with an excellent beach. On it we killed two wild pigs which served us as provisions for the trip, and we made another new canoe with three axes and two adzes, which we also had saved, our hands shedding blood because of the very hard wood we used. We spent days working on it, shaded by the trees of that forest, and since we lost the hooks and lines we were unable to fish and we made use of the palm cabbage of the Acrocomia palms, which after skinning and cutting into small pieces, we dried on the fire. After it was dry, we beat it on a stone, and we ate it in a mush using as a pan or pot a small alloy basin which we also had saved. The canoe finished, we continued our course and after three days we ran into a fallen tree along the edge of the river. We beached the canoes to search for some monkeys to eat to satisfy our great hunger, when we discovered the settlement of some Indians little more than one or two gunshots away. The settlement was large and had more than thirty or forty round huts. Having sighted this, we returned at once to embark; we fled with everyone paddling to escape being discovered by them. We went about four or five leagues downstream before stopping to sleep, constructing shelters in the forests on the left side where we found some palm cabbage. So great was the persecution of the bats that night that we slept little and it was very troublesome to free ourselves from them. By now we were naked and the minute we closed our eyes they bit into us to draw blood so that we awoke covered with blood, which caused us to leave that camp site much earlier than we normally would have.

From here we paddled downstream to where we came across a marmalade box genip whose fruit sustained us for two days. After we finished that fruit, our hunger was so great that we ate the seeds. But these affected us in such an adverse way that we thought ourselves dead and, using some small sticks, we aided nature in evicting the poison. We delayed at this point four or five days which we spent in search of some game to eat, and in order to get some fish we made a fine fishhook from the crossguard of a sword hilt, which we cut with the adze and sharpened with a stone. Using as a line a little wire, we pulled out quite a few fish. The fish were large, plentiful, and excellent and as abundant as in the sea. Here we also killed many saki monkeys, and roasted they served us as a new supply of food for the journey. We moved on downstream, and after some days the other canoe broke against a rock at the edge of a rushing current. Here we lost everything and since I did not know how to swim, I grabbed hold of the broken canoe and then taking firm hold on a vine I pulled myself up onto a rock reef. Something worse happened to one of my Indians who was pulled along by the rapids for more than two or three gunshots, and after we thought him to be dead, we found him seated on a large rock formation, at least a quarter of a league in length, which was in the middle of the river. Here we also lost our precious fishhook which a large and beautiful fish robbed from us and so we remained only with palm cabbage and the marmalade box genip—and these only when we could find them.

At this stop we repaired the canoe, and continuing downstream for two weeks, we were forced each night to sleep stretched out on the sands of the many islands in the river, also fearful of the innumerable Indians. What is worse, we could not fire a single shot to kill something to satisfy our hunger, which was not little. Here we saw various bars of other small rivers that from one or the other side flowed into the river on which we traveled. After passing these, we discovered, some leagues farther on, the bar of a great river which flowed from the right side. We slept that night between two bars. Leaving the following morning, we followed the shore of the river on the right side. The river here had an extraordinary width. We came upon a grove of babaçú palms and three Indians near the beach. One of my companions grabbed his gun, fired at one of them and wounded him. He also wounded the other Indians, who gave such screams and made such a horrible racket that it seemed to us as if Hell itself had opened up at that spot. We sought to avoid an attack, so we immediately crossed the river, fleeing while it was still possible. Here we feared to be lost again because the waves and tides were such, on crossing the current, that we very much feared they would submerge us. We arrived at an island very tired out and nearly dead. We pulled the canoes up on the sand at one point and then went to hide ourselves elsewhere so that if the Indians came looking for us they would not see us.

That danger over, we spent two days traveling without any sustenance other than the small coconuts and some palm cabbage which the palm trees provided us. Then we faced a new danger. We crashed against a rock reef in the middle of the river. The canoe in which I rode seemed lost because as it came off the rocks it was sucked into a whirlpool where, after seventeen or eighteen turns which the force of the water gave it, it spun free. The other had better luck and was thrown up against the shore. But everything came out all right. We slept that night on the shore of the same river next to a forest, very hungry and under a heavy rain that lasted all night. After two days of travel we killed a tapir that was so weak that it waited for the shot which killed it, and we ate it badly roasted. That night we found the trail of whites, which of course filled us with new courage. We saw a river, entering on the left side. Afterwards we learned it was the Araguaia because we were navigating the Tocantins. We followed the path because it ran along the edge of the river and from there we floated for three days among eight islands and we were perplexed because we could not locate the channel that we should follow. We searched for land, and we wanted to beach our canoes on some rocks near it but we could not because the water was so shallow.

We spent four days there searching for some palm cabbage or game, which was scarce, and, as our hunger increased, I sent my mulatto out to kill something to eat. He returned empty handed but with the certainty of having found a real path belonging to a white. I grabbed my gun and, nude as I was, I followed that path accompanied only by the Paulista, and less than four leagues away we caught sight of a recently constructed mission of the Reverend Fathers of the Jesuit Company. Seeing us naked and with arms, one of the fathers immediately fled and spread the news that the Manas Indians were there. These also use firearms which they obtain by trading with the Dutch, and they are our enemies. The officer in charge, who was stationed among the fathers, came running with all his men, armed and beating on boxes. Also, the mission Indians came hurrying with their bows and arrows. We threw our weapons on the ground and clapped our hands as a sign of peace. The Reverend Father Marcos Coelho, the superior of the mission, came to speak with us at once; and seeing that we were Portuguese, he took us with him, with extraordinary happiness and love; and when he heard us recount what we had endured, he could not hold back his tears. As soon as he learned that we had more companions, he ordered some of his Indians to go look for them in one of the canoes. When they arrived, we were received with three joyous clangs, caused by striking a piece of iron with a stone, because the small chapel had no other bell.

In this first and affectionate lodging, we began to satisfy our hunger. There was no lack of beans and fish, and as everything was seasoned, our stomachs did not stop reacting to it for a long time. This pleasantness lasted only two weeks because at the end of that time the officer in charge, Domingos Portella de Mello, sent us on to Pará, a journey of twenty days. When we arrived at Pará Governor João da Maia de Gama learned of it, and he came down to the port to see us. Hearing us tell about the tragic events of the trip, he would not believe us. He intended to arrest us until we could prove whether or not the Indians that we brought with us were ours or were fugitives from the same expedition from which we had deserted. I answered him that I had catechized the Indians and that, if catechized they confessed they were not ours, he could punish us; and notwithstanding the misery in which he saw us because we were all naked with our skin clinging to our bones, he left us to stay on the same beach and canoe port without resolving anything and with no more sustenance and shelter than the chips of wood and tree bark of the royal boatyard could give us.

However, immediately the following morning, private citizens of the town, the Reverend Canon João de Mello and others, made up for the unkind behavior of their Governor by coming to find us on the beach of the boatyard. Taking pity upon the miserable condition in which they found us, they took us to their homes. I went to the home of the Reverend Canon João de Mello; José Alves went to the home of Manoel de Góes with his brother; Manoel d'Oliveira went with João de Souza, a native of Basto, and João da Matta went with João de Silva, a native of Guimarães. After some months in Pará I fell ill of a fever that threatened to take my life, and my condition was so badly degenerated by malaria that I was anointed. I remained sick for eight months and during that time two of my slaves died, one of bubo and the mulatto of a poison that a Tapuya Indian gave him. Thus I embarked for Maranhão with only two. Of these I still keep one because it was necessary to sell one in order to buy two horses to carry me to Minas Gerais. I spent, on the road, just under ten months, and from the time we left the great Fearless until God brought us to Pará, four months and eleven days.

I recall that before we arrived at the whirlpool, when we fled from the Indians about whom I spoke above, because the river was so wide and we were nearly dead of exhaustion, we tied the two canoes together and let them drift. Everyone slept except me. Fearful and cautious, I kept vigil all night, and it paid off because, hearing a roar farther ahead in the same river, I woke up the men shouting that we were nearing a waterfall and for that reason we put in at an island. As soon as it was dawn, we saw the danger we escaped at night, because the waterfall was horrible and so high that it measured 500 palms and it fell among large rocks that made it even more formidable and with so many waves, mist, and splashing that it appeared like an inferno. We passed by it on the rocks and pushed the canoes through the channel. They came out below the falls, full of water and with holes. We took them from the water and mended them as best we could. We continued on our way. These are, Reverend Sir, the works, miseries, and the great advantages that I got out of the new mines of Goiás, etc.

Minas Gerais—Passagem das Congonhas, August 25, 1734
JOSÉ PEIXOTO DA SILVA

❁

16. Expansion to the South: New Roads and New Pastures*

After expanding first into the north and then into the interior, the Luso-Brazilians moved southward. As Lisbon came to realize the importance of the Rio da Prata network as a primary means of communication with the interior of the continent, a determined effort was made to win control of the northern bank of that river. In 1680, the Portuguese founded Colônia do Sacramento directly across the estuary from the Spanish town of Buenos Aires. That new outpost was not only the farthest extension southward of Portuguese

....

* Translated from a document printed in the *Revista do Instituto Histórico e Geográphico Brazileiro*, LXIX, Part I (1908), 255-259.

America but also a sharp challenge to Madrid. Rivalry between the two Iberian nations for control of the Prata added to the importance of South Brazil in Portuguese colonial policy with the consequence that the governments, both in Rio de Janeiro and in Lisbon, encouraged the opening and peopling of the south. Thanks to excellent climate and soil, the region soon became a thriving center for livestock raising. The document printed below tells of the increase in cattle-raising in the area and of the opening of roads for the dual purpose of supplying the distant outposts and of facilitating the marketing of the livestock.

You asked me for information about the new road which I opened through the wilderness to the town of Curitiba, the advantages which will result from it, and also its drawbacks. I would be able to carry out this task better if I had with me a map which I made of that road and gave to His Excellency, the Count of Sarzedas, Governor and Captain-General of the Captaincy of S. Paulo, but without it I will do the best I can from memory, certain that your generosity will excuse my errors.

It is well known that for lack of livestock, principally horses, it has not been possible to take full advantage of the great and rich treasures which Divine Providence has blessed and enriched the vast domains owned by His Majesty in this America and that his vassals have had to spend a disproportionate amount of their funds for the few animals there are because of their high value.

In an effort to remedy this situation, Antônio da Silva Caldeira Pimentel, who was governor of S. Paulo, decided to open a road so that by means of it cattle and horses from those interior pastures could be brought into S. Paulo and Minas Gerais for the benefit of the vassals and the increase of the Royal Treasury of His Majesty.

Opposed to this project were various inhabitants of the islands of Santos, of Paranaguá, and of Curitiba, as were the inhabitants of the town of Laguna and of Santa Catarina. These latter opposed because they were living isolated, either because of their crimes or other such motives, as though in an independent kingdom with no obedience nor any fear of justice, and they were fearful that the opening of a new road would cause them to lose their liberties. The others opposed it because as owners of some small farms in the countryside around Curitiba they feared their land might decrease in value, and to avoid that they published some false information that the land was worthless; they also wanted to persuade us that since those lands bordered on Spanish-dominated villages we could be invaded by the Indians under Spanish control.

Despite all this opposition, General Antônio da Silva Caldeira decided to push ahead with his plan to penetrate the wilderness, beginning in Rio Grande de S. Pedro. For this task he dispatched Sergeant-Major Francisco de Souza e Faria, and he ordered that he be assisted with whatever aid he might need from the Royal Treasury, and he gave him ample orders so that the municipal governments and local militia authorities would assist with the manpower or whatever else that he might need from them.

At this time, I was in the new Colônia do Sacramento. When I received news of the project, I set out to see its progress; and upon arrival in the town of Laguna, I found the said Francisco de Souza with some followers. But he had been prevented from carrying out his orders because the leading militia officer of the town, either for the motives already mentioned or out of deference to the inhabitants of the towns of Santos, Paranaguá, and Curitiba with whom he was related, did not give his cooperation. He was having trouble particularly in recruiting workers whom he would hire during the day only to have them flee at night. Seeing him in this state, I took care to find a solution for him. First I helped to reconcile the said Francisco de Souza with the military authority to whom he was not speaking, and with good luck he became more cooperative and agreed to furnish the necessary workers in February of 1728.

Leaving him at this time, I returned to Colônia. I took care to gather a herd of horses and mules to travel over the new road, and with the idea that I would find it finished, I left that town with a herd of 800 head, and I arrived at this port at the end of October of 1731. Moving northward I found various persons with a large number of animals ready to use the said road; and in spite of having certain news that the explorers had gone out, no one was emboldened to do so. They behaved thus because they said that the road badly needed to be improved and reconstructed. . . .

I went to Santos and S. Paulo to speak with General Antônio da Silva Caldeira and with new orders for an expedition from the said General to get additional reinforcements of men, arms, tools, and munitions which he liberally supplied me. Returning and following the routes of the first explorers, I began at the Araranguá River with a pilot and sixty-odd persons. During most of the expedition and until I left the mountains, I spent a great deal of time making improvements on the road, which necessitated much time because of the very dense woods, hills, rivers, streams, and swamps across which it was necessary to build bridges and footbridges.

With this work completed, I divided our group into three parts which between mine and the two others numbered nearly three thousand horses and one-hundred-and-thirty-odd persons. On the way I set up camp and ordered a scouting party to examine the path of the first explorers; and seeing that in a short distance ahead it became exceedingly rough because it remained always in the mountains and because it was not the most direct route, I determined to find another which stuck more to the pasture lands. Fearing a long delay, I had the foresight of taking with me about 500 head of cattle which I ordered pastured in those fields, and in this way I continued my task which I concluded after spending about thirteen months on it. At times and in parts, I covered the same ground as the road or path of the first explorers. I arrived at the town of Curitiba leaving behind a road in good condition with footbridges, river canoes, and more than 300 bridges so that it now takes a man on foot only a month to cross what delayed me for thirteen.

The highlands present a pleasant sight with their expansive fields crisscrossed by many streams of crystalline waters flowing to the west and forming various wide rivers which doubtless merge into the great Rio da Prata. These highlands contain many kinds of wood, good forests, and a great many pines.

As soon as one reaches the highlands, he encounters cattle along the road as far as the cross called Tapes, because of one found there by the first explorers; but entering the interior one encounters a large number of the said cattle in the expansive fields which are shut in by the mountains; and in the far distance are the lands of villages operated by the Fathers of the Company of Jesus, and they are separated by a deep gorge in the mountains filled with a thick woods, and it is there the said Fathers a few years ago with much work and by force of muscle and ax opened a road to permit the first cattle to pass through which I know because I ordered two of my group, in whom I trust, to go examine it.

. . .

Nature shaped and created those lands into perfect pastures for the raising of livestock, and in addition to that, the area is extremely healthy. During all the time that I spent in that wilderness, there was not a single bloodletting nor did more than one person die, and he was ill before we entered that area. The fields are abundant in game to hunt, honey, and edible pine seed and very fertile for every kind of plant as I learned when I experimented in the fields of Coritibanos where I lingered for awhile.

Above all this area promises much wealth and not a little increase in the Treasure of His Majesty because the horses that were in my herd alone paid to the Treasury more than ten thousand cruzados. . . .

❁

17. The Treaty of Madrid*

The principal result of the bandeirante activity was to expand the boundaries of Portuguese America far beyond the arbitrary line of the Tordesilhas Treaty. In their search for Indian slaves and gold, the Luso-Brazilians had spilled over the confines of the east coast into the north, west, and south with no challenge except at Colônia. That expansion had been facilitated to a large extent by the union of the Iberian crowns between 1580 and 1640, when, to all intents and purposes, boundaries between Spain and Portugal in South America were ignored. As the eighteenth century progressed, the two monarchs resolved to recognize the obvious. They agreed to abandon old and unrealistic boundaries and to sign a new treaty recognizing the status quo. The Treaty of Madrid, signed in 1750, is one of the most important documents in Brazilian history, because it established in South America the principle and precedent of uti possidetis for solving frontier controversies. When borders were in doubt, the demarcation line was and would be drawn to favor the nation whose citizens effectively held the territory in question. Such a principle gave legal sanction to Portuguese control of the vast regions explored and protected by the bandeirantes west of the Tordesilhas lines. Later, Brazil would use the principle to definitively mark its nine-thousand-mile border. The line drawn as a result of the Treaty of Madrid was, in its general shape, remarkably similar to the present-day boundaries of Brazil.

....

* From *Statement Submitted by the United States of Brazil to the President of the United States of America as Arbitrator*, III (New York: The Knickerbocker Press, 1894), 3-8.

The Most Serene Kings of Portugal and Spain, wishing effectively to consolidate and make closer the sincere and cordial friendship they profess for each other, have considered that the means most conducive to the attainment of so salutary a purpose are to remove all pretexts and clear away all impediments that may in future impair it, and particularly such as may arise with reference to the Boundaries in America of the two Crowns, whose Conquests have advanced with uncertainty and doubt, *because, until now, the true Boundaries of those Dominions, or the position in which must be imagined the Divisional Line, which was to be the unalterable principle of the demarcation for both Crowns, have not been ascertained. And considering the invincible difficulties which would arise if this Line had to be marked with the requisite practical knowledge,* they have resolved to examine the reasons and uncertainties that may be urged by both parties, and, in view of them, to conclude an agreement to their mutual satisfaction and convenience.

On the part of the Crown of Portugal it was alleged that, inasmuch as it was to reckon the one hundred and eighty degrees of its demarcation from the Line to the East, the other one hundred and eighty to the West remaining for Spain; and while each one of the Nations was to make its discoveries and establish its Colonies within one hundred and eighty degrees of its demarcation; nevertheless it is found that, according to the most exact and recent observations of Astronomers and Geographers, beginning to count the degrees to the West of the said Line, the Spanish Dominion at the Asiatic extremity of the South Sea extends to many more degrees than the one hundred and eighty of its demarcation; and that consequently it has occupied a much larger space than any excess attributed to the Portuguese can amount to in that which perhaps they may have occupied in South America to the West of the same Line, and at the beginning of the Spanish demarcation.

It was also alleged that by the Deed of Sale with an agreement as to repurchase (com pacto *de retrovendendo*) entered into by the Attorneys of the two Crowns at Saragossa on the 22d of April, 1529, the Crown of Spain sold to the

Crown of Portugal all that by whatsoever means or right appertained to it to the West of another imaginary Meridian Line, through the Velas Islands,[1] situated in the South Sea, at a distance of 17° from Maluco,[2] with the declaration that if Spain allowed and did not prevent its subjects from navigating to the Westward of the said Line, then the agreement as to repurchase should at once be rescinded and become void; and that when any Spanish subjects, through ignorance or through necessity, should pass within the Line, and discover any islands or lands, whatever might be so discovered should belong to Portugal. That notwithstanding this convention, the Spaniards subsequently proceeded to discover the Philippines and, in fact, settled therein shortly before the union of the two Crowns, which took place in the year 1580, and on account of which the controversies between the two Nations caused by this contravention ceased; but when they had again separated, the conditions of the Deed of Saragossa gave rise to a new title by which Portugal may claim restitution of or equivalent for all that the Spaniards had occupied to the West of said Line, in violation of that which had been capitulated in the aforesaid Deed.

As to the Territory of the Northern bank of the River Plate, it was alleged that, because of the foundation of the Colônia do Sacramento, a controversy arose between the two Crowns, relative to Boundaries: that is to say, as to whether the lands upon which that fortress was built, were to the East or to the West of the Boundary Line agreed upon in Tordesilhas; and, while this question was being decided, a provisional Treaty was concluded at Lisbon on the 7th of May, 1681, by which it was agreed that the aforesaid fortress should remain in the possession of the Portuguese; and that they should have in common with the Spaniards the use and benefit of the lands in dispute. That by Article VI of the Treaty of peace, concluded at Utrecht between the two Crowns, on the 6th of February, 1715, His Catholic Majesty ceded all action and right he may have had to Colônia and

....

[1] Marianne or Ladrones Islands.
[2] Moluccas Islands.

its Territory, the Provisional Treaty being abolished by virtue of cession. That whereas by virtue of the same cession the whole of the disputed Territory was to be delivered to the Crown of Portugal, the Governor of Buenos-Ayres contrived to surrender only the fortress, saying that by Territory he only understood what was within cannon-shot of it, reserving to the Crown of Spain all the other lands in dispute, on which was afterwards founded the Fortress of Montevideo and other establishments: That this interpretation of the Governor of Buenos-Ayres was manifestly opposed to what had been agreed, it being evident that the Crown of Spain, by means of its own cession, could not be placed in a better position than that in which it was before, in regard to the same thing that it had ceded; and that both Nations, having by the Provisional Treaty been left in common possession and enjoyment of those Plains, there is no more violent interpretation than to suppose that, by means of the cession of His Catholic Majesty, they were vested exclusively in his Crown.

That inasmuch as that Territory belongs to Portugal by a title different from that of the Boundary Line defined at Tordesilhas (that is to say, by the agreement made in the Treaty of Utrecht, in which His Catholic Majesty ceded his right under the old demarcation), such Territory ought, independently of questions concerning that Line, to be entirely surrendered to Portugal, together with everything which might newly have been built upon it, as having been erected upon foreign soil. Lastly that, assuming that His Catholic Majesty had reserved the right of offering an equivalent, to the satisfaction of His Most Faithful Majesty, for the said Colônia and its Territory, nevertheless as many years had elapsed since the expiration of the terms fixed for this offer, every pretext or motive, even apparent, for delaying the cession of the same Territory has ceased to exist.

On the part of the Crown of Spain it was alleged that as a Line from North to South was to be imagined three hundred and seventy leagues West of the Cape Verde Islands, in accordance with the Treaty concluded at Tordesilhas on the 7th of June, 1494, all the land that might lie within the three hundred and seventy leagues from the said islands to the place where the Line ought to be laid down, belongs to Portugal, and nothing more in this direction; because the one hundred and eighty degrees of the demarcation of Spain must be reckoned thence Westward: and, although, because it is not stated from which of the Cape Verde Islands the three hundred and seventy leagues are to be reckoned, a doubt has arisen, and this point is of great interest, seeing that they are all situated East and West with a difference of four and a half degrees; it is certain also that, even if Spain yielded, and consented that the reckoning should begin from the most Westerly, which is named Santo Antão, the three hundred and seventy leagues would scarcely extend as far as the City of Pará, and other Colonies, or Portuguese Captaincies founded formerly on the coasts of Brazil; and as the Crown of Portugal has occupied the two banks of the River Amazonas, or Marañon, up as far as the mouth of the River Javarí, which flows into it by the Southern bank, it clearly follows that it has encroached upon the territory of the Spanish demarcation to the extent of the distance of the said City from the mouth of the said river, the same being the case in the interior of Brazil with regard to the advance inward made by this Crown to Cuyabá and Matto Grosso.

With regard to Colônia do Sacramento, it was alleged that, according to the most accurate Maps, the place at which the Line ought to be imagined does not reach by a long distance the mouth of the River Plate; and, consequently, the said Colônia with all its Territory lies to the West of it, and within the boundary of Spain, without prejudice to the new right under which the Crown of Portugal retains it by virtue of the Treaty of Utrecht, since restitution by an equivalent was stipulated therein; and although the Court of Spain offered the equivalent within the period prescribed by Article VII, that of Portugal did not accept it; on which account the period was extended, the equivalent being, as it was, proportionate; and the not having admitted it was more though the fault of Portugal than that of Spain.

These reasons having been seen and examined by the two Most Serene Monarchs with the replications that were made on both sides, proceeding with that good faith and sincerity which is so becoming in Princes so just, so friendly, and who are related, wishing to maintain their Subjects in peace and quietness, and recognizing the difficulties and doubts which in all time would complicate this controversy, if it had to be decided by means of the demarcation adjusted in Tordesilhas, both because it was not stated from which of the Cape Verde Islands the three hundred and seventy leagues was to be reckoned, and on account of the difficulty of determining on the coasts of South America the two points on the South and North from which the Line was to begin; on account, also, of the moral impossibility of establishing accurately through the center of the same America a Meridian Line; and, lastly, on account of many other almost insurmountable difficulties which would occur in the way of preserving without controversy or encroachment a demarcation regulated by Meridian Lines; and considering at the same time that the said difficulties were perhaps in the past the chief cause of the encroachments set out by both parties, and of the numerous conflicts which disturbed the peace of their Dominions; they have resolved to put an end to past and future disputes, and to forget and desist from all actions and rights that they may have by virtue of the said Treaties of Tordesilhas, Lisbon, Utrecht, and the Deed of Saragossa, or of any other grounds whatever which may influence them in the division of their Dominions by a Meridian Line; *and it is their will that for the future the same shall not be further considered, the Boundaries of the two Monarchies being reduced to those which are specified in the present Treaty, it being their desire that two purposes shall be carefully secured by it: The first, and principal one is that the Boundaries of the two Dominions shall be defined, taking as landmarks the best known spots, so that they may never be mistaken or give rise to disputes, such as the sources and courses of rivers, and the most remarkable mountains: The second, that each party shall remain in possession of that which it holds at the present time, with the exception of mutual cessions, which shall be mentioned in the proper place;* which cessions shall be carried out for mutual convenience, and in order that the Borders may be as little subject to controversy as possible.

18. The Omnipresent Fear of Slave Rebellion

When the Indian proved to be a recalcitrant or erratic worker, the Portuguese sought a new labor source, and it did not take them long to discover that the African slave was well suited to Brazil. From the mid-sixteenth century on, particularly after 1570, increasingly large numbers of slaves were imported from Africa until, before very long, the blacks outnumbered the whites. Not always docile, the Negro slave occasionally threatened the tranquillity of the colony. Escaping into the hinterlands from the towns and plantations, the fugitive slaves established their own settlements known as quilombos, the most famous and strongest of which was Palmares, which lasted throughout most of the seventeenth century in Alagoas. At other times, the slaves would revolt against their masters. The minority white population greatly feared those insurrections, and rumors of such uprisings periodically disturbed the peace of colonial society.

*

SIXTEENTH-CENTURY SLAVE REVOLT*

One of the earliest notices of a slave revolt comes from an English traveler at the end of the sixteenth century. His terse report appears below.

Out of Angola is said to bee yeerely shipped eight and twentie thousand slaves and there was a rebellion of slaves
....
* From Samuel Purchas, *Hakluytus Posthumus or His Pilgrims* IV (London: Wm. Stansley, 1625), 1243.

against their Masters, tenne thousand making a head and barracading themselves, but by the Portugals and Indians chased, and one or two thousand reduced.

*

WARNING OF A SLAVE REBELLION*

Colonial documents contain frequent reference to actual or feared Negro rebellions and illustrate the precautions the governors took to discourage and prevent such rebellions. An eighteenth-century memorandum to the king describes a plot in the south.

Presented herein to Your Majesty are two letters of April 20 and June 21 of last year [1719], written to you by the Count of Assumar, Dom Pedro d'Almeida, Governor and Captain-General of the Captaincy of São Paulo and the lands of Minas, in which he gives account to Your Majesty of the uprising which the Negroes intended to make in that land, trusting in their number and in the foolish confidence of their masters, who not only entrusted to them every type of arms but also winked at their insolence and crimes and of the means which he used in order to prevent the slaves from carrying out their intent and to free those inhabitants from such a threat; and also letters of the city officials of Villa Rica and São Joseph and of the people of São João de 'El Rey, written to Your Majesty on the same subject and declaring that the Negroes failed because of the great activity of the Count-Governor, who took all the measures expressed in these cited letters which, with this one, are presented in the royal presence of Your Majesty.

....

* Translated from "A Memorandum to the King," dated January 8, 1720, in Archivo do Estado de São Paulo, *Publicação Oficial de Documentos Interessantes para a Historia e Costumes de São Paulo,* LIII (São Paulo: Imprensa Oficial, 1931), 191-192. Printed by permission of the Archivo do Estado.

After having examined these letters the Crown Attorney responded that in accordance with the information given, the Governor had, with great energy and prudence, avoided a situation frought with servile malice, which, if it had taken place, certainly could have been the end of Minas and all the whites who live there, and it is for that reason that thanks are owed to him; and he should be ordered to pass sentence immediately, as their crimes merit it, on the guilty Negroes who have been captured and to take all necessary measures to apprehend the others who were involved in the plot. However, because the punishment now of some is not sufficient to repress the malice of the rest, it will be necessary to use other means to prevent in the future similar events so characteristic of the cunning of the Negroes, principally in Minas, where for every white there are more than twenty or thirty Negroes. It seems necessary to order by an Alvará in the form of a law that no Negro, slave or free, can use any offensive or defensive armament of any kind or material, neither may he carry it nor may he keep it in his dwelling and should he do so he will incur the death penalty, which will be in effect even when he is accompanying his master, except at day and along the road when the master can take two or three slaves armed only with swords; and this is in order not only to avoid the encouragement of the Negroes to similar insolence but also the great robberies and crimes which they commit. . . .

*

PRECAUTIONS AGAINST
NEGRO SLAVE REBELLIONS*

A letter written by the Governor of Pernambuco on August 3, 1814 illustrates conditions in the north at this time and

....

* Translated from a letter of the Governor of Pernambuco, in Gilberto Freyre, *Nordeste* (Rio de Janeiro: José Olympio, 1937), pp. 227-283. Printed by permission of the publisher.

shows precautions which governors took to discourage and prevent slave rebellions.

My Lord—On the 27th of May [of 1814] a rumor was spread in this town [Recife] that the blacks were planning an uprising for the Feast of the Holy Ghost, although the proofs of this did not stand up under examination. So great was the fear caused by rumors of similar events in Bahia and so much did they ring in the ears of the slaves that I could not fail to take some measures to quiet these fears and to let the slaves themselves know the prompt punishment they would have if they attempted such a thing.

On the same day, the 27th, I ordered the soldiers of the militia troops to take over all guard duties so that the regular line regiment, which remained under arms in the barracks, would be free for special duty. I ordered the artillery regiment to march from Olinda in the quiet of the night between the 28th and 29th so that at dawn they appeared in formation in the Praça do Carmo. I ordered those two regiments to remain under arms throughout the three holy days and sent strong patrols into all the suburbs and neighboring districts. I ordered searches made in some houses under suspicion. The result of all these precautions was exactly as I had hoped, which is to say, the greatest peace and quiet after a period of fear and the greatest respect and not a little fright among the slaves in spite of recommendations I made that no violence be practiced against them.

❈

19. Pombal's Advice on How Best to Govern Brazil*

The Marquis of Pombal, who governed the Portuguese Empire from 1750 to 1777, first as the foreign minister and later as the prime minister of the weak José I, belonged to that group of eighteenth-century rulers known as the benevolent despots. In previous diplomatic missions to European courts, Pombal had assimilated many ideas about foreign governments and their operation, and he reflected those ideas in his action and thought. Following the mercantilist philosophies of the age, he manifested a deep interest in Portugal's largest and richest colony, Brazil, and sought to encourage its well-being as a necessary measure for Portuguese economic growth. As one of his many appointments, he named his brother as captain-general of Maranhão and then sent him a lengthy letter of political advice. In that intriguing document, the Marquis set forth his political philosophy, most of it wise and worthy of the efficient and energetic prime minister. He had never visited Brazil, but obviously he had formulated definite ideas about how it should be governed and how this differed from governing Portugal. Have care in Brazil, he cautioned, "because that country increases in everyone the spirit of ambition and the relaxation of virtues." Codified in this letter is Pombal's philosophy for the good government of colonial Brazil.

After having informed yourself about the territory you are to govern, its climate, products, and fruits, the best way to get

....
* Translated from *A Moral Como Base de Organização* (Rio de Janeiro, 1936).

there and the most comfortable means of travel, it seems just to me that you should also instruct yourself about the kind of people you will govern and the best way to rule and conduct yourself in order to avoid any of the difficulties which befall those who must learn by experience and who, when they find themselves in command, err unintentionally while trying to do right. The people you will govern are obedient and loyal to the King, his generals and ministers. As such, it is certain they will appreciate a prudent, affable, modest, and courteous governor.

You should govern with justice and peace because both of those virtues increase the public well-being. Whoever believes that fear rather than kindness makes his subjects obey is deluding himself because good sense teaches that all forced obedience creates violence, whereas voluntary obedience guarantees security.

The Captains-General assume the high power of the King and thereby have a dual role. Knowledge of this should make you an example of predicate virtues so that your subjects will not see the shadow of the copy belying the brilliance of the original which is pure and perfect. Through you they all will know that the King is merciful and that he sent you as a father, not as a tyrant, which is precisely the example you see practiced by the Royal Minister. There will be cases in which you must be rigorous against your own will. It is precisely as we learn from the doctors: you cauterize the sore or cut off the arm in order to save a life. In the same manner, he who governs in order to save the health of the State threatened by a defective member must cut off that member to avoid contaminating the health of the other members. Weigh in the balance of reason your benevolence which diminishes neither the respect of authority nor the just severity of the laws, because this equilibrium is the art of a successful government. The authority conferred upon you by the King never must serve to avenge your passions; it is an abuse of power to use the sword of justice for other ends than for what it is intended.

I doubt if there is anyone who knows how to execute these virtues. However, make every effort to achieve those heroic and invincible goals. Maintain the respect of your territory for the authority of the King and punish anyone who attempts to lessen it. Learn how to disguise and forget your own personal injuries. Adulators are known neither by the clothes they wear nor the words they speak. Nearly all who hear them behave like King Ahab who only esteemed the prophets who spoke to him of those things which pleased him, and because Micah, on one occasion, told him unpleasant things, he immediately ordered him from his presence with hatred. Almost everyone who governs desires to be praised and always listens with pleasure to the eulogies made to him.

This type of man and of enemies are found everywhere, and you also will find them in your government. Get rid of them at once for they are moral poison. The Holy Scripture says that men who govern should have their ears covered with thorns so that when the adulators approach they will be injured and flee. In law, there is a crime which the jurists call stellionatus, a crime of trickery, whose etymology derives from a name for a type of lizard which does not kill with its venom but only stupefies its enemies causing various kinds of effects on their minds. Punish these "lizards" and refuse to give them attention so that you are left alone to work freely and they do not paralyse your senses or your mind. You are going to head a government so new that you are the fourth general to go there. Imitate the first one in all that you believe pleased the people and was useful to the King and to the State. Alter nothing by force or by violence but use careful discretion in correcting inveterate customs even though they be shocking. The princes themselves have great difficulty in this task. Tiberius never was able to eliminate the illicit and public games introduced by Augustus; Galba ruled a brief time because he wanted to correct the indecency of Nero; and Pertinax wore the crown little less than a year because he wanted to reform the lax military establishment of his predecessor Comodus.

However, when reason permits it and it is necessary to banish abuses and to destroy pernicious customs for the benefit of the King, justice, and common good, be prudent and moderate because your method will accomplish more than your power. That doctrine comes from Aristotle and those who followed it never repented. In any resolution which you undertake, observe these three rules: prudence for deliberation, skill to carry out, and perseverance to bring to a conclusion. Do not resolve hastily the questions of government so that you have to make corrections immediately; it is better to move more slowly in order to make decisions after mature reflexion than to decide suddenly only to repent of the decision shortly thereafter. When in doubt obtain information, ask questions, and speak with those who are well informed on the subject. I do not mean that you ought to subject yourself to everyone but that you listen and carry out what you consider to be best. The officials you take with you will be of your own choice and of greatest importance to you; they will love you or despise you, applaud you or speak against you. They are domestic enemies when disloyal and prized companions when loyal; if they are not as they ought to be, they tell outside what goes on inside and they say inside what outside nobody would dream about; and what is more, since they are considered as loyal and truthful, everyone pays attention to what they say, thus they are able to seriously harm with their lies the innocent in order to take private revenge. The general must select carefully the officials he takes with him, especially to America because that country increases in everyone the spirit of ambition and the relaxation of virtues, especially in cases of charity, the dislike of which opens the door to vices and evils. By the hand of your servants do not accept petitions or requests even from those about whom you have the best opinion in order to prevent under the guise of such a petition favoring the personal interests and intense desires of one of your trusted courtiers. The lie is always well dressed; the truth is naked because it is innocent. The lie, because it is malicious, needs to be adorned in order to appear beautiful and the eyes fall in love with what they see and the ears with what they hear; in such cases the confidence that you put in your servant and in the information he gives about the petition he supports can easily incline you to favor his side and thereby cause you to offend the purity of justice and your rectitude. To prevent that (because experience is the best way to be sure) I advise you to order made a small box with an opening on top in which petitions can be slipped. Put that box outside the palace and only you should keep the key to open it at night in order to give decisions in the morning directly to each person. Receive nothing from the hands of one of your officials but receive only directly the petitions or requests.

Excluding your hours of precious and natural rest give audiences every day and on every occasion to whomever wishes to speak with you.

From the first information received, never be certain, even when they are followed by tears and the cause justified with the blood of the very complainer, because even that mask itself could deceive you. As nature gave you two ears, one should be for the accuser and the other for the absent defender. Listen to the afflicted who complains, hurt and offended, console him, but don't give him your word which should be done through the minister or another official. With maturity and rectitude make a decision which you will not repent later. With this method you will avoid also many false complaints usually made by those who frequently request things because the administrator decides hurriedly and punishes after the first accusation. When this happens and they trick you, punish the informer and also the complainer even if considerable time has passed. This not only satisfies justice but gives you self-respect and satisfaction and also makes an example which prevents similar situations. Do not permit violences of the rich against the poor. Be the defender of the humble because ordinarily the powerful are proud and wish to destroy and belittle the humble. This recommendation comes from both divine and human laws. Because you are a faithful executor of both, as a good Catholic and a good vassal, in so behaving you fulfill your duties to God and King. Every State is composed of more poor and humble than rich and opulent. It is better that the majority of the people know you as their father and proclaim you the defender of mercy than that the minority think of you as the protector of their temerity and glorify your rigor. It does not matter if they fail to incite you to take part in their violences because the very ones who now complain, knowing the justice which you dispense, soon confess the truth because virtue in itself has the characteristic of being recognized by the very ones who persecute and dislike it. There are many cases which, meriting punishment, first of all have to be prudently reprehended with words either because of the quality of the person or because of the nature of the offense. This is the occasion when you must call the offender aside and talk with him alone without witnesses, reprimanding him and forcing him to correct himself by the secrecy of the proceedings. Then, if he abuses your counsel, he forces you to punish him publicly and severely as an example to the others. That reprehension must be full of gravity and moderate words because these instill in the offender a certain spirit of shame giving rise to a desire for correction and to a respect for you. Your authority on many occasions is more efficient by the moderation with which you reprehend than by the severity with which you punish. The way you select to act on these occasions harmonizes authority and obedience.

Never offend with words or actions any of your subjects who come to petition because the superior has for punishment jails, irons, and officials to obey him. Never injure with words because men, if they have honor, feel less the weights of irons and privation of liberty than ignominious words of offense, and if they are not men of honor, it is useless to show violence of language. He who gives vent to his passions is a slave of them and undermines his own authority.

In all moments of peril and passion show yourself superior and unalterable because these two attributes of prudence and valor assure your subjects. As leader, regard it as discreditable to show your power on the weakness of miserable petitioners. I know of only three divinities whom the ancient people showed with blindfolds, as proof they were not blind, but in that way they used to make and to adore them: Pluto, god of wealth; Cupid, god of love; and Astraea, goddess of justice. Deny reverence to similar divinities and never permit your people to raise temples and take vows to them through the

King's officials because prejudicial to him who governs are blind richness, blind love, and blind justice.

❧

20. The Secret Instructions of Viceroy Lavradio to His Successor*

Pombal accelerated a tendency already under way in the colonial administration of Brazil: centralization and increase of royal power. He abolished the last remaining hereditary captaincies, made the State of Maranhão a part of Brazil, and restricted the prerogatives of the municipalities. At the same time, in his efforts to make royal power absolute he increased the power of the viceroy, the king's chief representative in the New World. Between 1640 and 1718 three governorsgeneral, because of their high nobility, bore the title viceroy. After 1720 every head of government in Brazil carried that title. Curiously enough, there is no known act which officially raised Brazil to the status of a viceroyalty. After the colonial capital was moved to Rio de Janeiro in 1763, some wellknown viceroys governed Brazil. One of the most outstanding was Luiz de Almeida Portugal Soares Deça Alarcão Silva Mascarenhas, second Marquis of Lavradio, who served from 1769 to 1779. Interested in agriculture, he transplanted coffee from Pará to southern Brazil. He also set a worthy precedent by leaving a letter of instructions to his successor. That letter is a source of vital information for an understanding of Brazil in the late colonial period.

....
* From N. Andrew N. Cleven, *Readings in Hispanic American History* (Boston: Ginn and Co., 1927), pp. 348-363.

Although the brilliant acquirements and distinguished talents of your Excellency may easily recognize whatever is of most importance in this Captaincy, and though your penetration may discover whatever be immediately necessary, by your inquiries, without the aid of the following diffuse and incomplete narration; yet as there may be some particulars with which you might for a long time be unacquainted, and towards which your attention will be required, in order that your cares and judicious measures may remedy my errors; the love which I bear to the royal service, and the interest which I take in the good of this people and in the good of the State, induce me to lay before your Excellency a narration of the forces of this Captaincy,—of the state in which I found it,—of its interests,—of the system which I have followed,—of the character of its inhabitants, and lastly, of the state in which I deliver it over to your Excellency. And if this my narration do not satisfy all the curiosity of your Excellency, you will be pleased to excuse me on account of this document being original, *i.e.* that I am the first who give an account to my successor of the Government which I deliver to him; this ceremony never having been before attended with any other formality than that of reading the Patents, or "Cartas Regias," of their Majesties to the individuals appointed, and to those deposed. This was all the instruction which I myself received, and I was thus obliged to lose much time ere I could trace out a path in which I could travel with perspicuity.

.   .   .

I found the troops in good order as far as regards evolutions, and that they were well provided for, but I found the jurisdiction materially altered, since the Lieutenant-General had overstretched his authority. The Viceroys were dissatisfied, but they permitted his usurpations and vented their spleen only in complaints, for which he cared but little. He acted with asperity towards the troops and his officers, and carried into execution the regulations even in points wherein they are prejudicial in this country, both to the life of men and to the State. Now the season for exercise selected in

Europe on account of the coolness of the weather, is in America the hottest period of the year, and is also the rainy season, from which cause I found many sick, that many others had lost their lives, and that others again had thus contracted maladies which had disabled them for the service. He consented to no more marriages than were permitted by the terms of the regulations, and as the armed force comprehends a great number of people in this country, he thus checked the means which might concur to the augmentation of the State. This excess of jurisdiction on the part of the Lieutenant-General, the consequent discontent of the Viceroy, the severity with which the troops were treated, and their loss of life and health, had given rise to so much intrigue and partiality, that every thing was in the greatest confusion, and there were so many deserters, that from these various motives the regiments were much diminished.

. . .

That district[1] is a highly important one, and worthy of the particular attention of your Excellency; its immense plains are extremely fertile, and the sugar-cane and all kinds of vegetables flourish there. It has also much excellent timber, admirable balsams, oils, and gums, and many other precious drugs, with all of which commerce might be increased. It also possesses excellent mines of gold, which may be of great utility to the State when His Majesty shall be informed of their situation, and permit them to be worked by the people. It has many navigable rivers in which even now a good commerce is carried on. For many years it was the general asylum of all malefactors, thieves, and assassins, who sought refuge there, and were allowed so much liberty that they felt no actual subjection; but lived in idleness, cultivating no more than was necessary for their subsistence. It has been extremely difficult to reduce them to order. I found, however, that this had been facilitated by the Viceroys, my predecessors, and by following in their steps both commerce and agriculture have increased under my government, as your

....
[1] The district of Campos dos Goitacazes.

Excellency will see from the annexed relation of the Colonel of Militia; but as these people have had such a bad education, it is necessary for the present to avoid giving them any power or authority, which may fill them with vanity, and lead to disastrous consequences.

I have followed the system of conceding many grants of land to people of this Capital who go to settle there,—I have sent for many of the inhabitants here, that I might speak to them,—I have retained them here for some time, in order that they might be witnesses of a people living in a state of subjection, and that they might observe what respect and obedience is paid to the magistrates, and other individuals in authority; and during all the time that they have remained here I have made them feel their dependence as much as possible. Finally, when I have again sent them away, I have always rendered them some benefit, and they have thus been gradually civilized in such a manner that those horrible disorders, which were once a daily source of disquietude to the Governors of this Captaincy, have no longer existence.

The greatest care ought to be taken that no attorneys, public writers, or other people of unquiet spirits, go to establish themselves there, since as the people have had a bad education, no sooner do they hear any turbulent individuals flattering them, and inciting them to insolence, than they immediately forget their duty, and range themselves under his banners. In my time this occurred in the case of an Advocate, José Pereira, who appearing to me a pacific character, and in good circumstances, I made Judge relative to the grants of land. He, however, became the cause of such disorders, that even a revolt took place; in which, if I had not had recourse to extraordinary measures, the farms and establishments in progress there might have been utterly destroyed. I immediately sent for both this man and the individuals with whom he was in dispute; I threw them into a close prison, and treated them with the utmost severity, and with this proceeding intimidated the rest. Afterwards, on tranquillity being restored, I allowed them to return, in order that they might inform others how they had been treated, telling them at the same time, that in case of any further disturbances, I should make them responsible for every thing that occurred, so that they have henceforth taken the office of peacemakers, and quiet has been maintained.

I hope your Excellency will excuse me for having dilated on this head; but as I consider that district as one of the most important, I have deemed it requisite to do this, in order that your Excellency may be fully acquainted with its condition.

Of all these battalions, detachments were during the war sent to this Capital, and with these the fortresses were garrisoned. I also availed myself of this occasion to exercise the troops; and until they were perfected in their exercises, I continued this, and all the militia thus became qualified to serve efficiently in case of any attack. I ought also to inform your Excellency that I have had another still more cogent reason for bringing into the militia all the able-bodied men, and into the Ordenanças all such as are disabled; and this is to reduce these people in small divisions, under the command of respectable individuals appointed as their officers, and to keep these again in such subordination, that all may recognize the due authority of the person appointed by His Majesty to the government of this vast, prolific, and rich country, inhabited for the most part by people devoid of education, licentious in character, heterogeneous in caste, and unaccustomed to any subjection except to the Government and Magistrates. Unless, in the first instance, they be separated, and made to recognize other and more immediate superiors, who (though themselves the depositaries of the laws and orders of the Sovereign), give an example of obedience and respect, it is quite impossible to govern without disturbance.

Experience has shown this, since, in all the points where there has been neglect in reducing the people to this system, the disorders and tumults have been frequent, and not even the penalty of death has been able to diminish them; whereas, in all points where the system has been adopted, tranquillity has been maintained, disorders are less frequent, and the laws are more respected. I make these reflections, since your Excellency will find much opposition to the conservation of these corps. The Lieutenant-General has the greatest envy of them; for, without looking to their great utility, he is vexed to see men who are not soldiers in uniform, and desires to see a distinction made between their officers and those of the regular troops, without remembering that the former serve without remuneration. Many private individuals, also, who desire to live in liberty, and free from subjection, employ all the means in their power to throw off a yoke which is necessary for their own good.

· · ·

Having hitherto spoken to your Excellency relative to the situation and military forces of the Captaincy, I shall now proceed to treat of the political and civil body, the character of the people, and the system which I have followed. Your Excellency has the Court of Appeal, and the Magistrates composing it. Up to the present time its members have fulfilled their obligations in a distinguished manner, and I have had no complaints whatever of want of rectitude in their decisions. In this Capital there is also an Ouvidor[2] and a Juiz de Fora.[3] The Ouvidor, besides being of very limited capacity, has, by old age and ill health, been totally disqualified for the performance of the duties of his office. As he is not sufficiently strong to fulfil his obligations, he frequently employs Advocates to execute his task, and it has thus happened on several occasions that the same Advocate who has been employed by the defendant, has, on the other hand, acted as accuser, and subsequently passed sentence as Judge. The consequences of such proceedings must be clearly apparent to your Excellency, yet the whole is managed with so much art that it is almost impossible to authenticate the fact, since the Advocates signing law papers on the part of the Ouvidor, cause the papers of their clients to be signed by other Advocates, who thus earn a livelihood; and it is thus impossible either to prove or to rectify the irregularity. I however make

....

[2] A special magistrate [ed.].
[3] Circuit judge [ed.].

your Excellency acquainted with the circumstance, in order that you may adopt the measures which you deem the most expedient. The Juiz de Fora, at present here, bears a good character. A Judge for criminal causes is much wanted in this city, as your Excellency will afterwards see.

Some more Juizes de Fora are also necessary, and especially one for the district of Santo Antônio de Sá and the neighbourhood,—another for Campos dos Goitacazes,—another for the island of St. Catharine, and another for Rio Grande de San Pedro; it being necessary, before the nomination of these magistrates, that a scrupulous examination be instituted relative to their worth and talents. A knowledge of the laws and civil jurisprudence is not sufficient; they ought to be endowed with patriotism, and of a disposition which may give hope that they will endeavour to promote the prosperity and happiness of the people, both in appeasing their differences, animating their commerce and agriculture, and in opposing the sloth and erroneous prejudices which have led to the utmost indigence. The three Ouvidores required, viz., the one for this Capital, the one for the Captaincy of Espirito Santo and Campos, and the one for St. Catharine and Rio Grande, ought to be three active men who will carry through the beneficial measures already commenced by the Juizes de Fora of these districts. Without these magistrates, your Excellency will find it difficult to accomplish the augmentation and prosperity of this Captaincy. I have laboured nearly two years for this object; I have been tenacious, and I have not been checked by the doubts and difficulties which every instant presented themselves, yet as I have wanted support, I have done but little. In general the magistrates who come to this country (as far as my experience goes), think of nothing further than fulfilling the time for which they have been sent here, in order that they may afterwards claim promotion; and during the time of their residence, their only study is to accumulate all that they can, in order that on their return they may benefit their families. Not one of them speaks of the utility of which he has been, or of any useful establishment which he has aided: all bewail the misery and poverty of their districts, being moved to this compassion by the trifling revenue which they have drawn from their office.

As the salaries of these magistrates are small, their chief aim is not to retire, some with less property than others, and they seek to multiply their emoluments by litigation and discord, which they foment, and not only keep the people unquiet, but put them to heavy expenses, and divert them from their occupations, with the end of promoting their own vile interest and that of their subalterns, who are the principal concocters of these disorders. During nearly twelve years that I have governed in America, I never heard speak of a single Judge who endeavoured to reconcile litigants,—persuading them not to ruin themselves by continued and unjust pleas, and who did in this respect what is so often recommended in the laws themselves. I may also state that I never found any one useful establishment instituted by any of these magistrates, and having sent to several of them to obtain information on a matter of this kind, I found them so ignorant and unacquainted with all such topics, that I resolved never more to have any conferences with them. Being in the end convinced of these truths, and aware that I ought to interfere, I endeavoured on numberless occasions to become the mediator between contending parties, no matter whether poor or rich, labourers or merchants; I called them mutually into my presence and reconciled them, and others I induced to appoint arbitrators for the adjustment of their differences; and in this manner, in the shortest way, I endeavoured to cause them to live together quietly, and to prevent them from ruining each other. Certainly the magistrates complained that law-suits were fewer and that their places were worth less than before; but the people experienced the benefit; commerce and labour increased, and would have increased still more if the said Judges had not opposed my efforts by all the means in their power.

Unless your Excellency, in the absence of any further orders from his Majesty on this point, do not pursue the same system with myself, you may rely upon it, this Capital will be ruined in a very short time, since as soon as it is known that your Excellency will leave every thing to the judicial tribunals, new law-suits will arise every instant, many that are now regarded as at an end, will begin again; the Magistracy who can now accumulate little more than will suffice to pay their passage to the mother country, will again be enabled to enrich themselves as formerly, but the people will be ruined.

. . .

To avoid the recurrence of these abuses, I ordered that the coffer should be conveyed to the Mint, that the Treasurer should find sureties, that there should be certain days of payment, and that a code of regulations which I framed should be executed. Accordingly the state of the coffer is always known, individuals receive the amount of deposits immediately, and all loss is prevented. I gave in an account of all this to the Marquis de Pombal: and receiving no answer, I persisted in my decisions.

There was, moreover, in this city a terrible nuisance, occasioned by the Negroes arriving from the coast of Africa. As soon as they were disembarked they entered the city by the principal streets, though not only covered with filthy diseases, but naked, and being devoid of all instructions, they were in the habit of enacting the most disgusting scenes in the streets, before the houses where they were stationed. Respectable people could not appear with decency at the windows, and yet the abuse was permitted under pretext that the owners of the slaves were spared expense of rent by exposing them in the street by day, and bringing them into their dwellings by night. This disorderly proceedings, it cost me a great deal of trouble to obviate, and nothing but the most extreme constancy enabled me to succeed.

My resolution was, that on slaves being disembarked in the Customhouse, they should again be sent in boats to the Valongo (which is apart from all the rest of the city), and that they should there be deposited in stores, or warehouses. Also, I decided, that the purchasers should never enter with more than four or five naked slaves into the city, and that those bought for the province of Minas, or for the plantations, should be retained in the square of St. Domingos, where there was every convenience for the object, until they were taken away from the city.

I paid a great deal of attention to the execution of this order, and, although with difficulty, I caused it to be carried into effect, the health of the inhabitants of the city improved, the slaves themselves were more easily cured of their maladies, and to-day all acknowledge the beneficial result of what I have done. The slave-owners, nevertheless, do every thing in their power to bring affairs into their former train: —regarding their complaints, your Excellency will act as you think proper.

I have now spoken to your Excellency of the military, political, and civil state of this capital, and have now only to address you regarding the character of the people, the merchants, their commerce, and my system of government. The general character of the inhabitants of those parts of America with which I am acquainted, is that of indolence, humility, and obedience. They are sober in their habits, yet they have at the same time great vanity and hauteur; but these defects are easily subdued. They are robust, support labor well, and follow the commands they receive; yet, unless they be commanded, they often remain in a state of inaction, until they are reduced to the most extreme indigence. Yet these very individuals, who are by themselves very easy to govern, sometimes become unmanageable, and give a great deal of trouble, on account of the Europeans, who have their establishments here.

. . .

Those who are here regarded as the richest merchants, as, for instance, Braz Carneiro Leão, Manoel de Costa Cardozo, José Caetano Alvez, and some others, have acquired their riches by commissions, and the consignment of vessels. As these men are very active, and have generally disposed of the merchandize sent to them, on good terms, and been diligent in procuring cargoes for their vessels, they are in good repute in Europe, and have thus acquired their capital. Though, however, these men are both rich and honourable, I cannot regard their houses as commercial houses, since they themselves are ignorant of their profession, and of the most approved methods of bookkeeping. At present, since the establishment of a commercial school, some clerks have been found who have put their books in better order; but this is only in a few instances. As these men are simple commission agents, they cannot forward the commerce of the State; since they are bound by the orders of their constituents, and can ship nothing without instructions. The exports thus consist exclusively of commodities which have been known for years, and all others are neglected. The commission agents here will not send any new commodities, since they have no orders for them, and they are too timid to send them on their own account. Thus your Excellency will perceive that, for the augmentation of the commerce of this Captaincy, the establishment of companies with partners, both in Brazil and in Europe, is necessary, or a more scrutinizing policy on the part of the merchants of Europe. Otherwise, it is impossible that commerce should increase, and your Excellency will have the disgust of seeing many precious and available articles of export utterly neglected. It was always my system, on all these points, to consider that every thing relating to the felicity, comfort, defence, and protection of these people, was my charge, and that I had a jurisdiction to interfere in all the foregoing departments, and take such measures as I regarded most conducive to the above ends.

In the municipal chamber I allowed the President and the Aldermen to govern according to their attributes, I meanwhile paying attention to all irregularities, and writing from time to time to the chamber to remind its members of their obligations. These my determinations or hints were, however, always ordered to be executed in the name of the chamber. I always followed the system of taking no notice whatever of the murmurs of the people. I always endeavoured to ascertain, without their perceiving it, when they were really aggrieved, and when I considered that they were, I endeavoured, as though insensibly, to amend my own resolutions, but always remained constant in my designs, feigning myself ignorant of what was said. Often, under other pretexts, I gave the complainants an opportunity of speaking to me, and, after having conversed with them freely, without allowing them to suppose me aware of their complaints, I led to the topic which had excited them, and, after repeating the objections which might be urged against my plans, I proceeded to answer them in such a natural manner, that they became convinced that I was right, and, being disabused, they imagined that I had chosen them for my confidants, never suspecting my real motives. As the good of the people has ever been my chief object, I endeavoured by all the means possible to avoid all prejudice to them, and at the same time to benefit their credit and reputation.

. . .

From what I have here said, your Excellency will perceive that His Majesty ought to be immediately made aware of the want of means in this Captaincy, both for the payment of the old debt, and the annual expenses. The public expenses increase daily, and the voluntary subsidy, the voluntary revenue, and the revenue arising from the estates of the Jesuits have ceased. Other branches of the revenue, as those of the Chancellorship and the duties on wines, have diminished; and others, such as the contract for the whale-fishery, and for salt, which ought to have doubled, have been lately sold at only a slight advance. Unless, indeed, some measures be taken for the relief of the Captaincy, your Excellency must necessarily contract a further debt of from 200,000 to 300,000 cruzados annually, and thus contribute to cripple commerce, and to depress industry still further.

The culpable negligence of the Secretary of the Junta, João Carlos Correia de Lemos, in conjunction with the malice which at times induced him to revenge himself on those who have complained of his delays, has prevented me from being enabled to draw out a formal account of the matter, fit to be presented to his Majesty. It has, moreover, appeared to me, that the statement ought to be presented in the name of the Junta de Fazenda, on account of its being the tribunal entrusted with the administration of this object. Not only, however, has the above-mentioned Secretary prevented this being done, but, by his idleness and the confused manner in which he keeps his accounts, he has been more than a year and a half in drawing out the accounts of the expenditure, since the commencement of the war, of the revenue during this time, of what we owe, and of what we are owed by the other Captaincies, according to what they ought to remit us, in comformity with the royal orders. Indispensable as is all this, I could never cause him to do it.

From what I have had the honour to say to your Excellency, you must perceive that I could not adhere to any fixed system; yet my chief objects were the preservation of the people in tranquillity and obedience, the promotion of their good, the arousing them from idleness, and the promotion of the interests of His Majesty; and, although I could never do what I wished from a want of means, I succeeded to a certain extent. I promoted the tranquillity and obedience of the people by the means already indicated; I promoted their good by forcibly compelling them to plant those products which are chiefly necessary for subsistence, such as maize and pulse; I threatened to take away their lands from them, unless they cultivated them diligently; I compelled the Colonels of Militia to give in exact statements on this matter, and thus led to a great increase both of these productions and of sugar. I promoted the culture of rice, and induced various merchants to assist and animate the labourers planters; in consequence, this article, which it was a short time ago necessary to purchase in Europe, is now so abundant that it is exported. I also forcibly compelled them to plant a portion of indigo, which was a shrub which grew uselessly in the forests, and for which nobody cared; and at the same time while I obliged them to cultivate it, I caused others to prepare the plant, paying them, however, for the indigo when prepared. In this manner I gave a material impulse to the cultivation of a new branch of commerce; but as it was a product little known, the merchants were afraid to purchase it, and as they offered but very low prices to the cultivators, it again retrograded. I stated all this to the Court, and His Majesty was pleased to order the quality of the indigo to be examined and divided into three classes, on each of which there was to be an established price, and that the whole should be purchased by the royal Treasury at the established rates, and no private individuals permitted to purchase the article. This was accordingly done; but I found that the expense might often exceed the resources of the Treasury, and the payments to the cultivators might thus be delayed, and the culture retarded. I also recollected that when people are obliged to dispose of an article to the royal Treasury, at stipulated prices, they always feel irritated, from a belief that they could obtain more from private individuals, and this might also be an inducement to abandon its cultivation. On this account, I represented to His Majesty, that it appeared to me that it would be well for the royal Treasury to make purchases; but that I should also recommend the cultivators to be left at liberty to make the best bargains possible with private individuals. They would thus be guaranteed from loss, since, when no private purchasers were found, the royal Treasury would pay them at established prices. My anticipations were verified; for, as the royal Treasury was straitened for means, payments to the cultivators were often delayed, without my being aware of it. Some merchants also induced them to believe that they could give them higher prices, and the result was so much vexation, that more than thirty cultivators abandoned this branch of industry altogether, and others prepared to follow their example.

It appeared to me that, until I received an answer to my representation, I ought to permit some merchants to make purchases, not, however, permitting that this should be done without my consent. They thus immediately began to purchase at higher rates than the Treasury, and the cultivators were encouraged to proceed; but those who had abandoned the business did not return to it. The merchants sent the indigo which they had purchased to Lisbon; but as it there came into competition with a quantity found in some prize vessels taken from the Spaniards, the price fell very much, and a remunerating rate could no longer be given. Finally, the last resolution of the Court arrived, whereby His Majesty gave the cultivators permission either to dispose of it to whom they thought proper, or to export it on their own account, and appointed, also, certain stipulated prices to be paid for it at the royal Treasury. I published a proclamation to this effect, and stated, that henceforward all cultivators would be reimbursed without the slightest delay, and that I myself would provide funds for the object. The consequence was, that not only was a large quantity bought, but the merchants again began to buy, and the cultivators, in some instances, proceeded to export the article on their own account. It is only thus, that commerce and agriculture can be promoted in these dominions. Unless the Sovereign encourage and indemnify the cultivators, nothing can be done; but your Excellency must be aware that these succours, far from being prejudicial to the interests of His Majesty, on the contrary, contribute to an increase of revenue.

About the same period, an individual named João Opmam brought under my notice a plant called Guaxima, capable of making excellent cordage and cables. It appeared to me, that this might be of the greatest utility, and I resolved on commencing a series of experiments, which I have answered as well as could be anticipated. In the first instance, cables were made, but the plant was cut in the wrong season, and prepared by unskilful and ignorant individuals, and the cable-makers neither knew how to twist the thread nor to pitch it. I nevertheless caused some of them to be used in the vessels of the squadron, where they were found almost, if not quite as good, as those of hemp. I gave an account of this discovery to the Court, and, by order of His Majesty, some lengths of this rope were made for comparison with the cordage of Riga. It cannot, however, excite surprise that this cordage, the preparation of which was not understood, should have been found inferior to that of Riga, which is superior to all other qualities known, therefore, in order to make a fair comparison, I ordered a rope to be bought in one of the shops in the city, and the strength of it tried with one of Guaxima, and as your Excellency was present during the experiment, you will recollect what was the result. Previous to this, I had ordered the cultivation of the plant and had constructed a ropewalk. The cultivators of the plant I paid at so much an arroba, and charged João Opmam to receive it, and to pay them from funds furnished by the Royal Treasury. In the meantime I occupied him in making cordage for the public service, in which he has since been employed without any wages or other recompense. I have permitted him to make and sell cordage to private individuals; but as he is very poor, he requires further encouragement, or the establishment must be abandoned. In consequence of the experiments made with these ropes, and those of Riga, the Court has decided in favor of the latter; yet, in the absence of a total prohibition, I have continued to promote the cultivation and production of the former, considering that, even in case of its inferiority, it may answer for ordinary purposes and in small vessels. The culture of this plant does not interfere with that of hemp. I have endeavoured to establish hemp also, but I had difficulty in procuring the seed, which I at last obtained in a casual manner from a French vessel, and which I ordered to be sowed with great care. The birds destroyed the greater part of the crop, but some seed was retained, and I sent it to the island of St. Catharine to be planted. At the time when the Spaniards invaded that island there were hopes of a plentiful crop, but all my hopes were frustrated. Having, however, heard, after the restitution of the island, that some persons had had the curiosity to preserve the seed, I ordered them to plant it again, in hope of realizing my former plans. I ought to inform your Excellency, that not only are there excellent situations for these plantations on the island of St. Catharine, but also in Rio Grande, Campos dos Goitacazes, and some places in the vicinity of the city, such as Santa Cruz.

. . .

The good success of mulberry trees in America induced me to make a plantation of them, and with great exertion I obtained silk-worms from Europe, which have multiplied abundantly. Some silk has been made, but my efforts to hit upon the best plan of raising the worm have been in vain. As this country has a similar climate to Asia, where the silk-worm succeeds, I have written there for instructions as to its treatment, but have not yet received an answer. When it arrives it will be placed in the hands of your Excellency.

Francisco Xavier is at present entrusted with the mulberry plantation, and the care of the silk-worms, and from him all the information which your Excellency may require can be obtained.

From all the districts I have sent for timbers, oils, balsams, gums, and shrubs, which I have transmitted to the court, in order that their virtues might be ascertained, and commerce promoted. The Minister of State informed me that many have already been examined, and some excellent dyes have been found amongst them; but, ere they had written to me explicitly on this point, the news arrived of my having the felicity to be substituted by your Excellency, and I therefore suspended all my measures under the certainty that your Excellency would act much more judiciously than I could. Such are the particulars of several of the plans which I attempted to carry into execution.

My self-love does not blind me to the point of inducing me to defend all my resolutions as judicious; I did what I could, and what my limited talents permitted me, and I never omitted any labours which appeared likely to prevent my falling into error. Your Excellency will act with more discretion, and, by correcting my imperfections and mistakes, will bring about that felicity of the people which I have ever desired, and still desire.

. . .

In the last place, it is necessary that I speak to your Excellency regarding the conclusion of the treaty, which I ordered to be executed on receipt of the last orders from the Court. I named Jozé Marcelino as first Commissioner, and of this I informed the Spanish general. I named as Commissioner to take account of the prisoners, military stores, provisions and effects appertaining to His Majesty and his vassals, and taken by the Spaniards during the interim elapsing from the date of the Treaty of Paris in 1763 to the present time,—Lieutenant-Colonel Vicente Jozé de Velasco Molina, and as his substitute Major Pedro de Silva. I requested from the General of Buenos Ayres, a counter-nomination, but as it was his object to delay the conclusion of the treaty, although it is far from being disadvantageous to him, he has evinced much bad faith and insincerity, procrastinating as much as possible, yet pretending that the delay occasioned was much against his inclination, in the face of evidence to the contrary. This your Excellency will see evinced in despatches and papers of Velasco, and the replies to them. With regard, however, to the demarcation of limits, nothing can be done at present from a want of means. In the first place, the instruments necessary for the operation are wanting, and, secondly, geographers are wanting to be divided and sub-divided into different companies. Many doubts will necessarily arise on account of the incorrectness of maps, and the formation of establishments in the interior will be necessary for the sustenance of the individuals employed. Your Excellency will perceive that I was devoid of all the necessary and indispensable means for the object: all that I could do was to nominate Jozé Marcelino as my first Commissioner, which nomination I made rather to satisfy the Spaniards in appearance, than with the idea of availing myself of his services. His pride and his incapacity alone unfit him for any office wherein sincerity is required, and his interference could lead only to continual doubts, discord, and embarrassment. Engineers and instruments are also wanting, and I was supplied only with orders from the Government. The opinion of Francisco João Rocio regarding the demarcation appears to me extremely correct, and I should recommend both him and the Colonel Rafael Pinto Bandeira to be employed on occasion of the demarcation. The latter is in fact so well versed in the geography of the country, that he may be said to have the map of it in his head. By means of these two men, the Court may be assured that all doubts will be resolved, while unless they be employed, difficulties will arise, time and money will be thrown away, and our sincerity will be distrusted.

What I have had the honour of repeating to your Excellency in the foregoing document, is what appears to me most essential regarding the present state of the Government, and regarding also what I have done. All my errors your Excellency will amend, with that wisdom and prudence which is characteristic of your distinguished talents, and thus will the people under your charge be enabled to enjoy all the good fortune possible, and your Excellency all the glory which I desire.

May God guard your Excellency.

[Signed] MARQUIS DE LAVRADIO

Rio de Janeiro,
19th of June, 1779.

❀

21. Observations on Life in Minas Gerais During the Gold Mining Era*

To the casual observer, Minas Gerais in the eighteenth century was a center of fabled wealth. Its very name conjured up visions of gold and diamonds. More realistically, Minas Gerais was a trouble spot—in every sense of the term. A burgeoning population interested in mining and not farming created a dire food shortage in which agricultural products sold at outlandish prices. As adventurers from all over the empire rushed in, lawlessness became a way of life. Corruption among venal governmental officials was commonplace. Commenting on the unhappy state of affairs in 1780, José João Teixeira Coelho, who had spent eleven years in that captaincy in the service of three governors, wrote an "Instruction for the Government of the Captaincy of Minas Gerais," which was a sober portrayal of some aspects of life in that El Dorado during the gold mining era.

....

* Translated from the *Revista do Instituto Histórico e Geográphico do Brazil*, XV, No. 3 (1852), 375-377, 382-383, 454-459.

The Poverty of the Miners

Without means and burdened with debt, the miners cannot undertake costly projects; in the majority of cases, because of their poverty, they are content to be simple prospectors. They know that in some places on their lands rich lodes and veins of gold lie hidden. However, because its excavation requires investments beyond their abilities, they show no enthusiasm to carry out projects for which they do not have the capital. They know that the banks and bed of the stream of Carmo contain much gold, but as this cannot be obtained without great expenditure, which one miner, and even many, cannot afford, the gold remains untouched.

At other places, because there is no one able to control the waterfalls, drain the deep water, or dig away hills, there exists the same inability to get at the natural resources. The presence of hostile Indians along other rivers likewise prevents gold mining. Lately along the Rio das Velhas many projects have been abandoned because the miners did not have enough equipment to encourage them to carry on, and they frequently failed to complete their work during the dry season so that when the rains fell the swollen streams washed away equipment and the deposits being searched for gold.

If some miners own the necessary number of slaves for mining along the river banks, they divert part of that number for other tasks because they show no talent as prospectors. They are able to get a small quantity of gold with which to pay the necessary expenses, but they become discouraged because the return is so small and do not fully pursue their vocation.

Other miners, having just enough Negroes for the mining of gold use some of them to work in the fields which lessens the production of gold, and so they extract less gold than they might if all the Negroes were at work looking for gold.

Lack of Negroes, Monopoly of Them, and Taxes on Them

There is a severe shortage of slaves in the captaincy of Minas Gerais because there is no systematic method of obtaining them along the African coast and because in Rio de Janeiro there is a monopoly over the slave trade.

In 1779, when I was in Rio de Janeiro, two shiploads of Negroes arrived in the port, and immediately a group of merchants bought the entire cargo.

These merchants, as they own all the Negroes, are arbiters of their price, and the miners who are poor and find the Negroes expensive do not buy as many as they need. For that reason they never are able to run their mining operation at full capacity.

There is no doubt that a miner with fifty slaves and a yearly production of 1,000 oitavas[1] would be able to double his production with one hundred slaves and the same thing would happen proportionally with the other miners. A more systematic exportation of slaves from Africa and an abolition of the monopoly in order to reduce the price of slaves are matters which deserve particular attention.

There is no doubt that slaves are cheaper than they were in former times. Even so, they are expensive because the mining industry no longer enjoys the same prosperity it did in the past. The easy gold has been removed, and now it is necessary to work harder in more difficult places to excavate less gold.

The taxes on slaves are excessive because in addition to what they charge in Africa, it is still necessary to pay the following: in Rio de Janeiro each Negro on landing, 4$500 réis;[2] for documents and transactions, 500; on crossing the Parahyba and Parahybuna Rivers, 160; and to the soldiers that guard them, 40; for each one shipped beyond the Parahybuna, 640; as some of the slaves are detained because of sickness and do not proceed with their group, it is necessary to pay an additional 640; and to register their entrance into the province is another 3$000 réis.

In addition to these charges, in Rio de Janeiro it is neces-

....

[1] An *oitava* equals 3.586 grams.
[2] The basic monetary unit is the *real* (plural réis). 1,000 réis is expressed as 1$000 and is called a *milreis*. The value of the milreis has varied considerably over the years [ed.].

sary to pay to the secretary of the police 40 réis for each Negro. There have been differences in this practice over the last decades. At first it was required to pay 40 réis for each passport which might include one person or many if they were a family group. Later the Viceroy Conde da Cunha suspended those payments. During the succeeding administration once again a charge of 40 réis a passport was made, but four or five years later it became necessary to pay 40 réis per person no matter whether they were alone or a part of a family. The practice of paying for each Negro is current today.

For more than twenty years a subsidy of 4$800 was paid for every Negro but that subsidy has ended.

All these taxes on Negroes, as well as the other reasons given, raise the price of slaves and make it difficult for the miners to buy as many as they need. None of the miners has a sufficient number. This is a constant and known fact to which I can attest because I have visited the principal mining regions of Villa Rica, Sabará, and Rio das Mortes.

It is calculated that each year about four thousand Negroes enter Minas Gerais. Subtracting from that number the slaves needed for household and field services there remains but a handful to work in mining, and by these calculations alone it is possible to see that the mines are underworked.

Poor Mining Methods

Governor Antônio de Albuquerque Coelho de Carvalho in a letter written to His Majesty on August 7, 1711, spoke of the necessity of establishing regulations for gold mining and of using the knowledge of science to increase production. His recommendations have not been implemented and the miners go about their work according to their own caprices. Not one single engineer came to Minas Gerais to direct the mining operations. The miners learn from experience, but they are far from perfect because they follow no principles.

For this reason they have dug mines which are useless and invested large sums with no return.

The mistake of mining on the top of the hill prior to excavating the gold at the foot of the hill is incomprehensible. Those lower sites became blocked with the dirt from the top of the hill, and the gold which existed in the lower sites remains forever buried beneath the earth where it cannot be reached.

It is amazing that the government created superintendents of agriculture for various regions of America and never appointed superintendents of gold mining to regulate the mines and the methods of their exploitation. This is a result of not informing His Majesty or his ministry of the aforementioned chaos.

These superintendents should be men with practical mining experience and given to such pursuits. The simple study of the laws of the Realm or of Roman law is not sufficient to make a superintendent of gold mining a useful man for a task which requires other knowledge.

If the miners of Rio das Velhas did not excavate on their own whims and if they were prohibited from working the mines without a minimum number of slaves, many of the mines would not fail to produce because of the lack of resources of the owners. Necessity would cause them to band together voluntarily to form one mining company capable of solving the problems which individually they could not solve, but there is no one in Minas Gerais who has jurisdiction to regulate the mining industry and to order others to work in it.

The results of all this are errors very prejudicial to public interests. Much of the gold is not extracted from the mines and many rich sites are covered up by other diggings.

The Lack of Police in the Captaincy of Minas Gerais and Some Injustices Which Need Prompt Remedy

The lack of police in the captaincy of Minas Gerais disturbs order there. The majority of the inhabitants of this captaincy either have come directly from Europe or are born of Europeans. They arrive here excited and with the hope of advancing their fortunes. The majority of them were either criminals or persons who at home had no more than what they earned with their hoe or by the offices they held. These men, who in Portugal were the scum of the masses and the despair of the elite, come to this enormous land of freedom to make themselves insolent and to play the role of nobles.

Governor Antônio de Albuquerque Coelho de Carvalho already made this complaint in the letter he wrote to His Majesty on August 7, 1711. And what would he say if he could see the conditions in Minas Gerais today?

What sort of education can men of that kind give to their children? What virtues do they have which serve as examples for their own children? All of them refer to themselves as distinguished men and for that reason they deprecate work, living in idleness and thereby depriving the State of hundreds of workers.

In all the captaincy of Minas Gerais there is not one white man nor one white woman who wants to work, for they persuade themselves that to labor is to compete with the slaves. In such a way hundreds of male and female slaves must work at domestic tasks and abandon work in the mines or panning gold.

This presumption and idleness of the whites is being transferred to the mulattoes and Negroes because once they are freed they do not want to work anymore, and as necessity obliges them to look for sustenance by illicit means both the men and women take part in the vices characteristic of their different sexes.

Those mulattoes who are not total idlers find employment as musicians of whom there are so many in the captaincy of Minas Gerais that certainly they exceed the number in all Portugal. But what good is such an overabundance of musicians to the State?

The protectors of orphans,[3] following in every respect the pernicious practices already described, take no care to hire out and to apprentice the orphans in their districts, as they are required to do by law. They only take care to get hold of the gold which might belong to some of those orphans for their own coffers by using various tricks such as the testi-

....
[3] Juiz dos orfãos [ed.].

mony of third persons that the money is being spent for the upkeep of the orphans.

The Count of Valladares attempted to remedy these deep-rooted evils, but the lack of jurisdiction diminished his great zeal for the conservation and improvement of the captaincy.

The governor, who has a patriotic spirit and who wants to fulfil his obligations, ought to report these wrongs to His Majesty so that he could put a halt to these acts prejudicial to both the royal interests and those of the people.

I shall speak now of those judges who have jurisdiction over the property of the dead and those absent from the captaincy of Minas Gerais.[4] This is a subject which demands considerable discussion but I shall be brief and limit myself to pointing out only the most notable abuses of these judges.

The justices of the peace of the juridical districts of Minas Gerais serve as purveyors of the dead and absent in virtue of the authority granted to them by the Conscience Board.[5] The rules by which they govern are incomplete and the orders that have been decreed to make up for that lack are infinite and some contradictory.

This contradiction and diversity of orders causes some judges to use one rule sometimes and another at other times according to the case. The people feel the vexations of rapid legal action which is unfavorable to them, and being ignorant of the law they do not know that there also exist rules favorable to their side of the case.

The decisions of the High Court of Rio de Janeiro, which have been handed down in these matters, are famous and do little honor to the purveyors.

The poverty-stricken masses have no resources to dispute the jurisdiction of those justices when they are told that they will not receive custody of the inheritance. Even if they would appeal the decisions, the appeals are received only on the basis of restoration, and the sequestration of the goods of the inheritance proceeds pending a judgment on the competence of the judge.

....

[4] Juizos dos defuntos e ausentes [ed.].
[5] Mesa da Consciência [ed.].

The executors of a will or the administrators of inheritances are obliged in this manner to make compromises with the treasurers handling the property of the absent, giving to them certain means or certain sums necessary to disentangle the inheritances.

. . .

The Count of Vallardares wanted to stop these injustices. Such action, prompted by the extortions of the judges in charge of the affairs of those absent, is authorized by the clamors of the people. In one particular case, the Count knew perfectly well that the inheritance of the Franças of Congonhas do Campo was extremely important, and while it wasted away in custody by order of the judge, one of the heirs had to go around begging alms, which I saw with my own eyes, at the same time that his goods were in the hands of the treasurer because of a corrupt bribe.

I must mention another famous case which I witnessed. A keen-witted Negro slave was imprisoned in Mariana. He belonged to João da Silva Coura, an inhabitant in the vicinity of that city. He ended up in the court of the absent as an unclaimed property as it appeared that he belonged to no one. It was as if that slave were a cow or a beast or some animal that could not respond to questioning as provided by specific formalities of the law. But the Count of Vallardares learned of this matter after some time and he ordered that slave to be returned to his proper master who took him back into custody.

Besides this, the treasurers of the property of those absent from the captaincy have in their power for many months the slaves which form part of an inheritance, and they do not hesitate to make use of them in domestic service or they put them to work mining or send them into the forests for firewood and into the pastures for hay, both of which are sold for profit. On top of this it is necessary to pay for the food and clothing of the slaves held in custody.

As to the furniture passed on as an inheritance, those same treasurers make use of them to decorate their homes or for other purposes, and in this way the goods deteriorate.

Those same treasurers, when they go with the secretaries of the courts to make inventories of the goods of the deceased, describe the furniture of greatest size and least importance and they do not mention the valuable pieces. This is an easy theft abetted by the purveyors who do not visit the homes of the dead at once prior to ordering an inventory of their goods.

There is yet another method by which the treasurers and the other officials with authority rob the goods left by the dead or the absent.

After making the inventories of the inheritances, it is necessary to appraise the goods described in it. The treasurers in collusion with the appraisers assign the lowest possible prices to the goods or furniture that they want for themselves. These evaluations are kept secret, and the bidders can get the goods only if they offer a price superior to the appraisal price, which the public does not know, and the bidders are never willing to offer very much. However, the treasurers who know which goods, farms, and furniture bear ridiculously low appraisals boldly bid a third more than the evaluated price and still buy cheaply. This is the reason for keeping the appraisals secret from the bidders.

.   .   .

As to the executors of wills one cannot count in the captaincy of Minas Gerais more than two who do not rob the inheritances in their care. I could make a catalogue of them because I know many of them but it is not necessary because these are known and public facts.

.   .   .

It is certain that there have been and are in this captaincy many honorable and disinterested judges, but not all of them are so. In order to avoid doubts and extortions it is best to issue some new regulations to prevent the evil and the ambitious from doing injustices and corrupting the good.

❦

22. Intellectual Achievements of Colonial Brazil

All was not conquest and discovery, sugar and gold. In the coastal cities and in some mining towns, an intellectual elite was contributing to the literary and scientific growth of the colony. While historians chronicled the developments of the New World, poets, too, flourished in the tropics. They read their compositions to one another or circulated them in manuscript form or, if they were lucky (or rich), had them published in Lisbon.

*

THE POETRY OF GREGÓRIO DE MATTOS

One of the foremost bards was the satirical Gregório de Mattos (1633-1696), who, not hesitating to incorporate words of Indian and African origin into his poems, was one of the first to write in the Brazilian vernacular. In the first poem, he uses his acrid pen to ridicule the Portuguese immigrant to the New World. The second poem reveals his more philosophical nature.

PORTUGUESE OF THE REALM*

Is there a miracle more strange—
Hear me well, you who have ears—
Than a man from Lisbon or Minho Province,
A Kingdom worthy, who in our midst appears?
Some lad who flees his father's wrath,

....

* From Samuel Putnam, *Marvelous Journey* (New York: Knopf, 1948), pp. 63-64. Reprinted by permission of the publisher.

A criminal who here must roam;
Or else he comes that he may eat,
For there is nothing to eat at home.
Barefoot, naked save for his rags—
Ah, there upon the wharf he springs;
And a few lice and filthy bags
Are all the capital he brings.

THE SUN IS BORN AND LASTS BUT A SINGLE DAY*

The sun is born and lasts but a single day;
Dark night follows upon the light;
Beauty dies amidst the gloomy shadows
And joy amid continued grief.

Why, then, if the sun must die, was it born?
Why, if light be beautiful, does it not endure?
How is beauty thus transfigured?
How does pleasure thus trust pain?

But let firmness be lacking in sun and light,
Let permanence flee beauty,
And in joy, let there be a note of sadness.

Let the world begin, at length, in ignorance;
For, whatever the boon,
It is by nature constant only in its inconstancy.

*

JOSÉ BASÍLIO DA GAMA'S EPIC POEM

O URUGUAI†

José Basílio da Gama (1740-1795) *represents the epic poets of the period. His O Uruguai sings of the heroism of*

....

* From Isaac Goldberg, *Brazilian Literature* (New York: Knopf, 1922), p. 45. Reprinted by permission of the publisher.
† From Samuel Putnam, *Marvelous Journey* (New York: Knopf, 1948), pp. 84-85. Reprinted by permission of the publisher.

the Indian struggling against the European. As the selection below, taken from that romantic epic, demonstrates, he belonged to a growing school of poets and writers who lavishly praised the beauty and virtues of Brazil. Thus, they were creating a feeling of nativism, the forerunner of patriotism.

How pleasing is the scene that meets the eye!
In the immensity of space that lies below,
A broad expanse of fields carved here and there
With tremulous rivulets—how very bright
The fountains and how crystalline the lakes,
Where the wanton wind sprinkles with morning dew
Light-lifting wings of birds that ride the air;
The gracious slopes, deep valleys, and the dense
And tufted groves, a verdant theater
Where one may well admire the lavishness
Nature has here produced. The patient earth
Shows its plow-torn bosom and the various plants
Join hands to form a long woven avenue
Down which the yearning gaze goes wandering, lost,
As through the shades of greenery from afar
White-gleaming huts are glimpsed with temple spires.

*

ROCHA PITTA'S HISTORY OF
PORTUGUESE AMERICA*

The colony's historians set down the heroic episodes of the New World. One of the best known early historians was Sebastião José da Rocha Pitta (1660-1739). In 1724 he became a member of the Brazilian Academy of the Forgotten in Bahia, the first of many literary and scientific societies established in imitation of the European academies. As his

....

* Translated from *História da América Portuguesa* (Bahia: Imprensa Económica, 1878), pp. 3-4, 47-50, 54-55, 453.

project, he wrote a History of Portuguese America, *which shows the same native love for Brazil that is so apparent in many poems by other writers of the same era. Some selections from the* History *appear below.*

Of the New World . . . Brazil comprises the major part. It is a vast region with favored terrain. On its soil grow all fruits; in its subsoil exist all treasures. Its mountains and coasts abound in pleasant air. Its fields give the most useful food; its mines, the finest gold; its tree trunks, the smoothest balsam; its seas, the most select amber. It is an admirable country, rich in every respect, where prodigiously profuse nature sacrifices herself in fertile produce for the opulence of the monarchy and the benefit of the world by shooting forth its sugarcane to be squeezed into nectar and by giving as its fruits ripe ambrosia, the liquor and meat the cultured populace offered to its false gods.

In no other region is the sky more serene or the dawn which greets the day more beautiful; the sun in no other hemisphere has such golden rays nor the nocturnal reflections more brilliance; the stars here are more benign and always joyous; the horizons where the sun rises and sets are always bright; the waters, whether in the fountains of the countryside or in the aqueducts of the city, are the purest anywhere; in short, Brazil, where the mighty rivers surge and flow, is an earthly paradise. A salubrious climate dominates, benign stars inspire, and gentle breezes blow making this land fertile and well populated by uncountable numbers of inhabitants even though the land lies beneath the Torrid Zone so discredited and regarded as uninhabitable by Aristotle, Pliny, and Cicero. . . . It is here that my happiness takes flight given wings by my love of my country and propelled into the air by its greatness.

To begin, we will describe the very powerful Province of Bahia, which, although it was not the first settled, derives its greatness from its dignity: it is the capital of the State. . . .

The site on which the City of S. Salvador, Bahia de Todos os Santos (two names, one given by the first discoverer and the other by the first Captain-General) was built became the capital of the State not only by choice but also because nature selected it as the superior position in Brazil, just as Constantinople is in [Turkey], Rome in Italy, Lisbon in Iberia. . . .

The sky which covers it is the gayest; the stars which illuminate it, the clearest; the climate which envelopes it, the most benevolent; the airs which refresh it, the purest; the fountains which water it, the most crystalline; the fields which embellish it, the most pleasant; it possesses delightful plants, leafy trees, healthy fruits, and temperate seasons. . . .

The city with its prolonged shape extends along a great plain elevated above the sea. The city rises above the sea ports below, which are connected to it by wide streets. It has two gates, one at the south and the other at the north, near which are located the famous churches of Nossa Senhora da Ajuda and Misericordia which has connected to it a magnificent retreat for women and the majestic Mother Church and close by are the great Archepiscopal Palace, the new church of S. Pedro da Irmandade dos Clerigos, the church, college and classrooms of the Company of Jesus and the sumptuous church and convent of S. Francisco.

The city is divided into six districts: Portas de S. Bento, Nossa Senhora da Ajuda, Praça, Terreiro, S. Francisco, and Portas do Carmo. In addition there are others, but they are outside of the walls which we mentioned. Two public plazas increase the beauty of the city. The Plaza of the Palace is 162 feet square, containing 26,244 square feet of area. Along one side is the majestic Palace, home of the Captains-General; across from it is the Treasury; on the left side is the City Hall and the jail; on the right side is the High Court. Six handsome streets connect it with all parts of the city.

The second plaza, known as Terreiro de Jesus, is 350 feet wide and 228 feet long, comprising an area of 79,800 square feet. It is dominated by a church belonging to the college of the Fathers of the Company of Jesus, from which the square received its name, and on all sides it is embellished with attractive buildings which make it such a pleasant sight. Seven streets connect it to all the districts of the city. The street of S. Francisco begins at the plaza and ends at the convent of the same name. It is 310 feet long and 74 feet wide with an area of 19,840 square feet. This street is lined with noble homes equal in height and construction with the finest homes to be found anywhere. . . .

Marvellous country homes and estates for commercial farming and recreation fill the countryside around the city. The abundant grass, the fruit trees, the gardens of herbs, flowers, and vegetables make this area not only a pleasant spectacle for the eyes but also a treat for all the senses. . . .

The area around the city is so well cultivated and populated that if we described it in detail we would need many pages and not a few numbers. Therefore, in order to reduce the narrative we will say only that there exist 150 sugar mills, some propelled by water, others by horses, producing each year 15 or 16,000 crates of sugar, each crate weighing many pounds. . . .

There are many factories to boil down and prepare the sugar, others to manufacture liquor from it. There are large areas planted in tobacco, various fields devoted to manioc, others for orchards and gardens. For all these crops there are overseers and experts whom the inhabitants hire to run the farms. The number of persons who inhabit this area, where the greater part of the nobility reside, the laborers, the slaves who work both in the fields and in the homes, exceed the number given as 100,000 souls admitted to confession because there are still others who are not admitted to the Sacraments.

The commerce which results from these valuable crops and from the arrival of ships from the ports of Portugal, other overseas conquests, and other provinces of Brazil to trade one product for another make this port a fair for all merchandise, an emporium of all riches, and it could be a port for all the goods of the world if the interests of the State and of the Monarchy did not prohibit trade and navigation with foreign nations for whom there is no lack of hospitality when their ships do arrive in this port in need of supplies, water, or repairs and ask for whatever is necessary to continue on their journey. However, the most severe penalties prohibit the inhabitants from buying their goods or selling them ours. In everything else pertaining to the preparation of their ships with water, refreshments, and supplies they are courteously and affectionately treated and served.

· · ·

Our Portuguese America (and principally the Province of Bahia), which in the production of resourceful sons can compete with Italy and Greece, never possessed Academies, established in all well ordered nations, which purify the subtleness of the geniuses and separate youthful vigor from an idleness contrary to the virtues and origin of all vices. The Viceroy could not permit in Brazil the lack of this touchstone to the inestimable gold of his talents, worth far more than all the gold of Minas Gerais. He created a very learned Academy which meets in his presence in the Palace. Persons of the highest rank and intelligence of Bahia have become members. Very erudite men have presided over it. They have treated wise and grave matters for which they wrote elegant and witty verses. The Academy continues its progress with the hope that under such high protection these works will reach the press as a reward for the toil involved.

· · ·

*

THE LITERARY SOCIETY OF
RIO DE JANEIRO*

The Literary Society of Rio de Janeiro, one of the most famous of the eighteenth-century Brazilian academies, was founded in 1786. The general interests of its members and the themes of its sessions are indicated in the report, printed
....

* Translated from the *Revista do Instituto Histórico e Geográphico Brasileiro*, XIV (1882), Part I, 69-76.

*below, of its president, José Joaquim de Atahide, given at the
celebration of the Society's first anniversary.*

Good fortune, which, despite my unworthiness, conferred on
me the duty of president of this society, now obliges me to
inform you of the accomplishments of this laudable organization. The constant experience of many centuries has
shown that from literary societies and academies has come
the greatest progress and resulted the major advances of science. Since these are some of the most inestimable treasures
of kingdoms and empires and the learned vassals a part of
the principal share of the glory of monarchies, who would
doubt that they are the most worthy objects of the attention
of the great princes?

With wise providence our well beloved monarch, whose
memory we nostalgically remember, reformed education and
clearly manifested to all the protection and encouragement
which learning received from him. His august daughter, who
now reigns, followed the example of her father.[1] How could
she be so virtuous, as she is universally recognized to be, if
her royal mind was not stimulated by the love of the sciences?

Now, in this present century, everyone has well understood the enlightenment and knowledge of such useful institutes, which is why our sovereign founded and protects the
Royal Academy of Sciences of Lisbon. In truth, gentlemen,
there is nothing more interesting to man than to understand
his body, what surrounds it, what constantly influences it,
the duty imposed on him by the state of society, the reason
he was born, the recognition that he owes to the author of
his being and preservation, if man is to blame the majority of
the time or if he is blameless for lack of necessary instruction
because he does not devote the diligence which he ought to
instructing himself in the things he ought most to know,
from where does he come that he does not know the advan-

....

[1] The speaker is referring to Maria I who reigned from 1777 to
1816 and her father, José I, 1750-1777 [ed.].

tages which are linked to the fulfilment of his obligations. What other object could he have in mind other than the public good and his own instruction?

You cannot doubt, gentlemen, that men are much more useful to their fellowmen when they fully understand their obligations. Therefore, it is necessary that they be educated and enlightened. What horrors have disappeared from the face of the earth as ignorance has been banished and as the instruction of science has clarified thinking. It is exactly as the ghosts which haunt the night disappear with the first rays of sunlight!

Man is born with passions which misdirect him and he needs instruction to guide himself. He is born ignorant and he needs education. It is not necessary to cast one's eyes toward the cultured nations; it is sufficient to see the difference between individuals and to note the great advantages which accrue from the cultivation of the arts and the application of science. Make a comparison in our own respect, and clearly you will see that the goal which this learned group proposes was not nor could not be other than instruction which results in public benefits. This was the just motive of its establishment and remains always the motivation of its literary efforts. I did not undertake to make this speech for any other reason than to give a summary of the interesting projects which this group has worked on in the brief space of less than one year. In it you will see with what zeal we have worked, what rewards we have reaped, what devotion to public good and the ardent desire of its advancement have animated us. It is the greatest proof that I can give in its favor. Listen to this.

First, before all else, desiring to sacrifice the best of our work to the greatest good of humanity, which is life and the preservation of good health, it was planned to deal with epidemics and endemic diseases of the country. Toward this end, we selected and took as our model the recommendable work of observations of Caligorne on epidemics and endemic diseases on the island of Minorca. However, since this work is found only in the English language, it was necessary to translate it, and the first part is now in Portuguese and we await momentarily the completion of the second part. Meanwhile, we are carrying out a physical and economic description or a political and natural history of our country. What a multiplicity of objectives such a work involves.

The geographical situation of the climate, the demarcation and limits of the land, whose history is being undertaken, waters, seas, rivers, the diversity of their sources, astronomical description of the meteors, temperature of the atmosphere, variety of the seasons, medical observations influenced by meteorology or at any rate by the varying seasons, a description of the three kingdoms of nature, etc. Obviously time is necessary to carry out such a project, and this is only the part relating to a physical description. I mentioned also an economic description which is no less complicated: a history of the peopling of the land, the governors, the courts, the politics, the laws, habits, and customs, agriculture, commerce, literature, military events, etc. The material will be spread out over a long period of time demanded by a work of this nature. Here are the reports that received consideration at our sessions.

On November 30th of last year, a report was read on the total eclipse of the moon which later was verified on February 3rd of this year. It noted, using our meridian, the exact and minute calculation of the eclipse and with the most accurate designs showed the diverse aspects of the moon at different phases of the eclipse, the beginning and end of the total and partial darkness, the beginning, middle, and end of the eclipse, the semi-diameter of the moon, the hourly movement, its latitude, its parallax, and a thousand other details which for the sake of brevity I omit but which confirm the well merited reputation of that science and of those professors who do honor to this society. After the holidays of December, January, and February, another was read in which an account was given of what had been observed during the time of the eclipse with such attention and minuteness that it noted the darkness or appearance down to the most detailed phases of this planet so that with good reason one could apply the fact or principle—*quam multa vident pictores in umbris, quae nos non videmos, quam multa quae nos fugiunt in cantu, exaudiunt in genere exercitati.*

Its merits are enhanced by the fact that these observations were made in a country where it never was attempted before or if it was it lies buried with the forgotten. What is more, the true longitude of Rio de Janeiro was established which until then was only doubtfully known. That is a great advantage for all nations whose ships should anchor here. What admiration mixed with confusion to see this difficulty conquered at last and to find defective the longitude made by the Abbot of Lacaille in 1751, as noted in the report. He was no less than a member of the Royal Academy of Science of Paris and came to this capital with precise orders to carry out the measurements. It will have to amend its book on the movement of the stars which is published each year in order to remove the error made by one of its astronomers and members. The advantages do not end here. Such observations will permit us to learn the longitude of Rio Grande, Mato Grosso, and Pará as the report points out. You can see the great usefulness which it has.

At this same time, another report was delivered on massaging, a method which, although simple, is efficient in many circumstances. Its author, after having related that it is a remedy recommended by Hippocrates and practiced by the most famous doctors of antiquity, recalls judiciously that its very simplicity caused us to forget it as a possible remedy. Proceeding in a good critical method, he gives his definition, makes his distinctions, cites many and good authorities, and presents a great many observations which confirm his success; he points out the different circumstances in which his method can be used and the best way of doing it; he shows how it is useful in humid countries, in rainy and wet climates, in swampy lands, on clients of flabby structure and on those whose languid circulation requires stimulation to make up for the defect of unhealthy air and to cure defective digestions and other things. He then proceeded to point out the advantages which his method could have for the inhabitants of this city and concluded by showing the caution one must observe. About such a simple remedy one could not say anything more or better.

Two more reports were given on March 22 of this year, one a physical consideration of the heat of the earth and the other on the interior fire of the earth.

In the first one, after having pondered the propagation of heat by means of the laws of refraction and reflection of the rays of the sun according to physical action, all explained and noted in such form that it made one realize the profound studies its author had made of this science, he went on to give account of the meteorological observations made in the month of February for a period of six successive years in which he showed by figures that this was the month of greatest heat in our country for the past six years and this has increased (with the exception of 1784 in which there was but a slight difference) the rains, thunderstorms, and evaporation. His work was well documented with the most careful attention to detail and he concluded with some intelligent remarks about the effects of heat on the human body.

In the other, on an internal fire in the earth, its author, after making reference to different opinions voiced on the subject, gave some reasons which caused him to disagree with the opinions of M. de Buffon about the formation of the universe. Since this point still is undecided in physics, he prudently concluded his report contenting himself with the glory of entering into this inquiry and indicating the great difficulties yet to be solved.

The society undertook the useful project of analyzing the waters of the Carioca River to understand by their contents the healthfulness or damage which could result from their use by the inhabitants of this city. In need of instruments for this project, a report was wisely and heedfully drawn up which showed the characteristics of the hydrometer or liquid-weigher, the care which should be employed with this instrument in order for the observations to be made with it to be exact. You must admire the prudence and sagacity of the report and the zeal evidenced in a search for the truth in this experiment. In the same report is found a drawing of the said instrument so well done that it faithfully shows the reasons for which it is constructed according to the laws of fluids.

Some of the members devoted themselves to analytical experiments of water which resulted in two excellent reports. In one of them, the author, having already written a short discourse on analysis by means of the senses, which for then seemed to him sufficient in order to be able to draw conclusions about ordinary water, saving perhaps the majority of experiments for the analysis of mineral water, reflected on the slight certainty of those who venture into new experiments. With what patience he carried out his project so worthy of praise without disturbing his laborious and busy duties as minister. Notice what nobleness animates those minds desirous of understanding the truth!

In the other, on the same subject, were reproduced many and diverse experiments made at different times by evaporation and the addition of various mixtures, all carried out so methodically and scrupulously that it reminded one of the work of Abby Resnel in the summary of the 4th canto of the Essay on the criticism of Pope—presumption is the characteristic of mediocre minds, doubt of oneself the characteristic of the elevated.

As you can see, it is the second part which I apply to the author of that report. Timidly and prudently he dares not to give his experiments as conclusive and reserves judgment for future inquiries.

Another report was presented by the same member on the method of making ink from the fruit of the annatto tree, in which, after having made some references to the usefulness which the French Americans have gotten from the cultivation of this seed, he describes the tree which produces it according to the system of Linnaeus and Adamson and he employs their method with the greatest possible perfection.

There were two more reports in which the dangers and benefits which accrue to the inhabitants of this capital from the use of sugarcane rum and spiritous liquors were examined in detail and the most efficient and appropriate means to combat the sickness which can result as a consequence of their use were discussed. The reports pointed out, first, what chemistry has shown in respect to liquors which result from spiritous fermentation. They discussed the most general doctrine and the most common language of all the doctors on the effects of those drinks and noted the diseases which have been observed to have their origin from such a cause. They indicated the remedies and desiring, if it were possible, to prevent the abuses of such drinks they pointed out the modifications which can be used under different circumstances and relative to the climate of the tropics.

I do not wish to exhaust your patience; from what I have already discussed you can well see the hopes which we ought to entertain for the future. Who can better employ his talents than in reports which might be of use to humanity? During such an elucidated century and under such a just and prudent government we can expect a great number of literary works.

The time will come when these fragments, which now are divided, will join together and unite in one meaningful body of knowledge: many separate truths, when they come to be a larger number, offer vividly to the spirit their correlations and their mutual dependence. The spirit which governs this society is a sincere love for truth; we enter into this undertaking because it represents to us the most conducive means to the object which excites us and it will be received with pleasure by all good citizens who love letters and are animated by the same sentiments.

The society keeps its door open to receive all good patriots who by means of cultivating the sciences and the arts seek to be useful to humanity. Yes, dear companions, redouble your efforts and if your diligence is not enough I ask that justice be done to your intentions. Your zeal for the public's happiness is pure and sincere. I pray to Heaven that our efforts make us worthy of the blessings which the happy reign of Her Majesty, may God grant her many years, and the wise and prudent government among us promise us and that among the monuments which announce to the future ages the facts of the present century there is a place for the Literary Society of Rio de Janeiro.

❄

23 . The Sentence of Tiradentes*

The first conspiracy against Portuguese rule took place in Minas Gerais toward the end of the eighteenth century. A group of the intellectual elite began to think in terms of Brazil's independence, and they discussed impractical plans to effect it. The conspirators were motivated partly by the ideas of the Enlightenment and partly by a resentment of the way the mother country drained off the mineral wealth of their captaincy and left them poor and backward. When word spread that Portugal planned to collect back taxes, the plotters redoubled their activity in the early months of 1789. The plans of these romantic and unrealistic poets never passed the hypothetical stage. All agreed that Brazil should be independent. Beyond that, they did not concur. Some were republicans, others monarchists; some advocated the abolition of slavery, others favored the institution. While they debated, an informer reported their meetings to the governor who promptly ordered their arrest. The trial in Rio de Janeiro dragged on throughout 1791, and the sentence was not handed down until April 18, 1792. Only one of the death sentences was carried out, that of the leader, Joaquim José da Silva Xavier, more picturesquely known by his profession, Tiradentes or "the Toothpuller." The principal result of the brutal execution was to create a martyr to Brazilian independence. Thereafter, Tiradentes acquired a more significant place in history than his impractical plans merited.

....

* Translated from Lúcio José dos Santos, A Inconfidência Mineira (São Paulo: Escolas Profissionaes do Lyceu Coração de Jesus, 1927), p. 615.

Therefore, they condemn the criminal Joaquim José da Silva Xavier, known as Tiradentes, formerly second lieutenant of the troops in Minas Gerais, to be paraded with hangman's noose and public proclamation through the public streets to the place of hanging, where he will be executed, and that after death his head will be cut off and taken to Villa Rica where in the most public place it will be fastened to a tall pole until consumed by time; his body will be divided into four quarters and fastened to poles along the road to Minas at Varginha and Sevolas, where the criminal carried on his infamous practices, and the rest at places of greatest population until consumed by time. They declare the criminal infamous and his sons and grandsons infamous and his goods confiscated and the house in which he lived in Villa Rica will be leveled and the ground salted so that nothing more can be built there; and if they do not belong to him, they will be appraised and the owner paid from the confiscated goods, and on that same spot will be placed a sign to preserve forever the infamy of this abominable criminal.

❦

24 . The Economic Complaints of the Brazilians

*

AZEREDO COUTINHO ON ECONOMIC REFORMS

José Joaquim da Cunha de Azeredo Coutinho was born in Brazil and became well acquainted with its economic problems by managing the family sugar plantations and visiting

*the gold fields of Minas Gerais. In 1775 he went to Coimbra
University, newly reformed by Pombal, for his advanced education. During his prolonged stay in Portugal, he wrote
three important essays on economics, influenced by the ideas
of François Quesnay and the French physiocrats, which organized and expressed many of the economic desires of the
Brazilians. His writing is particularly significant because he
applied the ideas as well as the methods of the thinking of
the Enlightenment to Brazilian economic problems. Azeredo Coutinho's most important essay,* An Essay on the
Commerce and Products of the Portuguese Colonies in
South America, *was first published in 1794. Reprinted below
are selections from this work.**

The salt trade being prohibited throughout Brazil, the exclusive privilege for this useful branch of commerce is farmed
out to one individual, who pays for it the sum of 48,000,000
of Réis, every year, into the Royal treasury. This farmer gets
annually from Brazil ninety-six millions of Réis, of which
forty-eight millions go to the queen's treasury, and an equal
sum remains for himself, his agents, and receivers, even after
deducting all the principal expenses of the salt, including
freight and carriage. But much more considerable are the
profits he draws from the interparts of those districts, where
the herds are more numerous, the demand for salt consequently greater, and the price of that article enhanced in
proportion to the expense of carriage, over the many mountains, which are there to be met with.

On account of the vast sum of money which is thus every
year drawn from Brazil, for the sole purpose of enriching the
individual, to whom the salt trade has been farmed out, all
the rest of the inhabitants of those countries are made losers;
at least their gain is materially prejudiced by the monopoly.

....

* From José Joaquim da Cunha de Azeredo Coutinho, *An Essay
on the Commerce and Products of the Portuguese Colonies in
South America, Especially the Brazils* (London, 1807), pp. 7-13,
118-121.

The whole commerce of Portugal, indeed, is made to forfeit, by this abuse, infinite emoluments and advantages, which would otherwise accrue to it, from a greater abundance of salt fish, butcher's meat, bacon, cheese, and butter, that would be preserved and brought to market. Thus the royal treasury, for the sake of the comparatively paltry consideration of forty-eight millions of Réis a year, robs itself of much larger sums, which the duties of these products would fetch, but for the factitious dearness of salt.

Unless flesh and fish can be salted or preserved, the marine of Portugal will never attain any great degree of importance; there will never be many cargoes for ships, never many seamen, never a nursery for their instruction. Thus the expense of freight will always be very high; sugar and all other colonial products, will consequently remain very dear; and the colonists will be deprived of a fair competition with foreigners, who bring the same products to the markets of Portugal, but can afford to sell them cheaper, as they can ship them at a much lower freight.

. . .

A single ship, with manufactured goods, from the mother country to Rio Grande, might, for instance, take on board all the wearing apparel, and other articles of luxury, requisite for the inhabitants of those happy plains. But it would be impossible for the same ship to take in at once, and convey from thence the amount of the value of her cargo; either in money—for there is none at all in those countries, nor can there be any, since there is no commerce—or in produce, as it would weigh infinitely heavier, and is by far lower, in price, than the goods coming from the mother country. A handkerchief, for instance, is sold for more, at Rio Grande, than a fat ox, and is of no weight at all, compared with the animal.

In order to carry back produce of equal value with the first cargo, the ship from the mother country would be obliged to return to the colonies, twice, or three times, in ballast, consequently with expenses exceeding the returns. The ship would thus always remain debtor, without being able to settle the account, or she would be otherwise forced to place the charges of freight, for two or three voyages, on the goods of a single voyage; which might fairly be said to be pulling up by the roots the commerce of the colonies, and, by the same inference, that of the mother country itself.

On the other hand, such articles might be exported to those colonies, as would equal, as nearly as possible, both in weight and value, the different sorts of colonial produce, which would be taken in return. The mother country has, I believe, no article better calculated for this purpose than salt. This alone can make up the cargo of a ship from the mother country, and procure her a freight from the colonies, on her passage home.

If the salt trade to Brazil were once made free, the super-abundance of that charming country would no longer be the prey of tigers, and that of its coasts the food of sea monsters. The fisherman, the herdsman, the husbandman, the merchant, would reciprocally lend a helping hand. They would, in concert, supply Portugal with meat, fish, bread, cheese, butter, and other necessaries. This trade would pour millions of additional revenue into the royal coffers. And Portugal would possess a mine of inexhaustible treasure, richer than the mines of Potosí.

. . .

Beside the various sorts of wood, useful in building ships, there are in Brazil several others. . . .

But owing to the high price of freight, and the many duties, which must be paid, on the importation of Brazilwood into Portugal, a great part of the value of those noble products are lost to the country from which they are drawn, or they are smuggled into the mother country, or left to spoil in the forests, in which they grow.

With regard to freight, its price must fall, the more commercial navigation increases; but the latter, too, as soon as the laborers are allowed the free sale of their wood, must gain additional vigor, in proportion as the abundance of products is multiplied. On the other hand, if the duties of importation be not taken off, Portugal will not be able to effect anything beneficial in the timber trade, or rather it will become prejudicial to the state, owing to the powerful competition of foreigners in the same branch of commerce.

The dearness of brazilwood, occasioned by these means, in Portugal, will facilitate the importation of foreign timber. This will, of course, give to the revenues of the country a blow doubly severe, by the wilful suppression, in the first place, of the produce of the country, and, in the second, by the money paid for the same articles to foreigners.

Foreign wood not only contains, for the most part, more resin, and is consequently more combustible, and more dangerous in fires, but is also less lasting than that of Brazil. The duties on the importation of this wood should, therefore, be taken off, for the purpose of getting a larger quantity of a commodity, so much better in quality, and so much less dangerous, where fires break out.

The suppression of the duties on all the importation of brazilwood cannot, at all, be deemed a loss to the royal treasury. Those who harbour such an idea, are, to the great prejudice of the public welfare, grossly mistaken.

. . .

*

COMPLAINTS OF THE
MERCHANT CLASS OF BAHIA*

A little over a decade after Coutinho's essay was published, the municipal government of Bahia, cognizant of the increasing economic dissatisfaction in the community, requested the leading citizens to suggest and codify desired economic improvements which should be made. In turn, the city officials promised to present the recommendations to the Portuguese government. The responses revealed the influence Adam Smith enjoyed among the colonial elite. One of the

....

* Translated from João Rodrigues Brites and others, *Cartas Económico-Políticas* (Bahia: Imprenta Oficial do Estado, 1924), pp. 27-28, 49, 78, 84-85.

most intelligent and cogent answers was made by João Rod-
rigues de Brito in a letter dated May 28,1807. Excerpts from
that letter are given below.

I have observed diverse causes, which, in my opinion, retard
the progress of agriculture in this country, and many of them
are easily remedied without diminishing the present state of
the royal income which must be respected. I will speak here
only of the principal reforms needed. As, according to the
best economists, everything that a government can do for the
good of agriculture falls under the chief headings of Liberties, Improvements, and Instruction, I will classify the
needed reforms in conformity with this division. I will speak
first of difficulties arising from the lack of Liberty for the
agricultural worker to employ his labor and his capital in the
manner he judges most suitable. Secondly, I will speak of
the inconveniences which come from the lack of proper Improvements which aid the exercise of that Liberty. By Improvements, I refer to roads, bridges, and other works and
institutions which by diminishing expenses and obstacles to
communication and transportation increase as a result the
profits of the farmer. Thirdly and lastly, I will mention the
difficulties which result from the lack of necessary Instructions to the farmers so that they can take advantage of those
Liberties and Improvements.

In order for the farmers to achieve the full liberty which
the well-being of agriculture demands, it is necessary for
them to have; 1) the liberty to grow whatever crops they
deem best, 2) the liberty to construct whatever works and
factories they judge necessary for the good of their crops, 3)
the liberty to sell in any place, by any means, and through
whatever agent they wish to choose without heavy taxes or
any bureaucracy, 4) the liberty to sell to those buyers who
offer the highest prices, and 5) the liberty to sell their products at any time when it best suits them. Unfortunately, the
farmers of this captaincy enjoy none of these liberties at the
present time.

. . .

The first thing that the government of any country ought to encourage is the construction and preservation of bridges, river ferries, roads, canals, footbridges, etc., for the transportation of the crops and consumers' articles of the farmer and ports, wharfs, and docks for their export and import.

These works are totally absent and we are reduced to those facilities which nature herself offers us or which the industry of some private individual at his own cost creates when some exclusive privilege does not impede him, as is happening at the Joanes River which has no bridge because a monopoly granted to a certain religious to let cattle swim across and to ferry men across on a raft. What a pity! What a shame! Right here in the environs of this populous city! Not only does the governor lack the duty of establishing ferries or building bridges but he makes obstacles to their creation. . . .

The Liberties and Improvements given to the farmers for the exercise of their industry will be of slight advantage if they are not instructed in the best methods of taking advantage of them.

. . .

In order to remedy the evils arising from the lack of instruction it is necessary to order that everyone of both sexes learn how to read, to write, and to count by establishing schools and a good system of studies and by honoring and encouraging those who distinguish themselves in studies, principally in economics which being the most important subject is the least known. . . . But all these beneficial instructions will amount to little and fail to spread human knowledge without the liberty to think freely and to publish those thoughts by all the means known, principally the press.

❀

25. The Royal Order
Opening the Ports*

The Napoleonic invasion of Portugal in late 1807 forced the Braganzas to flee their imperial capital, bag and baggage, to the distant New World colony. In early 1808, much to the delight of the colonists, the prince-regent, later João VI, and the royal family disembarked in Bahia prior to proceeding to Rio de Janeiro. It is the first and only example of a ruling sovereign transferring his residence from Europe to America. Attending to the petitions of his joyous subjects in the former colonial capital, João listened attentively to a request of the Governor of Bahia, the Count da Ponte, prompted by the brilliant Brazilian economist, José da Silva Lisboa, to throw open the ports to world trade and thereby end the rigorous Portuguese restrictions and monopolies on external trade. The prince-regent assented to the request in a royal order, which, according to historian Américo Jacobina Lacombe, "represents the economic independence of the colony." Certainly it marked the beginning of a new era in Brazilian economic history. In 1808, ninety foreign ships entered Brazilian harbors; in 1815, authorities registered the arrival of 217; and in 1820, the number had risen to 354.

Count da Ponte, Member of My Council, Governor, and Captain-General of Bahia. Friend. I, the Prince Regent, send you greetings as one whom I esteem.

Attending to the remonstrance which you sent to My

....

* Translated from Pinto de Aguiar, A Abertura dos Portos do Brasil (Bahia: Progresso, 1960) pp. 109-110.

Royal Person concerning the interruption and suspension of the commerce of this captaincy with the consequent grave prejudice it does to My Vassals and to My Royal Treasury because of the critical situation in Europe and wishing to give to that important matter prompt attention capable of remedying the ills it does, I am pleased to order provisionally and temporarily, until I formulate a general law which will effectively regulate the matter, the following:

First: In the Custom Houses of Brazil shall be admitted all and whatever produce, fabrics, and merchandise transported either in foreign ships of powers which are at peace and harmony with My Royal Crown or in the ships of My Vassals, by paying upon entrance a tariff of twenty-four percent, namely, twenty in direct duties and four in special gift duties as already established. The charges shall be regulated by a customs list or laws because up to now each one of the said Custom Houses has made its own regulations. Wines, liquors, and olive oil henceforth will be charged double duties. Second: Not only My Vassals but also the above mentioned foreigners can export to any ports which seem to benefit commerce and agriculture because I sincerely desire to encourage trade in all and whatever colonial produce and products with the exception of brazilwood or other products notably scarce. Produce leaving the country shall pay the same duties already established in the respective captaincies. Royal Letters and other Orders which until now prohibited trade between My Vassals and foreigners are suspended and without vigor. Execute all this with the zeal and activity I expect of you.

Bahia, January 28, 1808.

THE PRINCE.

❀

26. The Royal Order Revoking the Prohibition of Manufacturing*

For centuries, the government in Lisbon had forbidden manufacturing in the overseas possessions. In conformity with classic mercantilistic philosophy, the colonies were to supply the raw materials and the metropolis was to furnish the manufactured goods. Accordingly, Brazil's economic role had been to send mineral and tropical exports to Portugal. The consequence of that policy had been the encouragement of monoculture and large landholdings. In 1808, with Portugal occupied by the French, João found it necessary to reverse the traditional colonial policy and to give impetus to the establishment of manufacturing in Brazil.

I, the Prince Regent, make known to one and all: That desiring to promote and further the national wealth, and one of the sources of it being manufacturing and industry which multiply, improve, and give greater value to the provisions and products of Agriculture and the Arts and increase the population by giving work to many laborers and by furnishing means of subsistence to many of My Vassals, who, for lack of such means, would be left to the vices of idleness, and that wishing to remove all obstacles which might diminish or frustrate such advantageous benefits, I am pleased to abolish and revoke all and every prohibition which exists to this respect in the State of Brazil and in My Overseas Domains. Henceforth, it shall be legal for any of My Vassals in any area in which they live to establish any kind of manufacture, with-

....

* Translated from Pinto de Aguiar, *A Abertura dos Portos do Brasil* (Bahia: Progresso, 1960), pp. 111-112.

out any exception, to make goods in large or small quantities as best suits them. I do therefore annul the Royal Order of January 5, 1785 and any other laws or orders which contradict this decision without making individual and express mention of them. Therefore, I command the President of the Royal Council, Governors, Captains-General, and other Governors of the State of Brazil and of the Overseas Domains and all the Ministers of Justice and other persons to whom knowledge of this is important to carry out and to fulfill this My Royal Order and to disregard those laws which I have hereby revoked and annulled. Given in the Palace of Rio de Janeiro on

April 1, 1808.

THE PRINCE.

27. The Decree Elevating Brazil to a Kingdom*

During the thirteen-year residency of João VI in Rio de Janeiro, Brazil changed greatly. Established for the first time in the colony were naval and military academies, schools of medicine, printing presses, a botanical garden, a fine arts academy, a public library, and a bank. Textile factories were built and the iron and steel industries begun. Increased exports of sugar, coffee, cotton, tobacco, rice, hides, and hemp were sent to European ports. Remarkable internal progress urged the elevation of Brazil to a higher status than viceroyalty. External pressures also demanded such a promotion.

....

* From R. Walsh, *Notices of Brazil in 1828 and 1829*, II (Boston: Richardson, Lord, & Holbrook, 1831), p. 290.

The Congress of Vienna became particularly annoyed that the Braganzas insisted on living in a lowly and distant vice-royalty after Lisbon had long since been freed from the French. Talleyrand suggested that if João continued to remain in Brazil he at least ought to raise it to the status of a kingdom. For those internal and external reasons, the prince-regent elevated Brazil to a kingdom on December 16, 1815. It was then on an equal footing with Portugal. In effect, the king thenceforth reigned over a dual monarchy.

D. João, by the Grace of God, Prince Regent of Portugal and the Algarves, in Africa and Guinea, and of the Conquest, Navigation, and Commerce of Ethiopia, Arabia, Persia, and India, &c. make known to those to whom this present Letter of Law shall come, that there being constantly in my royal mind the most lively desire to cause to prosper those States which the Divine Providence has confided to my sovereign rule; and giving, at the same time, its due importance to the magnitude and locality of my domains in America, to the copiousness and variety of the precious elements of wealth which it contains; and knowing besides how advantageous to my faithful subjects in general will be a perfect union and identity between my kingdom of Portugal, the Algarves, and my dominions of Brazil, by raising them to that grade and political class, which, by the aforesaid proposition, they ought to aspire to, and in which my said dominions have been already considered by the plenipotentiaries of the powers which form the Congress at Vienna, also in the Treaty of Alliance concluded on the 8th of April in the current year, as in the final treaty of the same Congress; I am therefore minded, and it is my pleasure, to ordain as follows:

1st. That from the publication of this Letter of Law, the State of Brazil shall be elevated to the dignity, preeminence, and denomination of the Kingdom of Brazil. 2dly. That my kingdom of Portugal, the Algarves, and Brazil, shall form from henceforth one only and united kingdom, under the title of The United Kingdom of Portugal, Brazil, and the Algarves. 3dly. That for the titles inherent in the crown of

Portugal, and of which it has hitherto made use in all its public acts, the new title shall be substituted of Prince Regent of the United Kingdoms of Portugal, Brazil, and the Algarves, &c.

Given in the Palace of Rio de Janeiro, the 16th of December, 1815.

THE PRINCE
MARQUES DO AGUIAR.

❀

28. Instructions for the Guidance of the Prince Royal as Regent*

King João VI—he officially ascended the throne in 1816 following the death of his demented mother—made no secret of his affection for Brazil. Somehow he felt more at home in the tropics than he ever had in Europe, which was incomprehensible to those on the other side of the Atlantic. His Portuguese subjects and the English government clamored for his return to Lisbon. Yet he tarried. Making one excuse after another, he postponed his departure until he could do so no longer. In April of 1821, with many regrets, he took leave of the Kingdom of Brazil, the land he had done so much to transform. Young Prince Pedro, heir to the Braganza throne, remained behind as regent. Prior to embarking, João sent him the following instructions to guide his administration of Brazil.

....

* From *British and Foreign State Papers, 1820-1821* (London: J. Harrison, 1830), pp. 970-971.

The Prince Royal of the United Kingdom shall take the title of Prince Regent, and my Lieutenant, in the Provisional Government of the Kingdom of Brazil, with which he is to be charged.

This Government shall consist of the Conde dos Arcos, Minister and Secretary of State for the Interior of the Kingdom of Brazil, and for Foreign Affairs; the Conde da Louza, Dom Diogo de Menezes, Minister and Secretary of State for Finance; the Secretaries of State, *ad interim*, Camp Marshal, Carlos Frederico de Caula, for the War Department; and Major General of the Fleet, Manoel Antônio Farinha, for the Department of the Marine.

The Prince Royal shall form his decisions, in the Council composed of the two Ministers of State, and the two Secretaries of State (*ad interim*) and those decisions shall be registered by the Minister or Secretary of State, to whose Department the responsibility thereof shall belong.

The Prince Royal shall possess every power for the Administration of Justice, Finance, and internal Government; he may pardon Criminals who may have been capitally convicted, and commute punishments. He shall decide on all questions relating to the public Administration.

He shall appoint to all places in the Law, in the Courts of Justice, or in the Department of Finance, which are now or may become vacant, and to all Civil and Military Employments: the Persons named, by virtue of his Decree, shall enter upon the exercise or enjoyment of their places, offices, or employments, immediately after the Payment of the New Duties; although their respective Commissions require my Royal Signature, which is indispensable to Letters and Patents; for the prompt expedition whereof, the Prince shall not only be empowered to sign Alvarás,[1] by virtue of which such Letters shall be granted, but also to concede those dispensations, which, according to custom, are granted to the Possessors of such Letters.

He shall also appoint to all Benefices, whether with or without cure of souls, and to other Ecclesiastical Dignities,

....
[1] Royal decrees [ed.].

with the exception of Bishopricks; but he may propose to me, for the same, such Persons, as he may consider worthy of them.

He shall be empowered to declare War, offensive or defensive, against any Enemy which may attack the Kingdom of Brazil, should the circumstances be so urgent as to make the waiting for my Royal Orders a serious prejudice to my faithful Vassals of this Kingdom; and for the same reason, and under similar circumstances, he may conclude Provisional Treaties, or Truces, with the Enemies of the State.

Finally, The Prince is empowered to confer, as honourable favors, upon such Persons as he shall judge worthy of the distinction, the Badges of the three Military Orders, of Christ, St. Bento de Aviz, and St. Thiago da Espada; he may grant to them the immediate use of the Insignia, and the usual dispensations for their vows.

In the unforeseen and unhappy event of the death of the Prince Royal (which may God forbid), the Regency of the Kingdom of Brazil shall pass directly to the Princess Royal, his wife and my much loved and valued Daughter-in-Law, who shall govern the Kingdom, aided by a Council of Regency, composed of the Ministers of State, of the President of the Council of State, of the Chief Justice, and of the Secretaries of State (*ad interim*) for the Departments of War and Marine. The eldest Minister of State shall be President of this Council, and this Regency shall enjoy the same powers and authorities as those enjoyed by the Prince Royal. *Palace of Boa Vista, 22d April, 1821.*

With the Signature of His Majesty.

II

IMPERIAL PERIOD

❄

---

29. The Declaration of Brazilian Independence*

With lack of foresight, the Côrtes in Lisbon sought to reduce Brazil to its pre-Napoleonic status as a colony, to recall
Pedro, and to undo the progress of the preceding decade and
a half. The Brazilians would not tolerate such arrogance.
Under the able direction of his adviser, José Bonifácio de
Andrada, the prince began to sever the ties binding the two
kingdoms. On January 9, 1822, to the delight of a delegation
claiming to represent the people, he replied to an order of
the Côrtes to leave at once for Europe with the now historic
words, "I shall remain." On May 4th he decreed that no act
of the Côrtes was to have force in Brazil without his approval, and he accepted the title of Perpetual Defender of
Brazil nine days later. The climax to these and other events
came on September 7th of that year, when Pedro declared
Brazil's independence. No congress assembled; no military
junta deliberated; no crowds agitated. Unlike the declarations of independence of the rest of the nations of the hemisphere, the Brazilian separation was the result of the proclaimed wishes of a single man, Dom Pedro. As it happened,
the personable young prince was abreast of public sentiments

....

* Translated from F. Assis Cintra, *D. Pedro I e o Grito da Inde-
pendência* (São Paulo: Companhia Melhoramentos, 1921), pp.
211-213. Printed by permission of the publisher.

so that in his solitary act he was expressing the will of the majority. He chose to make this declaration of independence in the countryside after having received by special courier some distressing correspondence on the situation in Lisbon. He issued no decree; he drew up no solemn document. His declaration was verbal. Fortunately several of the courtiers who were in the royal party at the time set down in diaries or in letters their memories of that historic day on the banks of the Ypiranga River. Thanks to their afterthought, a description of events surrounding the Grito de Ypiranga, the Brazilian declaration of independence, has been preserved. Of the several accounts, the best written, the fullest, and seemingly the most accurate is a letter of Father Belchior Pinheiro de Oliveira, a confidant of the prince and an eyewitness to the Grito.

The Prince ordered me to read aloud the letters brought by Paulo Bregaro and Antônio Cordeiro. They consisted of the following: an instruction from the Côrtes, a letter from D. João, another from the Princess, another from José Bonifácio and still another from Chamberlain, the secret agent of the Prince. The Côrtes demanded the immediate return of the Prince and the imprisonment and trial of José Bonifácio; the Princess recommended prudence and asked the Prince to listen to the advice of his minister; José Bonifácio told the Prince that he must choose one of two roads to follow: leave immediately for Portugal and make himself the prisoner of the Côrtes, as was the situation of D. João VI, or remain and proclaim the independence of Brazil becoming either its Emperor or King; Chamberlain gave information that the party of D. Miguel, in Portugal, was victorious and that they spoke openly of the disinheritance of D. Pedro in favor of D. Miguel; D. João advised his son to obey the Portuguese law. D. Pedro, trembling with rage, grabbed the letters from my hands and crumpling them up threw them on the ground and stomped on them. He left them lying there, but I picked them up and kept them. Then, after buttoning up and arranging his uniform (he had just been to the edge of the stream of Ypiranga agonized by a painful attack of dysentery), he turned toward me and asked: "What now, Father Belchior?"

I quickly responded, "If your Highness does not declare himself King of Brazil, you will be made a prisoner of the Côrtes and perhaps disinherited by them. The only course is independence and separation."

Accompanied by me, Cordeiro, Bregaro, Carlota, and others, D. Pedro silently walked toward our horses at the side of the road. Suddenly he halted in the middle of the road and said to me, "Father Belchior, they asked for it and they will get it. The Côrtes is persecuting me and calling me an adolescent and a Brazilian. Well, now let them see their adolescent in action. From today on our relations with them are finished. I want nothing more from the Portuguese government, and I proclaim Brazil forevermore separated from Portugal."

With enthusiasm we immediately answered, "Long live liberty! Long live an independent Brazil! Long live D. Pedro!"

The Prince turned to his adjutant and said, "Tell my guard that I have just declared the complete independence of Brazil. We are free from Portugal."

Lieutenant Canto e Melo rode toward a market where most of the soldiers of the guard remained. He returned to the Prince with them shouting enthusiastically in favor of an independent and separate Brazil, D. Pedro, and the Catholic Religion.

D. Pedro before the guard said, "The Portuguese Côrtes wants to enslave and to persecute us. Henceforth our relations are broken. Not one tie unites us!" And tearing from his hat the blue and white emblem decreed by the Côrtes as the symbol of the Portuguese nation, he threw it on the ground, saying, "Throw away that symbol, soldiers! Long live independence, liberty, and the separation of Brazil!"

We responded with a shout in favor of an independent and separate Brazil and another for D. Pedro.

The Prince unsheathed his sword, and the civilians removed their hats. D. Pedro said, "By my blood, by my honor, and with God's help, I swear to liberate Brazil."

"We all swear to it," shouted the rest.

D. Pedro sheathed his sword, an act repeated by the guard, went to the head of the crowd, turned, and rose up in the stirrups to cry, "Brazilians, our motto from this day forward will be 'Independence or Death.' "

Seated firmly in his saddle, he spurred his handsome horse and galloped, followed by his retinue, toward São Paulo, where he was lodged by Brigadier Jordão, Captain Antônio Silva Prado, and others, who worked miracles in order to cheer up the prince.

After dismounting, D. Pedro ordered his adjutant to go at once to the goldsmith Lessa and have made a small disk in gold bearing the words "Independence or Death" to be fastened on the arm with ribbons of green and gold.

Wearing the emblem he appeared at the theatre where my dear friends Alfêres Aquins and Father Ildefonso acclaimed him the King of Brazil.

Throughout the theatre were yellow and green ribbons. They hung from the walls, from the boxes, from the arms of the men and from the hair and dresses of the women.

❀

---

30. José Bonifácio on Negro Slavery and Civilizing the Indians*

Shortly after the declaration of independence, José Bonifácio directed his attention to one of the most perplexing problems facing the new nation: the incorporation of the Indians

....

* Translated from Octávio Tarquinio de Sousa (ed.), *O Pensamento Vivo de José Bonifácio* (São Paulo: Livraria Martins Editora, 1961), pp. 47-50, 60-64, 79-80, 87-88. Printed by permission of the publisher.

and Negroes into the Brazilian family. He was one of the first to demand an end to the slave trade and to advocate the preparation of the slave for gradual emancipation. He was also the direct heir to the Jesuit and Pombaline policies of Christianizing and civilizing the Indians. In both cases, the imperial minister was far in advance of his times. Although the slave traffic was ended in 1850, slavery abolished in 1888, and the Indian Protection Service established in 1910, some of the problems of acculturation and assimilation of those two groups, which he sought to answer, still remain unsolved. The following selection from Bonifácio's writings demonstrates his own attempts at their solution.

As a free citizen and a national deputy, two objectives, excluding the Constitution, seem to me to be of the greatest interest for the future prosperity of this Empire. The first is a new law to promote the general civilization of the Indians in Brazil. . . . The second is a new law concerning the slave trade and treatment of the miserable captives.

. . .

Why do the Brazilians continue to be deaf to the cries of reason and of the Christian religion and, I will add, of national honor and dignity? We are the only nation of European blood which still openly and publicly traffics in African slaves.

I also am a Christian and a philanthropist; and God prompts me to dare to raise my feeble voice in the midst of this august assembly in favor of the cause of justice and even of political sanity, the most noble and holy cause that can animate generous and humane hearts.

. . .

How can we have a long-lasting and liberal constitution in a country continually inhabited by an immense multitude of brutal and hostile slaves? Let us begin at once this grand work by the expiation of our old crimes and sins. Indeed, it is not simply a question of being just but we ought also to be penitent. We ought to demonstrate before God and our fellow men that we repent everything we have done over the centuries against both justice and religion and to shout our agreement that we will not do unto others what we do not want them to do unto us. It is necessary that the robberies, hate, and war which we encourage among the natives of Africa cease at once. It is necessary that our ports no longer be visited by ships bringing thousands and thousands of Negroes who die smothered in the holds of our ships, more closely jammed together than the cotton bales from our plantations. It is necessary once and for all to stop all these numberless deaths and torments which we inflicted and still do inflict on these unfortunates in our own land. It is time, then, more than time, that we end such a barbarian and bloody traffic; it is time, also, that we begin to gradually end slavery until its last vestiges have disappeared from our midst so that we will come to create within a few generations a homogeneous nation without which we never will be truly free, respected, and happy.

．　．　．

It is amazing that a commerce so contrary to the laws of human morality and to the holy writs of the Church and even against the laws of political sanity lasts so many centuries among men who call themselves civilized and Christians. They lie; they never were.

Civil society has as its primary base justice and as its principal goal the happiness of man; but what right does a man have to rob the liberty of a fellow man or, what is worse, of the sons of this fellow man or the sons of those sons? Perhaps someone will answer that to favor the manumission of slaves will be to attack the sanctity of property Do not delude yourself, gentlemen. Private property was sanctioned for the good of all and what is the good which a slave receives from the loss of all his natural rights when he becomes a thing and is no longer a person, to use the phrase of the lawyers? It is not the right of property that they seek to defend; it is the right of force because since man cannot be a thing neither can he become property. If the law ought to defend property much more ought it to defend the personal liberty of men who cannot be the property of anyone without attacking the rights of divine Providence which make man free and not servile and without attacking the moral order of societies which is the strict execution of all the duties prescribed by nature, by religion, and by political sanity.

. . .

This commerce in human flesh is a cancer which gnaws at the entrails of Brazil, a commerce, however, which nowadays is not necessary for the increase of agriculture or population once that, by wise laws, idleness of the white, the mixed bloods, and the freed is eliminated, once that the many slaves which we now have can, with the protection of a just government, mix freely and naturally with the other classes, once that they can raise and support their own children . . . once that through gradual emancipation of the slaves these immoral brutes are changed into useful, active, and upright citizens.

Stop once and for all this infamous traffic in African slaves; but with that step the end of the road is not reached. It is also necessary to seriously care for the improvement of the lot of the existing slaves and such care is just another step taken toward their future emancipation.

. . .

I repeat that I do not wish to see slavery suddenly abolished. Such an act would bring with it great evils. In order to emancipate the slaves without harming society it is essential first to make them worthy of their freedom. Reason and law dictate that they be converted gradually from vile slaves to free and active men. Then the inhabitants of this land will be changed from their cruelness, which they frequently manifest on this point, into Christians and just men, and they will gain much with the passage of time. They will put into free circulation dead capital which slavery absorbs. They will free their families from domestic examples of corruption and

tyranny. They will free their homes and their nation of enemies. Those who today have no fatherland can be transformed into our brothers and compatriots.

. . .

We must bear the blame for the increasing difficulties we
are having with the Indians. Our faults are many: the dis-
dain with which we generally treat [the Indians], the continuous robbery of their best lands, the services to which we
subject them paying them little or nothing daily, feeding
them badly, tricking them in the contracts of commerce that
we make with them, and taking them year after year from
their families and fields for governmental and private service,
and finally grafting onto them all our vices and evils without
communicating to them our virtues and talents.

If we desire, then, to overcome these difficulties we must
completely change our manners and behavior by understanding first what the wild Indians are and must be by nature in
order then to find the methods of converting them into what
we believe they should be.

. . .

Without new measures and institutions founded on justice and political sanity we never will be able to succeed in
catechizing and civilizing those savages. It is necessary to imitate and to perfect the methods the Jesuits used. By means
of kindness and good turns they brought a large number of
Indians into villages, and what is more, even the governors of
Goiás, by imitating them, made the Acroás, the Jovais, the
unconquered Caiapós, and the cruel Xavantes our friends.
And how did they do it? By giving liberty to the prisoners,
dressing them, encouraging them, and persuading them to
come live under the holy laws of the Faith. In spite of their
barbarity, they understood the kindness done and were not
insensible to the attentions given them by the great chiefs of
the Whites, as they called those governors. The very Botocudos and Puris, against whom cruel war was declared recently,
are becoming domesticated. In the province of Bahia, due to
the understanding method the governor uses to earn their

good will, the Botocudos live in peace with us, while, at the same time, in the Captaincy of Espirito Santo they wage a hard war against us despite our expeditions and military posts.

I have shown by means of reason and experience that in spite of the fact that the wild Indians are a race of lazy, inconsiderate men and to a large extent ungrateful and inhumane to us, they are nonetheless capable of civilization as soon as the proper methods are adopted and there is true constancy and zeal in carrying them out.

❁

---

31 . Statement of the Emperor on the Dissolution of the Constituent Assembly*

Another problem facing the new nation was the preparation of a constitution. Considering himself a liberal, Emperor Pedro I had promised his subjects to rule under a constitution. Therefore, he convoked a Constituent Assembly, which began to hold sessions on May 3, 1823. It appeared initially to be a liberal and highly motivated body. Unfortunately, the ninety deputies, mostly lawyers, judges, and priests, had little legislative experience and scant political finesse. When the Assembly began to criticize the Emperor and attempted to limit some of his powers, Dom Pedro manifested a distrust of and scorn for it. The lack of understanding and good will between the legislature and executive

....

* From *British and Foreign State Papers*, 1823-1824 (London: J. Harrison and Son, 1825), pp. 800-803.

*quickly developed into a contest to curtail each other's au-
thority. After the assembly gave vent to tirades of anti-
Portuguese hatred, the emperor, himself born in Portugal,
decided to dissolve it, claiming the deputies lacked discipline
and preached revolution. Troops sent to the assembly hall on
November 11, 1823 refused to admit the deputies. After
sending the assembly leaders into exile, the disillusioned
Pedro explained his action to the people in a public manifesto.*

Providence, which watches over the stability and preservation of Empires, had, in its profound wisdom, permitted
that, after the establishment of the Independence of Brazil,
and the union of all its Provinces, even the most remote, this
Empire should continue its progressive march towards con-
solidation and prosperity. The Constituent and Legislative
Assembly employed itself with assiduity, judgment, and activity, to erect, on a solid foundation, the Constitutional System in this vast Empire: on this firm basis rose successfully
the social edifice, and Foreigners formed so favourable an
opinion of The Brazilian Nation, as to believe that the principal Powers of Europe would speedily recognize the Independence of the Empire of Brazil, and would even be eager
to enter into political and commercial relations with it. This
brilliant prospect, which nothing seemed capable of obscuring, was suddenly darkened by a tempest that overcast our
horizon. An evil genius infused fatal designs into some rest-
less and ill-disposed characters, and fanned in their minds
the flame of discord. From that time it began to be clearly
perceived, that there was no uniformity of sound principles
on which Constitutional Governments ought to rest, in the
Assembly, and the harmony, arising from a distribution of
powers, which constitutes the moral and physical force of
such Governments, began to be disturbed. Various and continued attacks on the Executive Power, and the concessions
it made for the sake of harmony, weakened the force of Government, and secretly undermined it. The spirit of division
increased, the poison of distrust diffused itself, Parties were

artfully formed, and a disorganising Faction, which suddenly made its appearance, and was gaining strength, commenced to strike terror into the minds of worthy Men, who, prompted solely by their zeal for the public good and the purest love of their Country, trembled at the idea of future perils, which they anticipated, and even saw near at hand. Meanwhile those who meditated and framed subversive plans, calculated only for the accomplishment of their own ends, succeeded in gaining over some that were well-meaning and upright, with the flattering representation of more firmly establishing liberty, that sacred idol, desired by all, though most frequently ill understood; others, with persuading them that Government was manoeuvring to obtain despotic sway; and others again, perhaps with advantageous promises, exaggerated by the heated imaginations of the latter, till at last their malignity went the length of propagating the notion, that the perfidious and insidious project was resolved on of forming a Union with the Portuguese Government.

After framing these schemes, after devising and agreeing upon the means of realizing them, and after removing the difficulties which they supposed to be in their way, it was thought proper to proceed to the execution of the plot, and a time was fixed for it.

One of the means chosen as infallible, was to sow discord between the Natives of Brazil and of Portugal, partly through the agency of Newspapers, artfully instilling insidious sentiments, endeavouring to destroy the moral force of the Government, and threatening My Imperial Person with the examples of Iturbide, and Charles I, and partly through the instrumentality of Emissaries, tutored to uphold and disseminate seditious principles.

Having thus prepared the fermentation, from which was to burst forth the Revolutionary Volcano, the Faction which had gained the ascendency in the Assembly, availed itself for the fatal rupture, of a demand preferred by Citizen David Pamplona, a naturalized Brazilian, but, in reality, a native of the Portuguese Islands, who complained to the Assembly of having received some blows, inflicted on him by two Brazilian Military Officers, but born in Portugal, and who, by the

opinion of a Committee, was understood to have to seek redress in the usual way. Previous to this, and with the most
criminal anticipation, the Leaders of the above frightful Faction, aided by their Adherents, suborned Individuals from
the populace, to arm themselves with Poniards and Pistols,
and thus to strike terror into the Most Illustrious, Most
Honourable and Most Worthy Deputies of the Assembly,
who, faithful to their Oaths, desired only to discharge the
trust confided to them by the noble Brazilian Nation, and
delighted in maintaining the tranquillity required for the deliberations.

On that ill-fated Day, the most tragical and horrid Scenes
would have been acted, if, upon hearing the shouts, and perceiving the most extraordinary and most scandalous means
resorted to, The Illustrious President, with vigilant and con-
summate prudence, had not closed the Sitting, and thus prevented evils which would have broken forth with tremendous
Destruction from such a Volcano, engendered by the fury of
the Parties, by national hatred, by the thirst of vengeance,
and by the most inordinate ambition. Nothing short of it
was to be expected, from the large number of Persons posted
within and without the Assembly, to second the projects of
the terrible Faction; nothing less was to be apprehended,
considering the great quantity of Arms sold in abundance in
the City during the preceding Days, and judging by the
scandalous vociferations with which the Leaders of the nefarious Party were greeted and applauded on quitting the Assembly, notwithstanding My Imperial Presence.

This alarming Scene was repeated the next Day. Vehe-
ment and extravagant harangues of those belonging to the
above Faction, continued to fan the flame of discord, and
many of their Retainers in the galleries of the Assembly, and
without, would have aided the horrid results that must have
been the certain consequences of the premeditated Plans. To
this end it was insisted and carried, that the Sitting should
be declared permanent, under the specious pretext, that it
would be unfitting to close it, without the re-establishment
of tranquillity. To obtain this, I had already ordered the
Troops to proceed to, and draw up in the Field of St. Chris-

tovao, with the just view of affording perfect liberty to the Assembly, whom I caused afterwards to be informed of this Resolution, that they might take into consideration the just motives of it, and also how proper it would be to provide positive and peremptory Measures for restoring tranquillity. Without, however, taking any, they continued to debate with the same warmth and obstinacy, while, with an exaggeration of plausible pretexts, they sought the ruin of the Country, and their first and certain aim was My August Person, being, to this end, treated with disrespect by all the means which calumny and malignity could suggest.

The Revolutionary fury was not satisfied with this illjudged want of respect. They proceeded yet farther, and would have limited in the extreme the attributes belonging, by the very essence of Representative Governments, to the Head of the Executive Power, and which had been conferred upon Me by the Nation, as Constitutional Emperor and Perpetual Defender of Brazil; they even went to the extremity of proposing that either the whole, or a large portion of the Troops should be withdrawn to a great distance from the City, thereby to leave the Government without the necessary vigour and energy.

The danger of delaying Resolutions in critical cases, and even the fatal consequence of putting them off under the melancholy circumstances described; the horrible prospect of the occurrences that were impending; the despair of some, the pride and political fanaticism of others; the terrors and fears of every peaceful Citizen; the face of the Country in danger, and, finally, the apprehension of the ruin and subversion of the State, imperiously demanded the adoption of Measures equally prompt and efficacious, and remedies which, though violent to appearance, were alone capable of producing speedy and beneficial results.

And what Measure was it possible to take in a crisis so arduous and so fearful? What step was likely to stem the Revolutionary torrent, and by opposing its force, arrest it effectually? No other was left, nor was any so powerful as that of dissolving the Assembly. This, and the dismissal of the Ministers, are the preservatives against Public Commotions in Constitutional Monarchies. The latter was carried into effect, nor was there any other resource than that of directing also the former Measure, though to the greatest regret and grief of My Imperial Heart. On account of such powerful motives, and of the urgent necessity to save the Country, which is the supreme Law that justifies extreme Measures in cases of great danger, I ordered the Dissolution of the Assembly, by the Decree of the 12th Inst., which, at the same time, enjoins the Meeting of another, according to the public Law of the Constitution, to which I am solicitous and most happy to conform.

In that Decree, and in that of the 13th, which promulgated and enlarged it, are contained irrefragable proofs of the necessity which compelled Me to adopt so strong a Measure, and of how much I am desirous of restoring the Constitutional System, the only one which is capable of accomplishing the happiness of this Empire, and which was proclaimed by the Brazilian People. If such arduous and dangerous circumstances forced Me to chuse so violent a remedy, it ought to be remembered, that extraordinary evils demand extraordinary remedies, and that it is to be hoped and believed that they will never more be required. The Inhabitants of all the Provinces being confident of My Magnanimity and of My Constitutional Principles, and how much I am pledged to promote the happiness and tranquillity of the Nation, will take breath and recover from the commotion caused by this disastrous occurrence, which occasioned to Me likewise great pain; and will continue to enjoy the Peace, Tranquillity, and Prosperity which the Constitution gives and secures to them.

THE EMPEROR.

❀

---

32. The Constitution of 1824*

Pedro, with the aid of a Council of State, wrote a constitution for Brazil. An advanced and liberal document for the period, it provided for a highly centralized government with strong power in the hands of the emperor. In addition to the traditional three branches of government, there was a fourth, the poder moderador, *the moderating power, which gave the emperor authority over the three others. The Constitution of 1824 proved flexible enough to last throughout the imperial period. The following section contains excerpts from that constitution.*

TITLE I—*Of the Empire of Brazil, Its Territory, Government, Dynasty, and Religion.*

Art. 1. The Empire of Brazil is the political association of all Brazilian citizens. They form an independent and free nation which does not admit to any ties of unity or federation which comprise its independence.

Art. 2. Its territory is divided into Provinces in the form that they presently are found; they can be subdivided according to the exigencies of the State.

Art. 3. Its Government is Monarchical, Hereditary, Constitutional, and Representative.

Art. 4. The reigning dynasty is that of Dom Pedro I, present Emperor and Perpetual Defender of Brazil.

Art. 5. The Roman, Catholic, and Apostolic Religion will continue to be the Religion of the Empire. All the other

....

* Translated from *Constituição Política do Império do Brazil* (Lisbon: Impressão de João Nunes Esteves, 1826), pp. 3-4, 6-7, 12-15, 22-23, 27, 30-34, 39-44, 46, 50-51.

religions will be permitted to exercise their worship privately in houses designated for that purpose but without the exterior appearance of a church.

. . .

TITLE III—*Of the Powers and National Representation.*

Art. 9. The division and harmony of the Political Powers are the principal safeguard of the Rights of the Citizens and the most secure means of making effective the guarantees which the Constitution offers.

Art. 10. The Political Powers recognized by the Constitution of the Empire of Brazil are four: the Legislative Power, the Moderating Power, the Executive Power, and the Judiciary Power.

Art. 11. The representatives of the Brazilian Nation are the Emperor and the General Assembly.

Art. 12. All these Powers, in the Empire of Brazil, are delegations of the Nation.

. . .

TITLE IV—*Of the Legislative Power.*
Chapter I—Of the Branches of the Legislative Power and Its Powers.

Art. 13. The Legislative Power is delegated to the General Assembly with the sanction of the Emperor.

Art. 14. The General Assembly is composed of two branches: the Chamber of Deputies and the Chamber of Senators or Senate.

. . .

Chapter II—*Of the Chamber of Deputies.*

Art. 35. The Chamber of Deputies is elective and temporary.

Art. 36. It is the prerogative of the Chamber of Deputies to have the initiative on

1. Taxes.
2. Recruitment.

3. The designation of a new dynasty in event the reigning house becomes extinct.

Art. 37. Also to have initiation in the Chamber of Deputies are

1. An examination of the past administration and the reform of its abuses.

2. The discussion of proposals made by the Executive Power.

Art. 38. It is the prerogative of the same Chamber to initiate an indictment of the Ministers of State and Counselors of State.

. . .

Chapter III—*Of the Senate.*

Art. 40. The Senate is composed of members chosen for life and it will be organized by provincial elections.

Art. 41. Each Province will have as Senators half its number of Deputies; in the case that its number of Deputies be uneven, the number will be half of the lowest even number so that if a Province has eleven Deputies it will have five Senators.

Art. 42. The Province which has only one Deputy will elect one Senator also despite the aforesaid rule.

Art. 43. The Elections will be held in the same manner as for the Deputies but in triple lists so that the Emperor can select one-third of the total list.

Art. 44. Vacancies in the Senate will be filled in the same manner as for the first election in each respective province.

Art. 45. To be a Senator it is required

1. To be a Brazilian citizen and to have possession of his political rights.

2. To be forty years of age or older.

3. To be a person of knowledge, capacity, and virtues with preference given to those who have given service to the Nation.

4. To have an annual income from property, industry, commerce, or employment exceeding eight hundred thousand *réis*.

Art. 46. Princes of the Imperial House are Senators by right and will take their place in the Senate upon reaching the age of twenty-five.

. . .

Chapter V—Of the General Councils of the Provinces and their Powers.

Art. 71. The Constitution recognizes and guarantees the right of each Citizen to participate in the affairs of his Province which are immediately relative to his own interests.

Art. 72. This right will be exercised through the Municipal Councils and through the Councils to be entitled General Council of the Province which ought to be established in each Province where the Capital of the Empire is not located.

Art. 73. Each one of the General Councils will consist of twenty-one Members in the most populous Provinces as Pará, Maranhão, Ceará, Pernambuco, Bahia, Minas Gerais, São Paulo, and Rio Grande do Sul; and in the others, thirteen Members.

. . .

Chapter VI—Of Elections.

Art. 90. The election of Deputies and Senators for the General Assembly and of the Members of the General Councils of the Provinces is done indirectly. The active Citizens permitted to vote elect the Provincial Electors who in turn select the Representatives of the Nation and of the Province.

. . .

TITLE V—Of the Emperor.
Chapter I—Of the Moderating Power.

Art. 98. The Moderating Power is the key to the entire political organization and it is delegated exclusively to the Emperor as the Supreme Chief of the Nation and its First Representative so that he constantly can watch over the maintenance of the independence, equilibrium, and harmony of the other Political Powers.

Art. 99. The Person of the Emperor is inviolable and sacred. He is not subject to any responsibility.

Art. 100. His titles are "Constitutional Emperor and Perpetual Defender of Brazil" and he should be addressed as Imperial Majesty.

Art. 101. The Emperor exercises the Moderating Power.

1. By naming Senators in conformity with Article 43.

2. By convoking the General Assembly extraordinarily between sessions when the good of the Empire demands it.

3. By sanctioning the Decrees and Resolutions of the General Assembly so that they will have the force of law: Article 62.

4. By approving and suspending entirely the Resolutions of the Provincial Councils: Articles 86 and 87.

5. By postponing or adjourning the General Assembly and by dissolving the Chamber of Deputies in those cases in which the well-being of the State requires it; by convoking immediately another to substitute for it.

6. By naming and freely dismissing the Ministers of State.

7. By suspending the Magistrates in the cases provided in Article 154.

8. By paroling and by moderating the penalties imposed on criminals condemned by sentence.

9. By conceding amnesty in urgent cases or when counseled by humanity and the good of the State.

. . .

Chapter II—*Of the Executive Power.*

Art. 102. The Emperor is the Chief Executive Power and he exercises his office through the Ministers of State.

His principal prerogatives are:

1. To convoke the new ordinary General Assembly on the 3rd of June of the third year of the existing Legislature.

2. To name Bishops and to furnish Ecclesiastical Benefices.

3. To name Magistrates.

4. To supply the rest of the civil and political employees.

5. To name the Commandants of the Force of Land and Sea and to remove them when the service of the Nation demands it.

6. To name Ambassadors and other Diplomatic and Commerical Agents.

7. To direct Political Negotiations with Foreign Nations.

8. To make treaties of offensive and defensive Alliance, of Subsidy and Commerce, afterwards carrying them out, with the knowledge of the General Assembly when the interests and security of the State permit it. If the Treaties concluded in time of peace involve cession or exchange of Territory of the Empire or of Possessions to which the Empire has a right, they will not be ratified until they have been approved by the General Assembly.

9. To declare war and to make peace, sharing with the Assembly the communications compatible with the interests and security of the State.

10. To grant letters of naturalization in the form of Law.

11. To grant Titles, Honors, Military Orders, and Distinctions in recognition for services given to the State, the pecuniary grants depending on the approval of the Assembly when they are not designated and evaluated by Law.

12. To expedite the decrees, instructions, and regulations adequate for the proper execution of the Laws.

13. To decree the application of the funds approved by the Assembly to the various branches of public administration.

14. To concede, or to deny, sanction to the Decrees in Council and Apostolic Letters and any other Ecclesiastical Constitutions which are not contrary to the Constitution; and by preceding the approval of the Assembly they become the general will.

15. To provide all that might be necessary for the internal and external security of the State in accordance with the Constitution.

. . .

Chapter IV—*Of Succession to the Throne.*

Art. 121. The Emperor is a minor until he reaches the age of eighteen.

Art. 122. During his minority, the Empire will be ruled by a Regency which will devolve upon the Relative closest to the Emperor according to the order of Succession provided he be older than twenty-five years.

Art. 123. If the Emperor has no Relative with those qualifications the Empire will be governed by a permanent Regency named by the Assembly composed of three members, the oldest of whom will be the President.

. . .

Chapter V—*Of the Ministry.*

Art. 131. There will be various Secretaries of State. The Law will designate the duties of each and their number, joining them together or separating them as best suits the situation.

Art. 132. The Ministers of State will sign all the Acts of the Executive Power without which they cannot be executed.

. . .

Chapter VI—*Of the Council of State.*

Art. 137. There will be a Council of State composed of life-term Councilors named by the Emperor.

Art. 138. Their number will not exceed ten.

. . .

Art. 140. To be a Councilor of State it is necessary to possess the same qualities as a Senator.

. . .

Art. 142. The Councilors are heard in all business of a grave nature and general measures of Public Administration, principally on the declaration of war, the arrangements for peace, negotiations with foreign nations as well as on all occasions when the Emperor proposes to exercise any of the prerogatives of the Moderating Power indicated in Article 101 with the exception of No. 6.

. . .

TITLE VI—*Of the Judiciary Power.*
Only Chapter—*Of the Judges and Tribunals of Justice.*

Art. 151. The Judiciary Power is independent and will be composed of Judges and Jurors which take part in Civil and Criminal Cases in the manner determined by the Codes.

Art. 152. The Jurors will pronounce on the facts; the judges will apply the law.

Art. 153. Judges of law are permanent which is not understood to mean that they cannot be moved from one place to another in the time and manner determined by the law.

. . .

TITLE VII—*Of the Administration and Economy of the Provinces.*
Chapter I—*Of the Administration.*

Art. 165. There will be in each Province a President named by the Emperor, and he will be able to remove him when it is understood that such an action is convenient for the good service of the State.

. . .

Chapter II—*Of the Municipal Governments.*

Art. 167. In all the Cities and Towns now existing or to be created in the future there will be Municipal Governments which will have charge of the economic and political affairs of those Cities and Towns.

Art. 168. The Municipal Governments are elective and composed of the number of Councilmen which the Law designates, and the one who obtains the greatest number of votes will be President.

❀

33. Portuguese Recognition of Brazilian Independence*

In addition to assimilating diverse groups and preparing a constitution, a third problem facing the new government was to obtain recognition as an independent nation. The United States became the first to recognize Brazil when President James Monroe received José Silvestre Rebêlo in Washington in May of 1824. The European nations refused to accord recognition until the former mother country did so. Great Britain, desirous of obtaining the same favorable trade terms with Brazil it had enjoyed under the Treaty of 1810 signed with Portugal, began to apply pressure on Lisbon. Foreign Minister George Canning convinced the government of João VI to confer on a British subject, Sir Charles Stuart, the power to sign a treaty for Portugal recognizing Brazil's independence. The signing of that treaty on August 29, 1825, opened the way for immediate European recognition and for the welcoming of Brazil into the community of nations.

In the Name of the Most Holy and Undivided Trinity

His Most Faithful Majesty having constantly cherished in His Royal Mind the most lively desire to re-establish Peace, Friendship and good Harmony between Sister Nations, whom the most sacred ties ought to conciliate and unite in perpetual Alliance—in order to accomplish these important ends, as well as to promote general prosperity, and to secure the political existence and the future destinies of Portugal, in common with those of Brazil, and being desirous at once to

* From *British and Foreign State Papers*, 1824-1825 (London: J. Harrison and Son, 1826), pp. 674-678.

remove every obstacle that might impede the said Alliance, Concord, and Happiness of both States—by His Diploma of the 13th May of the current year, recognized Brazil as an Independent Empire, and as separate from the Kingdoms of Portugal and Algarve, and likewise His most beloved and valued son Dom Pedro as Emperor, ceding and transferring, of his own free will, the Sovereignty of the aforesaid Empire to his aforesaid son and his Legitimate Successors, and only taking and reserving for His own Person, the same title.

And these August Sovereigns accepting the Mediation of His Britannick Majesty for the adjustment of all preliminary questions regarding the separation of the two States, have named Plenipotentiaries, that is to say:

His Most Faithful Majesty names His Excellency the Right Honourable Sir Charles Stuart, Privy Councillor of His Britannick Majesty, Grand Cross of the Order of the Tower and Sword, and of the Order of the Bath.

His Imperial Majesty names the Most Illustrious and Most Excellent Luis José de Carvalho e Mello, of the Council of State, Dignitary of the Imperial Order of the Cross, Commander of the Orders of Christ, and of the Conception, and Minister and Secretary of State for Foreign Affairs; the Most Illustrious and Most Excellent Baron de Santo Amaro, Grandee of the Empire, of the Council of State, Gentleman of the Imperial Chamber, Dignitary of the Imperial Order of the Cross, and Commander of the Orders of Christ, and of the Tower and Sword—and the Most Illustrious and Most Excellent Francisco Vilella Barbosa, of the Council of State, Grand Cross of the Imperial Order of the Cross, Knight of the Order of Christ, Colonel of the Imperial Corps of Engineers, Minister and Secretary of State for the Naval Department, and Inspector General of the Navy:

And their Full Powers having been examined and exchanged, they have agreed in conformity, with the principles laid down in this Preamble, to the formation of the present Treaty.

I. His Most Faithful Majesty, recognizes Brazil as an Empire, independent and separate from the Kingdoms of Portugal and Algarve, and His most beloved and esteemed son

Dom Pedro as Emperor; ceding and transferring, of his own free will, the Sovereignty of the said Empire to His said son, and to His legitimate Successors; His Most Faithful Majesty only taking and reserving the same Title for His own Person.

II. His Imperial Majesty, in acknowledgment of respect and affection for his August Father and Lord Dom John VI., agrees that His Most Faithful Majesty shall, in His own Person, assume the title of Emperor.

III. His Imperial Majesty promises not to accept the proposals of any Portuguese Colonies whatever, to unite themselves with the Empire of Brazil.

IV. Henceforth there shall be Peace and Alliance, and the most perfect Friendship, between the Kingdoms of Portugal and Algarve, and the Empire of Brazil, with perfect oblivion of the past dissentions between the respective Nations.

V. The Subjects of both the Portuguese and Brazilian Nations, shall be considered and treated, in the respective States, as those of the most favoured and friendly Nation, and their Rights and Property shall be religiously guarded and protected; it being understood that the Owners of landed Property shall continue in the peaceable possession of such property.

VI. All property whether real or personal, and all interest in property, either sequestrated or confiscated, belonging to the Subjects of the Sovereigns of Portugal and Brazil, shall be immediately restored, as well as the profits already made thereon, after deducting the expenses of Administration; or their Proprietors shall be reciprocally indemnified, in the manner set forth in the 8th Article.

VII. All Vessels and Cargoes captured, belonging to the Subjects of either Sovereign, shall be, in like manner, restored, or their Proprietors indemnified.

VIII. A Commission named by both Governments, composed of an equal number of Portuguese and Brazilians, and established wherever the respective Governments shall think most convenient, shall be charged to examine into the matters provided for in the VIth and VIIth Articles: it being understood that those Claims ought to be preferred within the space of a year after the Commission is formed, and that, in the case of an equality of votes, the question shall be decided by the Representative of the Sovereign Mediator. Both Governments shall designate the funds from which the first liquidated Claims are to be paid.

IX. All the public Claims of the one Government upon the other shall be reciprocally received and decided, either by the restitution of the objects claimed, or by an indemnification for their just value. For the adjustment of these Claims, both the High Contracting Parties agree to conclude a direct and special Convention.

X. The relations of Commerce between the Portuguese and Brazilian Nations shall be immediately re-established, all the merchandize, reciprocally, paying a provisional duty, on consumption of 15 per Cent.: the duties of transhipment and re-exportation, remaining on the same scale as before the separation.

XI. The reciprocal exchange of the Ratifications of the present Treaty shall take place in the City of Lisbon, within the space of five months, or sooner if possible, reckoning from the day of the signature of the present Treaty.

In witness whereof, We the undersigned, Plenipotentiaries of His Most Faithful Majesty, and of His Imperial Majesty, in virtue of our respective Full Powers, sign the present Treaty with our hands, and affix to it the Seals of our Arms.

Done in the City of Rio de Janeiro on the 29th day of the month of August, in the year of our Lord Jesus Christ, 1825.

> CHARLES STUART.
> LUIZ JOSÉ DE CARVALHO E MELLO.
> BARON DE SANTO AMARO.
> FRANCISCO VILELLA BARBOSA.

❈

34. The Abdication of Pedro I

The first disenchantment with Pedro I appeared when he dissolved the Constituent Assembly. The loss of the Cisplatine Province (Uruguay) as a result of a costly war with Argentina, the humiliating treaties with Great Britain, particularly the forced promise to abolish the slave trade, the continuous appointment of Portuguese-born officials, and the preoccupation with Portuguese affairs, and the inability of the emperor to get along with the assemblies, further diminished the popularity of the impulsive Pedro. Events seemed to take a turn for the better on March 19, 1831, when he selected an all-Brazilian cabinet of moderates, a very well-received choice. However, the newly found popularity proved to be short-lived. On the 5th day of the following month, he capriciously replaced that cabinet with another, conservative and pro-Portuguese in its orientation. The opposition at once brought pressure to bear on him to bring back the March cabinet. He responded that it was his constitutional right to change ministers at will—legally it was true. Regardless of the legality of his act, the people and military demonstrated in the street for the reappointment of the former ministers.

*

THE ABDICATION*

In spite of the demonstration, the emperor remained adamant, retorting, "I will do everything for the people but nothing by the people." So saying, he abdicated on April 7th in favor of his five-year-old son, Pedro de Alcântara, and

....

* From *British and Foreign State Papers*, 1830-1831 (London: James Ridgway, 1833), p. 1301.

sailed immediately for Lisbon, leaving Brazil for the first time in the hands of the Brazilians.

Availing myself of the privilege which the Constitution gives me, I hereby declare that I have most voluntarily Abdicated, in favour of my well beloved and most esteemed Son, Dom Pedro de Alcântara.

Palace, Boa Vista, April 7, 1831—10th year of Independence, and of the Empire.

PEDRO.

*

THE REACTION*

The sudden decision of the emperor amazed the nation. No one had agitated for his abdication, only for a modification of some of his politics. The opposition found itself with the difficult task of explaining the events to the people. In the following proclamation to the nation, the assembly astutely explained the abdication as the beginning of a new era in national life in which the hated Portuguese influence would be eradicated. The young Brazilian-born prince, Pedro II, would be the hope of the nation and the symbol of its national unity. In effect, the abdication was a new declaration of independence for Brazil: "The Independence of our Country, and its Laws, will from this day be a reality."

An extraordinary event has taken place which baffles the calculations of human prudence; a glorious Revolution has been affected by the forces, and by the patriotic union of the People and Troops of Rio de Janeiro, without the shedding of a single drop of blood; a result never before witnessed, and

....

* From *British and Foreign State Papers*, *1830-1831* (London: James Ridgway, 1833), pp. 1301-1303.

which reflects honour on your moderation, and energy, and on the state of civilization to which you have arrived.

Brazilians! A Prince, badly advised, led on by violent passions, and by disgraceful and anti-constitutional prejudices, to a precipice, yielded to the public opinion so openly expressed, seeing that he could no longer remain Emperor of the Brazils.

The audacity of a party which was supported only by its name; the outrages which we suffered from a faction always averse to Brazil; and the treachery by which unpopular men, regarded as hostile to liberty, were suddenly elevated to the Ministry; placed arms in our hands. The tutelar genius of Brazil and the readiness with which the armed Force and the People hastened to the succour of their oppressed Country, deprived our enemies of their judgment and of their courage; they became alarmed, and the struggle was decided without the necessity of employing those arms for the shedding of blood. Dom Pedro I abdicated in favour of his Son, now Dom Pedro II, Constitutional Emperor of Brazil.

Deprived for some hours of a Government to carry on the public Administration, the first care of your Representatives, the Members of both Chambers, was to nominate a Provisional Regency, with the power prescribed by the Constitution. This Regency, whose authority will only last till the Meeting of the General Assembly, for the installation of which there are not at present a sufficient number of Members, was elected on the exigency of the moment, and there being no Administrative Government, the conditions of the CXXIVth Article of the Fundamental Law of the State could not be complied with. The persons, who have been named for that important office, possess your confidence. Patriots without a stain, they are ardently attached to our liberty, they will not allow it to suffer the slightest infringement, nor will they compromise with factions offensive to the Nation.

Fellow citizens! Rely on their care, and their zeal, but nevertheless do not slacken in your vigilance, and in your noble exertions. Patriotism and energy know how to unite themselves with moderation, when a People are possessed of the many virtues, which you have exhibited in this noble undertaking. Courageous in repelling tyranny, and in rejecting the yoke which the foulest treachery intended for you, you have shewn yourselves generous in victory, and your adversaries have turned pale with terror and with shame.

Brazilians! Your conduct has been above all praise; that detestable faction, which dared to insult us in our homes, has witnessed another proof of our greatness, in the moderation which we have observed after our victory. Adopted Brazilians, who have been urged to strife by perfidious suggestions, be assured that it was not a thirst for vengeance, but the love of liberty, which armed us; and that the security of your persons and property, will all be respected, whilst you obey the Laws of the magnanimous Nation to which you belong. The Brazilians hate tyranny, they abhor the idea of a Foreign yoke, but it is not their intention to hold a rod of iron over the conquered, or to avail themselves of their triumph in order to gratify rancorous passions. They have too much nobleness of soul to justify such an apprehension. Whenever traitors appear amongst us, Justice and Law only will punish them according to their crimes.

There are but few Members wanting to complete the number of the Representatives of the Nation, which is necessary to form the General Assembly, to whom you will have to look for those energetic measures which the Nation so urgently requires. Your Delegates will not forget your interests: this land is as dear to them as it is to yourselves. Brazil hitherto so oppressed, so humiliated by tyranny, is now the object of your and of their enthusiasm. Those whom you elect with your free choice, will not allow your glory, or your honour, to suffer the slightest stain. From the 7th of April 1831, has commenced our national existence; Brazil will belong to Brazilians, and be free.

Fellow citizens, we have a Country, we have a Monarch, the symbol of your union, and of the integrity of the Empire; who, being educated in the midst of us, will receive almost in the cradle the first lessons of American liberty, and will learn to love that Brazil which witnessed his birth: the woeful prospect of anarchy, and of the dissolution of the Provinces, which was presented to our view, disappeared as it were in an instant, and was substituted by a more cheerful scene. All, all is due to your resolution and patriotism, and to the courage of the Brazilian Army, which put an end to the wild dreams of tyranny.

That so noble a victory may receive no blemish, continue to shew that you are worthy of yourselves, and of that Liberty which rejects all excesses, and which delights only in noble and elevated sentiments.

Brazilians! we have no reason to blush at the name; the Independence of our Country, and its Laws, will from this day be a reality; the great obstacle which stood in the way of it has retired from amongst us; he has quitted a Country, where he would have given to us the scourge of a Civil War, in return for the Throne which we gave him. All now depends on ourselves, on our prudence, moderation, and energy; let us proceed as we have begun, and we shall be regarded with admiration amongst the most civilized Nations. Long live the Brazilian Nation! Long live the Constitution! Long live the Constitutional Emperor Señor Dom Pedro II. *Rio de Janeiro, 8th April, 1831.*

Bispo Capellao Mor.
President.

Luis Francisco de Paula Cavalcante de Albuquerque,

Secretary.

❀

35. Feijó Outlines His Political Philosophy*

The very liberal and ultra-nationalistic Father Diogo Antô-nio Feijó emerges as one of the most intriguing and powerful figures of the regency period, 1831-1840. First he served as Minister of Justice and then entered the Senate. When the Additional Act of 1834 reduced the number of regents from three to one, he was elected as that regent, an office he held until late 1837 when he resigned under pressure from the conservatives. He was—and is—a difficult man to understand, and the following letter of his is included to shed some light on his character.

The Conditions under Which I Accept the Ministry of Justice

1. The members of the Regency should work closely in harmony with the single purpose of increasing the prosperity of Brazil.

2. The ministers of the government will handle all matters relative to the hiring and firing of employees and the general or private business in the Council of Ministers presided over by the Regents. If any minister is in disagreement with the other members he must defend himself before the legislative chambers and the other ministers can censure the dissident minister in front of the chambers.

Each minister independently can execute the laws, seek

....

* The original of this document is found in the private archives of Dr. David Carneiro in Curitiba, Paraná, Brazil. It is translated and printed here with his kind permission.

clarifications, and give orders but must obtain ultimately the approval of the council.

3. Within the year if I find it necessary to leave the ministry for some time I will have the right to select my own substitute. However, should I be absent from the post more than four months, the Regency will have the right to name another minister if it desires.

4. If a minister resigns his post, an act which can occur only if he requests to leave or true public opinion demands it, his substitute will be approved by the council by a majority of votes of the Ministers and the Regents.

5. There will be a newspaper directed by me.

Statement of the Method I Intend to Use to Carry Out My Duty as Minister.

Persuaded that at all times and most assuredly during periods of unrest only firmness of conduct, hard work, and justice can sustain the Government and make it loved and respected and certain that prevarication and, above all else, lack of action by the employees are the cause of just complaints of the people, I will be rigorous and inflexible in making them assume their responsibilities. In my opinion the existing laws are inefficacious and the process incapable of achieving the desired goal; but experience will make the legislators wiser, will save the government from moral responsibility, and enable it to propose sagacious measures which will end all the present embarrassments.

As free government is that in which law rules, I will order the strict and careful enforcement of those laws regardless of any complaints of the Executive. After the clamors of the complainers have finally ceased, the nation will be grateful to those who labored for its prosperity.

Notice

My way of life: my personal life will not change but will continue in the same way it has in the past.

I will always take consolation in the fact that no matter

how unhappy the results might appear I am faithful to my principles and my conscience. I will be ashamed if I do not keep any of my promises. In testimony thereof I sign below and request the Regency to do likewise as proof of their acceptance of my conditions and of agreement with my statements.

Rio de Janeiro
July 4, 1831

DIOGO ANTÔNIO FEIJÓ.

❊

---

36. Proclamation of the Majority of Pedro II*

The most serious consequence of the regency period was the loosening of the ties of national unity. The experiments with federalism and the general weakness of the executive helped to fan regional sparks of discontent. Rebellions broke out in almost all the provinces at one time or another. The most threatening were the Cabanagem in Pará, 1835-1838; the Sabinada in Bahia, in 1837-1838; the Balaiada in Maranhão, 1838-1841; and the Farroupilha which started in Rio Grande do Sul in 1835 and lasted for a decade. Responsible statesmen of all political hues watched with horror as the centrifugal forces began to tear the nation apart. They looked to the young Pedro as the symbol of unity capable of holding Brazil together, but the constitution prevented him from ruling until his eighteenth birthday. As rebellion
....

* From *British and Foreign State Papers*, 1840-1841, XXIX (London: James Ridgway, 1857), 718.

spread, the legislature became convinced that it must act at once. Accordingly, it proclaimed Pedro to be of age on July 23, 1840 when he was only fourteen.

Brazilians!

The General Legislative Assembly of Brazil, recognizing the happy intellectual development of His Imperial Majesty Dom Pedro II, with whom Divine Providence has blessed the empire of Santa Cruz; recognizing likewise the evils inherent in exceptional Governments, and witnessing the unanimous desire of the people of this capital; convinced that this desire is in accordance with that of the whole empire to confer on the same august personage the exercise of the powers which belong to him by the Constitution, have considered it expedient from such weighty motives to declare him of age, in order immediately to enter on the full exercise of these powers as constitutional Emperor and perpetual defender of Brazil. The august Monarch has just taken the solemn oath determined by Article 103 of the Constitution of the empire.

Brazilians! The hopes of the nation are converted into realities: a new era has dawned: may it be one of union and prosperity: may we be worthy of so great a benefit.

❧

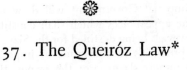

37. The Queiróz Law*

Under British pressure, Brazil had agreed to halt the importation of slaves in 1831. However, the Brazilian public was not then ready for such a move, and increased numbers of the unfortunate blacks continued to arrive on the aptly

....
* From *British and Foreign State Papers*, 1849-1850, XXXIX (London: Harrison and Sons, 1863), 1060-1061.

named tumbeiros (*floating tombs*). *As the economic emphasis shifted from sugar to coffee, as a middle class began to
emerge, and as it became increasingly desirable to attract
European immigrants, the Brazilians agreed that the nefarious traffic should be ended once and for all. Internal pressures culminated in the Queiróz Law of 1850 which closed
Brazil's principal source of slaves and provided an effective
and definitive abolition of the slave trade.*

We, Dom Pedro, by the Grace of God, and the unanimous
acclamation of the people, Constitutional Emperor and Perpetual Defender of Brazil, make known to all our subjects,
that the General Legislative Assembly has decreed, and we
have approved, the following Law:

ART. I. Brazilian vessels wherever found, and foreign vessels found in the ports, bays, anchorages, or territorial waters
of Brazil, having slaves on board, whose importation is prohibited by the Law of the 7th of November, 1831, or which
may have landed them, shall be seized by the authorities, or
by Brazilian ships of war, and considered importers of slaves.
Those which have not slaves on board, nor shall have recently landed them, shall, if appearances are found of having
been employed in Slave Trade, also be seized, and considered
as attempting to import slaves.

II. The Imperial Government will draw up regulations
specifying the appearances which shall constitute legal presumption of vessels being destined for the Slave Trade.

III. The principals in the crime of importing or of attempting to import slaves, are: the owner, the captain or
master, the mate, the boatswain, and the supercargo. The
accomplices are: the crew, and those who assist in the landing of slaves on Brazilian territory, or who assist in conceal-
ing them from the knowledge of the public authorities, or in
preventing their seizure at sea, or in the act of landing, if
pursued.

IV. The importation of slaves into the territory of the
empire is hereby considered piracy, and shall be punished by
its tribunals with the pains and penalties declared in Article

II of the Law of 7th November, 1831. The attempting and abetting shall be punished according to the rules of the Articles XXXIV and XXXV of the Criminal Code.

V. The vessels treated of in Articles I and II, and all boats employed in landing, hiding, or the fraudulent removal of slaves, shall be sold, with all the cargo found on board; and the proceeds shall belong to the captors, deducting one-fourth part for the informer, if any. And the Government, the prize being adjudged good, shall grant to the crew of the vessel making the capture, the sum of forty milreis for each African seized, which shall be distributed in conformity with the laws in that respect.

VI. All the slaves seized shall be re-exported at the cost of the State to the ports from whence they came, or to any other point out of the empire which the Government may think proper; and until this re-exportation shall take place, they shall be employed on work under the guardianship of the Government; in no case are their services to be conceded to private persons.

VII. Passports shall not be given to merchant-ships for the coast of Africa, until their owners, captains, or masters, have signed a declaration that they will not receive any slave on board of their vessels; the owner giving bond in a sum of money equal to the value of the ship and cargo; which bond shall not be cancelled unless they prove within eighteen months that they have strictly fulfilled the conditions of their declaration.

VIII. All seizures of vessels treated of in Articles I and II, as well as the freedom of the slaves captured on the high seas, or on the coast, before landing, or in the act of landing, or immediately after landing in barracoons and depôts on the coasts, or in ports, shall be tried and judged, in the first instance, by the Maritime Court, and, in the second instance, by the Council of State. The Government will fix by regulation the form of process in the first and second instance, and may create maritime judges in such ports as may be required; the judges of the respective districts serving of right as maritime judges, when appointed for that purpose.

IX. The maritime judges shall be equally competent to

try and sentence the accused mentioned in the IIIrd Article. From their decisions there shall be the same right of recourse and appeal to the superior courts as in the case of responsible public functionaries. The persons named in the IIIrd Article of the Law of the 7th of November, and who are not included in the IIIrd Article of this Law, are to be tried and sentenced in the ordinary judicial tribunals.

X. All provisions to the contrary are hereby revoked.

We command, therefore, all the authorities to whom a knowledge and the execution of the said Law belongs to execute the same, and to cause it to be executed, and thoroughly to observe that which is contained in it. Let the Department of Justice cause this to be printed, published, and distributed.

Given at the Palace of Rio de Janeiro, this 4th of September, 1850, 29th of the Independence and of the Empire.

[Sign manual of His Imperial Majesty.]
(L.S.) Euzebio de Queiróz Coutinho Mattozo Camara.

❋

---

38. The Standard of Living of the Worker in the Northeast in the Mid-Nineteenth Century*

At the time of independence, the population numbered roughly four million, of whom over a quarter were slaves. The two principal classes were the slaves and the slave-

....

* Translated from *Collecção dos Trabalhos do Conselho Geral de Salubridade Pública da Província de Pernambuco, 1849,* quoted in Gilberto Freyre, *Nordeste* (Rio de Janeiro: José Olympio, 1937), p. 237. Printed by permission of the publisher.

*owners, exactly as they had been throughout the colonial pe-
riod. Gradually the new nation developed its commercial and
manufacturing centers. The schools of law and medicine
graduated larger numbers of young whites and mulattoes. As
the small coastal towns began to grow, a new class timidly
began to appear in the cities, a group that was neither slave
nor slave-owner: the small merchants, the young professionals, the new military officers, the workers, and the artisans.
Crushed as they were in the economic vise between the large
mass of slaves below and the powerful slave-owners above,
their lot was not an easy one. One of the newspapers of Pernambuco in the mid-nineteenth century commented on the
lowly and difficult state of the free worker. Unhappily, the
questions posed therein were to be re-echoed over the succeeding decades, and the article could have appeared as easily
today as in 1850.*

The average daily wage of a man is 640 réis. Socially considered the man is the unification of three persons: husband,
wife, and son. He must bear the maximum load of work, the
work which will supply the other two.

Supposing that each one eats a pound of meat per day
. . . he will spend 300 réis on meat; if we add 80 réis for
flour and 20 for firewood, we will have the man spend 400
réis per day on food or about 12$000 milreis per month; and
as he must spend on housing about a third, more or less, of
what he spends for food, this comes to another 4$000 milreis
per month for a total of 16$000. He has left about four
thousand milreis to spend on holy days, during sickness, for
clothing, etc., which is impossible for a man who wants to
live hygienically and honorably. But as it is well known that
the poor live also with honor, it is interesting to learn how
this is done. Dry meat, salted and dry—and many times
spoiled—fish, flour without manioc, bad food, a hard bed,
an uncomfortable house, ragged clothing are the products
which the poor use. Even these come in limited amounts in
order not to exceed the budget.

Under such conditions the family can only suffer. It will

not have complete physical growth; its quantity of work will be less; its offspring will be deficient. From such a malnourished family comes the weak and cowardly soldier, the sensitive and powerless sailor. . . .

❀

39. The Problem of Large Landholdings in Pernambuco in the Mid-Nineteenth Century*

The problem of land distribution presented itself early and has remained unsolved. Thanks to the generous grants of the colonial period, the best land along the coast, where the majority has insisted upon living, had long since been distributed, and acquisition of land by the poor became nearly impossible in the underpopulated subcontinent. The following article, which appeared in a Recife newspaper in 1856, points out that the large landholdings formed a barrier to the economic growth of the nation. Most of what the article says is as true of contemporary Brazil as it was of imperial Brazil.

What future has the continuously growing population of the interior? Will the new additions devote themselves to agriculture? No. The more enlightened part will come here to Recife to seek its fortune, to solicit some ridiculous job. The rest will go to the towns and other centers of population and

. . . .

* Translated from "Abdalah-el-Kratif" in *Diario de Pernambuco* of March 24, 1856, quoted in Gilberto Freyre, *Nordeste* (Rio de Janeiro: José Olympio, 1937), pp. 247-249. Printed by permission of the publisher.

there spend a miserable life because among us there is no industry that offers the free worker security and regular pay.

. . .

And why do the youths of these unfortunate families, instead of entering into such precarious careers in public service, not take up farming? And for what reason, instead of learning the skills of a tailor, bricklayer, or carpenter, etc., do the sons of the less favored families not go back into the interior, why don't they become farmers? Why don't the inhabitants of the interior cultivate the soil? Why do those young people hunt out the towns? For all these questions there is but one answer and unfortunately it is convincing!

In the social state in which we live, the means of subsistence of the father of the family do not increase in proportion to the number of children, the general consequence of which is that the sons are poorer than their fathers and they possess less capital. Now, agriculture is closed by an insurmountable barrier to the less favored man, to anyone who does not have a certain amount of money. Agriculture is the chief source of production, the chief hope of our country. But since agriculture is closed by a barrier, it is necessary that that barrier fall, cost whatever it may.

And what is that barrier? Large landholdings. It is the terrible curse which has ruined and depopulated many other nations.

This region which extends along the entire coast of our province and inland for ten, twelve, or, at times, fifteen and eighteen leagues is divided into sugar plantations and properties whose dimensions vary from a quarter of a league square to two and three and even four and five leagues square.

Here, as the growing of sugarcane demands, a certain amount of land, which cannot be found everywhere, is devoted to the cultivation of the cane. Other parts of the plantation are dedicated to the woods that are necessary for sugar production, the pastures for the care of the oxen, and the gardens for the planting of manioc, indispensable for the feeding of the slaves. But still a major part of the plantations possesses vast extensions of uncultivated land that would be

especially well suited for the small farmer and which, if cultivated, would be sufficient to furnish abundantly flour, corn,
beans, etc., to all the population of the province and of the
neighboring provinces with some produce left over for exportation.

The proprietors refuse to sell these lands or even to rent
them. If you own thirty or forty *contos de réis* you can buy a
sugar plantation, but if you are poor and want to buy or rent
a small patch of land, you won't find any.

This is what makes the unproductive population of the
cities, increases regularly the number of solicitors of public
employment, and raises daily the crimes against property;
and the country becomes poorer day by day in consequence
of the increase of the number of consumers while the number of producers remains stationary or at best increases at a
much slower rate.

But the large landowners say that they are far from refusing the poor people the land they need to cultivate. They say
that when these landless poor ask for it they give them at a
small rental or at times gratuitously not only land to plant
but wood to build homes. That does happen but only at the
pleasure of the large landowner.

Anytime he wants to, for any caprice or because they refuse to vote for his candidates or for any reason, he can order
them off the land, and they have no recourse. How can you
ask these people to plant when they have no certainty of
harvesting? What incentive exists to induce them to improve
the land from which they can be evicted at any moment?

On the land of the large property holders they do not
enjoy any public right because they do not have any freedom; for them, the large landowners are the police, the
courts, the administration, in short, everything. The lot of
these unhappy people differs in nothing from the serfs of the
Middle Ages.

❀

40. The Treaty of the Triple Alliance*

Brazilian diplomacy, like that of the Portuguese, focused on the Prata region. Brazil lost control of the left bank of that fluvial network in 1828, the year Uruguay was created as an independent buffer between the jealous rivals of the river, Argentina and Brazil. Rio de Janeiro continued to keep a cautious eye on the area and frequently intervened indirectly and, at times, directly—such as in 1852 to overthrow Juan Manuel de Rosas. The small but militarily powerful Paraguay regarded the maintenance of Uruguayan integrity as a guarantee of its own independence and of a just balance of power in the area. When Argentina and Brazil threatened to intervene in Uruguay in 1864, Paraguay attacked Brazil and its puppet government in Montevideo. To do so, the armies of Francisco Solano López marched across Argentine territory. In response to that bellicose action, Argentina, Brazil, and Uruguay signed a treaty of alliance on May 1, 1865. The longest and bloodiest war in South American history was under way, and its consequences in Brazil would be profound.

The government of the oriental republic of the Uruguay, the government of his Majesty the Emperor of Brazil, and the government of the Argentine republic—the two last finding themselves at war with the government of Paraguay by its having been declared against them in fact by this government, and the first in a state of hostility, and its internal security menaced by the said government which violated the republic, solemn treaties, and the international usages of civ-

....

* From N. Andrew N. Cleven, *Readings in Hispanic American History* (Boston: Ginn and Co., 1927), pp. 650-655.

ilized nations, and committed unjustifiable acts after having disturbed the relations with its neighbors by the most abusive and aggressive proceedings—persuaded that the peace, security, and well-being of their respective nations is impossible while the actual government of Paraguay exists, and that it is an imperious necessity, called for by the greatest interest, to cause that government to disappear, respecting the sovereignty, independence, and territorial integrity of the republic of Paraguay, have resolved, with this object, to celebrate a treaty of alliance, offensive and defensive, and thereto have appointed to be their plenipotentiaries, to wit: His excellency the provisional governor of the oriental republic of the Uruguay: his excellency Dr. D. Carlos de Castro, his minister secretary of state in the department of foreign affairs; his Majesty the Emperor of Brazil; his excellency Señor Dr. F. Octaviano de Almeida Rosa, of his council, deputy to the general legislative assembly, and officer of the imperial order of the rose; his excellency the President of the Argentine Confederation; his excellency Señor Dr. D. Rufino de Elizalde, his minister and secretary of state in the department of foreign affairs—who, after having exchanged their respective credentials, which were found to be in good and due form, did agree as follows:

Art. 1. The oriental republic of the Uruguay, his Majesty the Emperor of Brazil, and the Argentine Republic unite in offensive and defensive alliance in the war provoked by the government of Paraguay.

Art. 2. The allies will concur with all the means they can dispose of, by land or on the rivers, according as may be necessary.

Art. 3. The operations of the war being to commence in the territory of the Argentine Republic, or on a part of Paraguayan territory bordering on the same, the command in chief and the direction of the allied armies remains intrusted to the President of the Argentine Republic, general-in-chief of its army, Brigadier General Don Bartolome Mitre.

The maritime forces of the allies will be under the immediate command of Vice Admiral Viscount de Tamandaré, commander-in-chief of the squadron of his Majesty the Emperor of Brazil.

The land forces of the oriental republic of the Uruguay, a division of the Argentine forces, and another of the Brazilian forces, to be designated by their respective superior chiefs, will form an army under the immediate orders of the provisional governor of the oriental republic of the Uruguay, Brigadier General Don Venancio Flores.

The land forces of his Majesty the Emperor of Brazil will form an army under the immediate orders of their general-in-chief, Brigadier Manoel Luís Osório.

Although the high contracting parties are agreed not to change the field of the operations of war, nevertheless, in order to preserve the sovereign rights of the three nations, they do agree from this time, on the principle of reciprocity, for the command in chief, in the event of those operations having to pass over to the oriental or Brazilian territory.

Art. 4. The internal military order and economy of the allied troops will depend solely on their respective chiefs.

The pay, victuals, munitions of war, arms, clothing, equipment, and means of transport, of the allied troops will be for account of the respective states.

Art. 5. The high contracting parties will afford mutually all the assistance or elements which they may have, and which the others may require, in the form to be agreed upon.

Art. 6. The allies pledge themselves solemnly not to lay down their arms unless by common accord, nor until they shall have overthrown the present government of Paraguay, and not to treat with the enemy separately, nor sign any treaty of peace, truce, armistice, or convention whatsoever, for putting an end to or suspending the war, unless by a perfect agreement of all.

Art. 7. The war not being against the people of Paraguay, but against its government, the allies may admit into a Paraguayan legion all the citizens of that nation who may choose to concur to overthrow the said government, and will furnish them with all the elements they may require, in the form and under the conditions to be agreed upon.

Art. 8. The allies oblige themselves to respect the independence, sovereignty, and territorial integrity of the republic of Paraguay. Consequently, the Paraguayan people may choose their government, and give to themselves the institutions they please, not incorporating it nor asking for a protectorate under any of the allies as a consequence of this war.

Art. 9. The independence, sovereignty, and territorial integrity of the republic of Paraguay shall be guaranteed collectively, in conformity with the foregoing article by the high contracting parties, during the period of five years.

Art. 10. It is agreed between the high contracting parties that the exemptions, privileges, or concessions, which they may obtain from the government of Paraguay, shall be common to all gratuitously, if they be gratuitous, and with the same compensation if they be conditional.

Art. 11. The present government of Paraguay being overthrown, the allies will proceed to make the necessary arrangements with the authority constituted, to insure the free navigation of the rivers Paraná and Paraguay in such manner that the regulations or laws of that republic shall not obstruct, hinder, nor burden the transit or direct navigation of the merchantmen and vessels of war of the allied states proceeding to their respective territory, or to territory not belonging to Paraguay, and they will take suitable guarantees for the effectiveness of those arrangements on the base that those regulations of fluvial police, whether they be for those two rivers, or likewise for the river Uruguay, shall be made by common accord between the allies and such other bordering states as shall, within the term to be agreed upon by the said allies, accept the invitation made to them.

Art. 12. The allies reserve to themselves to concert the measures most suitable in order to guarantee peace with the republic of Paraguay after the overthrow of the present government.

Art. 13. The allies will appoint in due season the plenipotentiaries required to celebrate the arrangements, conventions, or treaties, that may have to be made with the government that shall be established in Paraguay.

Art. 14. The allies will exact from this government payment of the expenses of the war which they have been themselves obliged to accept, as well as reparation and indemnification for the damages and injuries caused to their public and private properties, and to the persons of their citizens, without express declaration of war, and for the damages and injuries committed subsequently, in violation of the principles which govern the laws of war.

The oriental republic of the Uruguay will likewise exact an indemnification proportioned to the damage and injury caused to it by the government of Paraguay through the war into which it is forced to enter to defend its security, threatened by that government.

Art. 15. In a special convention shall be determined the manner and form of liquidating and paying the debt proceeding from the aforesaid causes.

Art. 16. In order to avoid the discussions and wars which questions of boundaries involve, it is established that the allies shall exact from the government of Paraguay that it celebrate definitive boundary treaties with their respective governments upon the following basis: The Argentine Republic shall be divided from the republic of Paraguay by the rivers Paraná and Paraguay, until meeting the boundaries of the empire of Brazil, these being on the right margin of the river Paraguay, the Bahia Negra.

The empire of Brazil shall be divided from the republic of Paraguay on the side of the Paraná by the first river below the Salto de las Siete Cahidas, which, according to the recent map of Manchez, is the Igurey, and from the mouth of the Igurey and in its course upwards until reaching its source.

On the side of the left bank of the Paraguay, by the river Apa, from its mouth to its source.

In the interior from the summits of the mountain of Maracayú, the streams on the east belonging to Brazil, and those on the west to Paraguay, and drawing lines as straight as possible from the said mountain to the sources of the Apa and of the Igurey.

Art. 17. The allies guarantee to each other reciprocally the faithful fulfilment of the agreements, arrangements, or treaties that are to be celebrated with the government that shall be established in Paraguay, in virtue of what is agreed upon by the present treaty of alliance, which shall always remain in its full force and vigor to the effect that these stipulations be respected and executed by the republic of Paraguay.

In order to obtain this result they do agree that, in the case that one of the high contracting parties should be unable to obtain from the government of Paraguay the fulfilment of what is agreed upon, or that this government should attempt to annul the stipulations adjusted with the allies, the others shall employ actively their exertions to cause them to be respected.

If these exertions should be useless, the allies will concur with all their means in order to make effective the execution of what is stipulated.

Art. 18. This treaty shall be kept secret until the principal object of the alliance shall be obtained.

Art. 19. The stipulations of this treaty that do not require legislative authorization for their ratification shall begin to take effect so soon as they be approved by the respective governments, and the others from the exchange of the ratifications, which shall take place within the term of forty days, counted from the date of said treaty, or sooner if it be possible, which shall be done in the city of Buenos Ayres.

In testimony whereof, the undersigned plenipotentiaries of his excellency the provisional governor of the oriental republic of the Uruguay, of his Majesty the Emperor of Brazil, and of his excellency the President of the Argentine Republic, in virtue of our full powers, do sign this treaty, and do cause to be put thereto our seals, in the city of Buenos Ayres, the first day of May, in the year of our Lord 1865.

C. DE CASTRO
F. OCT. DE ALMEIDA ROSA
RUFINO DE ELIZALDE

Protocol

Their excellencies the plenipotentiaries of the Argentine Republic; of the oriental republic of the Uruguay, and of his Majesty the Emperor of Brazil, being assembled at the department for foreign affairs, agreed:

1. That in fulfilment of the treaty of alliance of this date the fortifications of Humaitá shall be caused to be demolished, and it shall not be permitted that others of an equal nature should be erected, which might impede the faithful execution of that treaty.

2. That it being one of the measures necessary to guarantee peace with the government that shall be established in Paraguay not to leave arms or elements of war, those that are met with shall be divided in equal shares between the allies.

3. That the trophies and booty that may be taken from the enemy shall be divided between the allies who make the capture.

4. That the chiefs in command of the allied armies shall concert measures to carry what is here agreed on into effect.

And they signed this at Buenos Ayres on the first of May, 1865.

CARLOS DE CASTRO
RUFINO DE ELIZALDE
F. OCT. DE ALMEIDA ROSA

❀

41. The Decree Opening the Amazon to International Traffic*

With 25,000 miles of navigable water and three million square miles of drainage basin, the Amazon ranks as one of the world's greatest rivers. Most of it is located within Brazilian territory, but it serves also as a back door into Bolivia, Peru, Ecuador, Colombia, and Venezuela. For some decades, the United States and several European nations had been urging the imperial government to open to world trade that international highway into the interior of the continent. Eager to develop that distant region, the government finally acceded to the foreign requests on December 7, 1866, permitting the vessels of all nations to ply the Amazon River.

With a view to promote the aggrandizement of the Empire, ever facilitating its international intercourse more and more, and imparting animation to the navigation and commerce of its River Amazon, and to its confluents Tocantins and San Francisco, having heard the opinion of my Council of State, it is my will to decree as follows:

Art. I. The navigation shall be opened to vessels of all nations from 7th September, 1867, of the River Amazon, as far as the frontiers of Brazil; of the River Tocantins, as far as Cametá; of the Tapajoz, as far as Santarem; of the Madeira, as far as Borda; and of the River Negro, as far as Manáos.

II. On the same date fixed upon in Article I, the navigation of the River San Francisco, as far as the city of Penedo, shall be opened.

....

* From *British and Foreign State Papers, 1867-1868*, LVIII (London: William Ridgway, 1873), 551-552.

III. In those confluents of the River Amazon, as and in the parts of same where only one bank belongs to Brazil, the navigation, as far as concerns their respective limits and police regulations, will depend on previous arrangement with the boundary States.

IV. The present dispositions in no respect alter the observances prescribed by the Treaties in force with the Republics of Peru and Venezuela, in conformity with the regulations already dispatched for that purpose.

V. My Ministers and Secretaries of State will carry out the agreement treated of in Article III, through the proper departments, and will expedite the necessary regulations for the effective execution of this Decree. Let Antônio Coelho de Sá e Albuquerque of my Council, Senator of the Empire, Minister and Secretary of State for Foreign Affairs, so understand and cause it to be executed.

Palace of Rio de Janeiro, 7th December, 1866, 46th (year) of the Independence and of the Empire, with the sign-manual of His Majesty the Emperor.

ANTÔNIO COELHO DE SÁ E ALBUQUERQUE.

❁

42 . The Republican Manifesto*

The drama of the five-year struggle against Paraguay stirred the empire. New ideas were sought to solve old problems. One important source of those ideas was Auguste Comte and his positivism. The new bourgeois elite was particularly at-

....

* Translated from Djacir Menezes (ed.), *O Brasil no Pensamento Brasileiro* (Rio de Janeiro: Ministério da Educação e Cultura, 1957), pp. 499-500, 505, 510-517.

*tracted to his philosophy, and from its ranks came the
founders of the Federal Republican Party. The new party
denounced the monarchy and called for a federal republic in
a manifesto issued in December of 1870.*

In this country, which considers itself constitutional and
where only delegated, responsible powers should be able to
act, it happens, because of a defect in the system, that there
is only one active, omnipotent, perpetual power, superior to
the law and to public opinion, and it is, of course, the sacred
power, inviolable and irresponsible.

Privilege invades all aspects of society—in synthesis, it is
the fabric of our society and politics—privilege of religion,
privilege of race, privilege of intellect, privilege of position,
which constitutes all the arbitrary and hateful distinctions
that create in the bosom of civil and political society the
monstrous superiority of one over all or of a few over the
many.

Our country owes its moral decadence, administrative dis-
organization, and economic disturbances, which threaten to
devour the future after ruining the present, to the disequi-
librium of forces, to that atrophying pressure.

Despite a half century of existence as an independent national community, Brazilian society finds itself today facing
the problem of its political organization as if it had just now
emerged from colonial chaos.

. . .

A Chamber of Deputies subject to dissolution at the will
of the sovereign and a life-term Senate selected by the sovereign in no way can constitute the legitimate representation
of the country.

Liberty of conscience nullified by a privileged Church;
economic freedom suppressed by restrictive legislation; liberty of the press subordinated to the jurisdiction of the functionaries of the Government; freedom of association dependent on the pleasure of the authorities; freedom of instruction

infringed upon by arbitrary governmental inspection and by official monopoly; individual freedom subject to preventative imprisonment, to recruitment, to the discipline of the national guard, deprived of the full guarantee of habeas corpus; these are the conditions under the present system of government.

A sovereign, perpetual, and irresponsible power creates with a nod of the head the executive by selecting the ministers, the legislature by choosing the Senators and designating the Deputies, and the judiciary by naming the judges.

Such is in essence the political mechanism of the Constitution of 1824; such are the sophisms by means of which the Emperor reigns, rules and regulates.

. . .

In Brazil the desire to establish federalism takes precedence even over the democratic idea. The topography of our territory, the diverse zones into which it is divided, the various climates and the different products, the mountains and the rivers indicate the necessity of modeling administration and local government to accompany and to respect the very divisions created by nature and imposed by the immensity of our territory.

. . .

From 1824 to 1848, from the Federation of the Equator to the Revolution of Pernambuco, one can say that the electric current which passed through the Provinces shaking the social organism came from a single source—the desire for local independence, the idea of federation, the sentiment for provincial autonomy.

. . .

Provincial autonomy is for us Republicans . . . a cardinal and solemn principle which we inscribe on our banner.

Federalism based on the reciprocal independence of the Provinces, elevated to the category of States, linked only by the bond of the same nationality and by the solidarity of the great interests of representation and defense is what we adopt in our program as being the only means capable of maintaining the community of the Brazilian family.

· · ·

National sovereignty can only exist, can only be recognized and practiced in a nation whose parliament, elected by the participation of all the citizens, has the supreme direction and pronounces the final word in public business.

If there exists, in any constitution, an element of compulsion to the principle of democratic liberty, the national sovereignty is violated, it is null, incapable of the salutary effects of the modern formula of government—the government of all for all.

Another indispensable condition of national sovereignty is that it is inalienable and that only exercise of it can be delegated. . . .

From this principle it follows that when the people cede a part of their sovereignty they do so to create not a master but a servant, that is, a functionary.

The consequence of this is that the functionary has to be revocable, mobile, elective, the very essence of the formula of the modern state—the mobility of persons and the perpetuity of functions—opposed to which are the systems, such as the one ruling over us, exalting heredity, inviolability, irresponsibility.

· · ·

Strengthened by our right and by our conscience, we present ourselves before our fellow citizens resolutely waving the banner of the Federal Republican Party.

We are from America and we desire to be Americans.

Our monarchical form of government is in its essence and practice contrary and hostile to the right and to the interests of the American States.

The continuance of that form will be, in addition to the origin of oppression in the interior, the perpetual source of hostility and war with our neighbors.

To Europe we pass as a democratic monarchy which

neither inspires sympathy nor provokes adhesion. To America we pass as a monarchical democracy where the instinct and force of the people cannot predominate over the will and omnipotence of the sovereign.

Under such conditions, Brazil can consider itself an isolated nation, not only in the Americas but in the world.

We direct our efforts to end this situation by putting ourselves in fraternal contact with all peoples and in democratic solidarity with the continent of which we are a part.

❀

43. Descriptions of Slave Markets

Slavery remained the dominant factor shaping Brazilian society throughout most of the nineteenth century. The conditions surrounding slavery varied widely within the empire. In general, due to the inheritance of Portuguese law and customs, the slave was well integrated within the society. He enjoyed certain rights. One of the unique aspects of Luso-Brazilian slavery was that Negroes could work for money on the side and in that way buy their own freedom. Occasionally they formed their own mutual aid societies for such a purpose. One of the bylaws of the Negro Brotherhood of St. Anthony of Catagerona in eighteenth-century Bahia stated, "Chapter XIII provides that any member who is a slave, either male or female, shall whenever possible be helped financially by the brotherhood to secure his or her freedom." Even so, slavery at its best is an odious institution. One of its most despicable aspects was the slave market. Travelers to Brazil inevitably remarked upon it.

*

CONDITIONS IN THE MARKET *

Robert Walsh, an Englishman traveling in Brazil during the late 1820's, left the following description of the slave market.

The place where the great slave mart is held, is a long winding street called the Vallongo, which runs from the sea, at the northern extremity of the city. Almost every house in this place is a large warehouse, where the slaves are deposited, and customers go to purchase. These warerooms stand at each side of the street, and the poor creatures are exposed for sale like any other commodity. When a customer comes in, they are turned up before him; such as he wishes are handled by the purchaser in different parts, exactly as I have seen others feeling a calf; and the whole examination is the mere animal capability, without the remotest inquiry as to the moral quality, which a man no more thinks of, than if he was buying a dog or a mule. I have frequently seen Brazilian ladies at these sales. They go dressed, sit down, handle and examine their purchases, and bring them away with the most perfect indifference. I sometimes saw groups of well-dressed females here, shopping for slaves, exactly as I have seen English ladies amusing themselves at our bazaars.

. . .

The warerooms are spacious apartments, where sometimes three or four hundred slaves, of all ages and sexes are exhibited together. Round the room are benches on which the elder generally sit, and the middle is occupied by the younger, particularly females, who squat on the ground stowed close together, with their hands and chins resting on their knees. Their only covering is a small girdle of cross-barred cotton, tied round the waist.

....

* From Robert Walsh, *Notices of Brazil in 1828 and 1829*, II (Boston: Richardson, Lord and Holbrook, 1831), 179-181.

The first time I passed through this street, I stood at the bars of the window looking through, when a cigano came and pressed me to enter. I was particularly attracted by a group of children, one of whom, a young girl, had something very pensive and engaging in her countenance. The cigano observing me look at her, whipped her up with a long rod, and bade her with a rough voice to come forward. It was quite affecting to see the poor timid shrinking child standing before me, in a state the most helpless and forlorn, that ever a being, endued, like myself, with a reasonable mind and an immortal soul, could be reduced to. Some of these girls have remarkably sweet and engaging countenances. Notwithstanding their dusky hue, they look so modest, gentle and sensible, that you could not for a moment hesitate to acknowledge, that they are endued with a like feeling, a common nature, with your own daughters. The seller was about to put the child into all the attitudes, and display her person in the same way, as he would a man; but I declined the exhibition, and she shrunk timidly back to her place, and seemed glad to hide herself in the group that surrounded her.

The men were generally less interesting objects than the women; their countenances and hues were very varied, according to the part of the African coast from which they came; some were soot black, having a certain ferocity of aspect that indicated strong and fierce passions, like men who were darkly brooding over some deep-felt wrongs, and meditating revenge. When any one was ordered, he came forward with a sullen indifference, threw his arms over his head, stamped with his feet, shouted to show the soundness of his lungs, ran up and down the room, and was treated exactly like a horse, put through his paces at a repository; and when done, he was whipped to his stall.

The heads of the slaves, both male and female, were generally half shaved; the hair being left only on the fore part. A few of the females had cotton handkerchiefs tied round their heads, which with some little ornaments of native seed or shells, gave them a very engaging appearance. A number, particularly the males, were affected with eruptions of a white scurf which had a loathsome appearance, like leprosy.

It was considered, however, a wholesome effort of nature, to throw off the effects of the salt provisions used during the voyage; and, in fact, it resembles exactly a saline concretion.

Many of them were lying stretched on the bare boards; and among the rest, mothers with young children at their breasts, of which they seemed passionately fond. They were all doomed to remain on the spot, like sheep in a pen, till they were sold; they had no apartment to retire to, no bed to repose on, no covering to protect them; they sit naked all day, and lie naked all night, on the bare boards, or benches where we saw them exhibited.

. . .

A great number of those who arrive at Rio are sent up the country, and we every day met cofilas, such as Mungo Park describes in Africa, winding through the woods, as they travelled from place to place in the interior. They formed long processions, following one another in a file; the slave-merchant, distinguished by his large felt hat and poncho, brings up the rear on a mule, with a long lash in his hand. It was another subject of pity, to see groups of these poor creatures cowering together at night in the open ranchos, drenched with cold rain, in a climate so much more frigid than their own.

*

THE AUCTION*

A North American traveler, Thomas Ewbank, described a slave auction at mid-century.

I have repeatedly passed an auction store at the corner of Ourives and Ouvidor. Today printed bills were hanging by

....

* From Thomas Ewbank, *Life in Brazil or a Visit to the Land of the Cocoa and the Palm* (New York: Harper & Brothers, 1856), pp. 282-284.

the door. I took one and stepped in. A long table extended from near the entrance to the low box pulpit of the salesman. Behind it, a light iron railing cut off a portion of the store. The place was filled with new and secondhand furniture, old pictures, Dutch cheeses, Yankee clocks, kitchen utensils, crockeryware, old books, shoes, pickles, etc. . . . .

Vendues of these things are held here daily, and once or twice a week another variety of merchandise is offered. This was the case today—an assorted invoice of colored goods, arranged on benches behind the railing. The catalogue contained eighty-nine lots, and each lot had a corresponding number pinned to it, that purchasers, on running over the list, might compare the articles with their description. These goods were living beings. Every lot was a man or woman, a boy or girl. There were fifty-three males, most of whom ranged between eighteen and thirty years of age—carpenters, masons, smiths, and country hands. One was a sailor, another a caulker and boatman. There were two tailors, a coachman, a saddler, a sawyer, a squarer of timber (one expert with the adze), a shoemaker, cooks, a coffee-carrier, and a barber surgeon, who, like most of his profession, was a musician—"No. 19, one Rapaz, *Barbeiro, bom sangrador e musico*."

Of females, the oldest was twenty-six, and the youngest between seven and eight—washers, sewers, cooks, two dressmakers *"muito prendada"*—very accomplished. Others made shirts, dressed ladies' hair, etc. A couple were wet nurses, with much good milk, and each with a colt or filly, thus: "No. 61, one Rapariga, *con muito bom leite, com cria*." *Cria* signifies the young of horses, and is applied to Negro offspring.

They were of every shade, from deep Angola jet to white or nearly white, as one young woman facing me appeared. She was certainly superior in mental organization to some of the buyers. The anguish with which she watched the proceedings, and waited her turn to be brought out, exposed, examined, and disposed of, was distressing. A little girl, I suppose her own, stood by her weeping, with one hand in her lap, obviously dreading to be torn away. This child did not cry out—that is not allowed—but tears chased each other down her cheeks, her little bosom panted violently, and such a look of alarm marked her face as she turned her large eyes on the proceedings, that I thought at one time she would have dropped.

"Purchasers of pots and pot-lids," said Diogenes, "ring them lest they should carry cracked ones home, but men they buy on sight." If such was the practice of old, it is not so now: the head, eyes, mouth, teeth, arms, hands, trunks, legs, feet—every limb and ligament without are scrutinized, while, to ascertain if aught within be ruptured, the breast and other parts are sounded.

The auctioneer, a tall, black-whiskered man of thirty-five, was a master of his profession, if one might judge from his fluency and fervor. A hammer in his right hand, the forefinger of his left pointing to a plantation hand standing confused at his side, he pours out a flood of words. The poor fellow had on a canvas shirt, with sleeves ending at the elbows and trousers of the same, the legs of which he is told to roll above his knees. A bidder steps up, examines his lower limbs, then his mouth, breast, and other parts. He is now told to walk toward the door and back to show his gait. As he was returning, the hammer fell, and he was pushed back within the railing. Another, who had but four toes on one foot, was quickly disposed of.

The clerk next went behind the rails and brought forward a woman—a field hand. She was stout, and seemed older than reported in the catalogue. Dressed as sparely and plainly as the men, she too was examined, and told to walk to and fro. When near the door, a bidder interrogated her, but on what I could not comprehend. His last remark was translated plainly by her raising her skirt to expose her legs. They were much swollen. Two hundred and fifty milreis was the sum she brought.

44. The Law of the Free Womb*

It was becoming increasingly obvious that the Negro was contributing more than his share to the development of Brazil. In The Negro in Brazilian Literature, *Raymond Sayers synthesized that contribution in his statement, "The greatest sculptor, Antônio Francisco Lisboa, and the greatest novelist, Machado de Assis, were both mulattoes, as were the first important musician, Father José Maurício, and the first great engineer, André Rebouças." Because of the Negro's valuable role in the war against Paraguay, both on the homefront and on the battlefield, opinion began to coalesce among the more enlightened groups of society in favor of the gradual emancipation of the slaves. The logical step after the closing of the external source of slaves in 1850 was to put an end to the internal source. Accordingly, in 1871, the* Law of the Free Womb *(Ventre Livre) was enacted declaring free all children born to slaves. The legislation condemned slavery to eventual extinction and momentarily agitation for emancipation subsided.*

The Princess Imperial, Regent, in the name of His Majesty the Emperor Senhor D. Pedro II, makes known to all the subjects of the Empire, that the General Assembly has decreed, and that she has sanctioned, the following Law:

Art. I. The children of women slaves that may be born in the Empire from the date of this Law shall be considered to be free.

§1. The said minors shall remain with and be under the dominion of the owners of the mother, who shall be obliged

....

* From *British and Foreign State Papers*, 1871-1872, LXII (London: William Ridgway, 1877), 616-620.

to rear and take care of them until such children shall have completed the age of eight years.

On the child of the slave attaining this age, the owner of its mother shall have the option either of receiving from the State the indemnification of 600 dollars, or of making use of the services of the minor until he shall have completed the age of twenty-one years.

In the former event the Government will receive the minor, and will dispose of him in conformity with the provisions of the present Law.

The pecuniary indemnification above fixed shall be paid in Government bonds, bearing interest at six per cent. per annum, which will be considered extinct at the end of thirty years.

The declaration of the owner must be made within thirty days, counting from the day on which the minor shall complete the age of eight years; and should he not do so within that time it will be understood that he embraces the option of making use of the service of the minor.

§2. Any one of those minors may ransom himself from the *onus* of servitude, by means of a previous pecuniary indemnification, offered by himself, or by any other person, to the owner of his mother, calculating the value of his services for the time which shall still remain unexpired to complete the period, should there be no agreement on the *quantum* of the said indemnification.

§3. It is also incumbent on owners to rear and bring up the children which the daughters of their female slaves may have while they are serving the same owners.

Such obligation, however, will cease as soon as the service of the mother ceases. Should the latter die within the term of servitude the children may be placed at the disposal of the Government.

§4. Should the female slave obtain her freedom, her children under eight years of age who may be under the dominion of her owners shall, by virtue of §1, be delivered up, unless she shall prefer leaving them with him, and he consents to their remaining.

§5. In case of the female slave being made over to another

owner her free children under twelve years of age shall accompany her, the new owner of the said slave being invested with the rights and obligations of his predecessor.

§6. The services of the children of female slaves shall cease to be rendered before the term marked in §1, if by decision of the Criminal Judge it be known that the owner of the mothers ill-treat the children, inflicting on them severe punishments.

§7. The right conferred on owners by §1 shall be transferred in cases of direct succession; the child of a slave must render his services to the person to whose share in the division of property the said slave shall belong.

II. The Government may deliver over to associations which they shall have authorized, the children of the slaves that may be born from the date of this Law forward, and given up or abandoned by the owners of said slaves, or taken away from them by virtue of Article I, §6.

§1. The said associations shall have a right to the gratuitous services of the minors, until they shall have completed the age of twenty-one years, and may hire out their services, but shall be bound—

1st. To rear and take care of the said minors.

2ndly. To save a sum for each of them, out of the amount of wages, which for this purpose is reserved in the respective statutes.

3rdly. To seek to place them in a proper situation when their term of service shall be ended.

§2. The associations referred to in the previous paragraph shall be subject to the inspection of Judges of the Orphans' Court, in as far as affects minors.

§3. The disposition of this Article is applicable to foundling asylums, and to the persons whom the Judges of the Orphans' Court charge with the education of the said minors, in default of associations or houses established for that purpose.

§4. The Government has the free right of ordering the said minors to be taken into the public establishments, the obligations imposed by §1 on the authorised associations being in this case transferred to the State.

III. As many slaves as correspond in value to the annual disposable sum from the emancipation fund shall be freed in each province of the Empire.

§1. The emancipation fund arises from—

1st. The tax on slaves.

2ndly. General tax on transfer of the slaves as property.

3rdly. The proceeds of six lotteries per annum, free of tax, and the tenth part of those which may be granted from this time forth, to be drawn in the capital of the Empire.

4thly. The fines imposed by virtue of this Law.

5thly. The sums which may be marked in the general budget, and in those of the provinces and municipalities.

6thly. Subscriptions, endowments, and legacies for that purpose.

§2. The sums marked in the provincial and municipal budgets, as also the subscriptions, endowments, and legacies for the local purpose, shall be applied for the manumission of slaves in the provinces, districts, municipalities, and parishes designated.

IV. The slave is permitted to form a saving fund from what may come to him through gifts, legacies, and inheritances, and from what, by consent of his owner, he may obtain by his labor and economy. The Government will see to the regulations as to the placing and security of said savings.

§1. By the death of the slave half of his savings shall belong to his surviving widow, if there be such, and the other half shall be transmitted to his heirs in conformity with civil law.

In default of heirs the savings shall be adjudged to the emancipation fund of which Article III treats.

§2. The slave who, through his savings, may obtain means to pay his value has a right to freedom.

If the indemnification be not fixed by agreement it shall be settled by arbitration. In judicial sales or inventories the price of manumission shall be that of the valuation.

§3. It is further permitted the slave, in furtherance of his liberty, to contract with a third party the hire of his future services, for a term not exceeding seven years, by obtaining the consent of his master, and approval of the Judge of the Orphans' Court.

§4. The slave that belongs to joint proprietors, and is freed by one of them, shall have a right to his freedom by indemnifying the other owners with the share of the amount which belongs to them. This indemnification may be paid by services rendered for a term not exceeding seven years, in conformity with the preceding paragraph.

§5. The manumission, with the clause of services during a certain time, shall not become annulled by want of fulfilling the said clause, but the freed man shall be compelled to fulfil, by means of labour in the public establishments, or by contracting for his services with private persons.

§6. Manumissions, whether gratuitous or by means of *onus*, shall be exempted from all duties, emoluments, or expenses.

§7. In any case of alienation or transfer of slaves, the separation of husband and wife, and children under twelve years of age from father or mother, is prohibited under penalty of annulment.

§8. If the division of property among heirs or partners does not permit the union of a family, and none of them prefers remaining with the family by replacing the amount of the share belonging to the other interested parties, the said family shall be sold and the proceeds shall be divided among the heirs.

§9. The ordination, Book 4th, title 63, in the part which revokes freedom, on account of ingratitude, is set aside.

V. The Emancipation Societies which are formed, and those which may for the future be formed, shall be subject to the inspection of the Judges of the Orphans' Court.

Sole paragraph. The said societies shall have the privilege of commanding the services of the slaves whom they may have liberated, to indemnify themselves for the sum spent in their purchase.

VI. The following shall be declared free:

§1. The slaves belonging to the State, the Government giving them such employment as they may deem fit.

§2. The slave given in *usufruct* to the Crown.

§3. The slaves of unclaimed inheritances.

§4. The slaves who have been abandoned by their owners. Should these have abandoned the slaves from the latter being invalids they shall be obliged to maintain them, except in case of their own penury, the maintenance being charged by the Judge of the Orphans' Court.

§5. In general the slaves liberated by virtue of this Law shall be under the inspection of Government during five years. They will be obliged to hire themselves under pain of compulsion; if they lead an idle life they shall be made to work in the public establishments.

The compulsory labour, however, shall cease so soon as the freed man shall exhibit an engagement of hire.

VII. In trials in favour of freedom—

§1. The process shall be summary.

§2. There shall be appeal *ex officio* when the decisions shall be against the freedom.

VIII. The Government will order the special registration of all the slaves existing in the Empire to be proceeded with, containing a declaration of name, sex, age, state, aptitude for work, and filiation of each, if such should be known.

§1. The date on which the registry ought to commence closing shall be announced beforehand, the longest time possible being given for preparation by means of edicts repeated, in which shall be inserted the dispositions of the following paragraph.

§2. The slaves who, through the fault or omission of the parties interested, shall not have been registered up to one year after the closing of the register, shall, *de facto*, be considered as free.

§3. For registering each slave the owner shall pay, once only, the emolument of 500 réis, if done within the term marked, and one dollar should that be exceeded. The produce of those emoluments shall go towards the expenses of registering, and the surplus to the emancipation fund.

§4. The children of a slave mother, who by this Law became free, shall also be registered in a separate book.

Those persons who have become remiss shall incur a fine of 100 dollars to 200 dollars, repeated as many times as there may be individuals omitted: and for fraud, in the penalties of Article CLXXIX of the Criminal Code.

§5. The parish priests shall be obliged to have special books for the registry of births and deaths of the children of slaves born from and after the date of this Law. Each omission will subject the parish priest to a fine of 100 dollars.

IX. The Government, in its regulations, can impose fines of as much as 100 dollars, and the penalty of imprisonment up to one month.

X. All contrary dispositions are revoked.

Therefore, order all authorities to whom, &c. Given at the Palace of Rio de Janeiro, on the 28th September, 1871. 50th of the Independence and of the Empire.

PRINCESS IMPERIAL, REGENT.
THEODORO MACHADO FREIRE PEREIRA DA SILVA.

❁

45. The Trial of the Bishop of Olinda*

Until 1873, the relations between church and state had been harmonious. In that year the Bishop of Olinda carried out a papal order, unapproved by the emperor, to expel Masons from the lay brotherhoods of the Roman Catholic Church. Many devout Brazilian Catholics, including the clergy and the highest governmental officials, were Masons. Pedro II ordered the Bishop of Olinda to remove the penalty. His refusal to comply was a challenge to the emperor in the

....

* From *Papers Relating to the Foreign Relations of the United States . . .* 1874 (Washington, D.C.: Government Printing Office, 1874), p. 82.

*name of the pope. Regalism, one of the mainstays of nation-
alism and an ancient principle of the Portuguese kings inherited by the Brazilian emperors, was being attacked by the
Church. When the bishop adamantly declined to alter his
position, the government arrested and jailed him. The government's case rested firmly upon the political grounds of
supremacy of the civil law and royal courts over those of the
Church. The Bishop of Olinda was judged guilty and sentenced to four years of hard labor, although an imperial amnesty freed him in 1875. The full text of that sentence appears below. This controversy with the Church and the
resultant imprisonment of the bishop created many religious
enemies for the crown. In a mood of sullen resentment the
once-loyal Church withdrew its ardent support of the monarchy.*

Considering that the brotherhoods are associations of a mixed
nature; that the temporal and spiritual powers alike concur in
their organization, the statutes being approved in their spiritual part by the prelates, and confirmed by the government
or by the provincial assemblies (law of Sept. 28, 1828, art. 2,
§11,) and therefore subject to ecclesiastical jurisdiction in
their spiritual part, and to the civil and temporal jurisdiction
in all their exhibits;

Considering that the qualifications required for persons to
belong to such associations are not an object of a spiritual
nature; considering it is indispensable that, besides the will
of the founders, the two powers should concur in the establishment of regulations which are to govern these associations and to fix the rights and obligations of its members,
such regulations cannot be reformed or altered by one alone
of the two powers, without the cooperation of the other and
the intervention of the brotherhood (Resolution of the
council of state, January 15, 1867);

Considering that the declaration that a certain class, or
individuals, are incapable of belonging to such associations,
for reasons not set forth in the regulations, amounts to a
reform or alteration of them;

Considering that the accused ordered the Board of the Brotherhood of the Most Holy Sacrament of the parish of Santo Antônio to expel from its body a certain and determined person because he belonged to the society of Free-Masons, an association permitted by the laws of the empire; ordering likewise the expulsion of all other members who were in the same situation;

Considering that when the brotherhood refused to carry out such order, as being contrary to its engagements, the accused launched the penalty of interdiction, without proceeding to any inquiry, or even hearing the interested parties;

Considering that in this proceeding the accused usurped the jurisdiction of the temporal power, and furthermore, used notorious violence in the exercise of the spiritual power, ignoring, in the imposition of the very grave penalty of interdiction, natural right and the canons of the Brazilian church, which do not allow the condemnation of any one without a hearing, and without the observance of the rules of defense;

Considering that when the appeal to the Crown, authorized by decree 1911, of March 28, 1857, in conformity with preceding legislation, was taken, the accused denied its legality, and when the said appeal was decided, and the imperial resolution transmitted to the accused to be carried out, he not only disobeyed it, but incited the vicars to do the same, threatening them with the penalty of suspension *"ex informata conscientia,"* of which one who showed hesitation was a victim;

Considering that the accused, who, as a public employé, (additional act to the constitution of the empire, art. 10, §7,) should, in his high position, have been prompt and solicitous to fulfill, and cause his subordinates to fulfill, the laws of the country, rendered his formal refusal to obey a lawful order still graver by going so far as to declare heretical the matter of appeal to the Crown and the placet. (See his note of June 6, 1873);

Considering, lastly, that, for the reasons set forth, the present case is within the jurisdiction of the tribunal, and that the accused has by his course impeded and prevented the due effects of the order of the executive which were contained in those resolutions, as is fully proved in the papers, the court judges that the bishop, D. Vital Maria Gonsalves de Oliviera, has incurred the penalty of article 96 of the criminal code, and so sentence him to four years of imprisonment with labor and costs.

Article 96 of the criminal code reads as follows:

Obstructing or preventing in any manner the effect of decisions of the moderative or executive powers, which are conformable to the constitution and the laws. Penalty: Imprisonment at hard labor for from two to six years.

46. Maúa Encourages Immigration and the Extension of Credit*

With the extinction of the sources of slavery, Brazil had to look elsewhere for its laborers. The Viscount of Maúa urged that favorable national legislation encourage foreigners to immigrate to Brazil. Indeed, with the demise of slavery, the number of immigrants increased greatly. Between 1873 and 1886 about 22,000 arrived annually; between 1891 and 1900 nearly 112,000 entered each year. Maúa also tried to industrialize Brazil and thus break the hold of monoculture on the economy. To accomplish those ends, he advocated the establishment of credit banking. He himself founded several banking houses, but unfortunately his efforts were doomed to failure. He was too far ahead of his times. Perhaps he would have been more at home among the captains

....

* Translated from Visconde de Maúa, *Autobiografia* (Rio de Janeiro: Zélio Valverde, 1942), pp. 222-224, 227.

*of industry then remaking the United States, but he defi-
nitely was out of place in imperial Brazil.*

The only means [to overcome the labor shortage] . . . is to
import salaried workers by contracts in which they lease their
services and to decree the effective measures to regulate the
rights of both parties. Go seek those services in any country
of Europe if it is possible to obtain them at prices which our
industry can pay without ruining itself; and if that is not
possible, go seek them wherever they might be found. This
might be a temporary measure, but it is one of life or death.
The State, which was negligent, has the obligation at the
beginning of providing that undeniable necessity [workers];
later, private interest will take care of it.

. . .

They claim that in Brazil everything comes from the government and that individual initiative does not exist! And
how can it be otherwise when everything relating to capital,
beginning with the accumulation of it for any project of public or private good in which the freedom of its use ought to
be the regulating principle, immediately confronts very bad
laws and, when those are insufficient to discourage, undue
governmental intervention in the guise of a tutor? . . .
Credit either is in the hands of the privileged few or does
not exist outside the limits of individual means where its
action is necessarily weak in a new country which has not
had time to convert into capital more than a minimal part of
its natural resources. . . . Credit and capital formation in
Brazil find themselves besieged by oppressive financial legislation—this gives rise to the clamor for governmental intervention when necessity knocks on the door. . . . The productive element of the country cries aloud in unison for
credit and low interest rates. And all are dismayed that toward this end only unworkable laws have been passed. . . .
The country has facilities for credit in the interior and an
advantageous position for such an end in the exterior. I know
perfectly that CREDIT is not capital—however, who would

dare to argue that it does not create capital? We have, then, an excellent base to aid economic growth, not with paper money but with the use of credit.

❀

47. Witness to a Drought in the Northeast*

The flagellating droughts of the Northeast have been one of the great tragedies periodically plaguing Brazil. In the trail of the droughts come famine and misery and then the pestilence of smallpox and other diseases. Since early in the colonial period, chroniclers have mentioned that unhappy phenomenon which has stunted the development of a huge region. The North American naturalist, Herbert H. Smith, witnessed one of the most devastating of the nineteenth-century sêcas, the one which lasted between 1877 and 1879 and killed more than half the population of Ceará. Printed below are extracts from his descriptions.

My personal observations of this great calamity were confined to a part of December, 1878. I reached Fortaleza on the 19th of that month, when the death-rate from small-pox had gone down to about 350 per day. Aided by His Excellency, President Julip, and by Sr. Morsing, I was able, during the ten days of my stay, to make careful observations, both at Fortaleza and in the interior. It was not a pleasant subject; but as the facts I gleaned may have some historical value, I will epitomize them here.

....

* From Herbert H. Smith, *Brazil, the Amazons and the Coast* (London: Sampson, Low, 1880), pp. 421-428, 431.

At first I saw very few signs of the pestilence. The city streets were clean and neat; here and there I noticed refugees standing idly by the street corners, and some of these had small-pox scars on their faces. About the public storehouses there were carts and porters carrying provisions; no signs of starvation were apparent, for the people had been well fed since May.

I stopped to engage a room at the little hotel; the landlord, after some questioning, acknowledged that there were two small-pox cases in the house; but added, truly enough, that no better place could be found; the sick here were carefully isolated, and well cared for.

I was much impressed with the apparent indifference of the people to their danger. The pestilence was, indeed, a universal subject of conversation, but everybody seemed to rest in an easy fatalism or blindness; speaking of the daily death-rate as one tells of the killed and wounded in a battle —a real event, but far away. I did not hear of a single resident who left the town on account of the danger; there was the usual amount of dissipation and flirtation; the market square was crowded, and men drove hard bargains; in outward appearance the little city had hardly changed since 1876.

Later in the day, I walked out to the refugee camps on the southern side of the city. The huts were wretched beyond description; many were built of boughs, or of poles, covered with an imperfect thatch of palm-leaves, and patched up with bits of boards and rags. Here whole families were crowded together in narrow spaces; filthy, as only these Ceará Arabs can be; ragged, unkempt, lounging on the sands, a fit prey for disease. No measures had been taken to cleanse the camp; the ground, in many places, was covered with filth and refuse; water, obtained from a pool near by, was unfit to drink. If the pestilence was hidden in the city, it was visible everywhere in the camps. Half-recovered patients sat apart, but scarcely healed; in almost every hut the sick were lying, horrible with the foul disease. Many dead were waiting for the body carriers; many more would be waiting at the morning round. Yet here, among the sick and dying and dead, there was the same indifference to danger that I had noticed in the city. The peasants were talking and laughing with each other; three or four were gathered about a mat, gambling for biscuits; everywhere the ghastly patients and ghastlier corpses were passed unnoticed; they were too common to be objects of curiosity.

Most of these people had come from the interior with the great exodus, and they had been fed by the Government for eight or nine months. As easily managed as children, they were, like children, fractious and careless, and improvident. From the first, they should have been placed under rigid military discipline; with the guidance of competent persons, they should have been made to construct good houses, arrange the streets and sections, for their better government; cleanliness of body and surroundings should have been enforced under the severest penalties; and every able-bodied man and woman should have been employed in work of some kind. But Brazilians everywhere are neglectful of sanitary measures; witness the dirty, badly-drained Rio streets, where yellow fever walks unstayed; witness the epidemic that ran through the army during the Paraguayan war, carrying off far more than the enemy's bullets.

In the morning I walked farther away from the city, where the strips of woodland were as bare as a winter landscape at home, and only a few mandioc fields escaped the general ruin. Here and there I passed lonely huts. Once I stopped to ask for a drink of water, but the woman who was sitting before the door told me that she had none, for the nearest pool was half a mile away, and she was sick and could not go to fill the calabash. No doubt her story was true, for her face was scarlet with fever, and she complained of a throbbing headache, constant symptom of the dreaded disease. Within the hut were three children; one, like the mother, was suffering with fever and headache; another was covered with small-pox pustules; the third child, a baby, was just dying. A man who was passing brought some water to the hut. I suppose that the woman and children were carried to the lazaretto on the following morning, but among so many patients they could receive little care. The three hospitals were overcrowded, and the new patients could only come in as the daily deaths and few recoveries left the cots vacant.

There was a cemetery near the town, where the dead were buried decently, in separate graves. But this was the city ground, from which bodies of those who had died of smallpox were generally excluded. Two miles west of the city, a much larger ground received the pestilence dead. Every morning searchers examined the huts, and carried away the bodies; as they were not allowed to take their burdens through the streets, they carried them around, either on the southern side, by a little-used path, or along the beach. At sunrise, when I went to bathe in the surf, a constant procession of those body carriers was passing. Sometimes the dead were wrapped in hammocks and slung to poles; oftener they were simply tied to the pole, two or three, perhaps, together, and so borne by two or four carriers; child corpses were thrown into shallow trays which were carried on men's heads. By eight o'clock the stream had lessened; but all through the day the ghastly sight was repeated at intervals. People who lived near the beach became accustomed to this constant funeral, and gave little heed to it.

At the Lagoa Funda ground the dead were buried in trenches, twelve together; "Unless," said one of the overseers, "they come too fast for the diggers; then we put fifteen or twenty in, *conforme*." The man had been here so long that he regarded the bodies as so many logs. For myself, I was not yet educated to this point; sick and faint, I turned away from the horrible trench and the fetid air. The bodies were buried deep but under loose sand; two thousand of these trenches were poisoning the air, and the stench was almost unbearable. It is recorded of the London plague that men died in the pits they were digging; here the workmen had fallen dead, not from the disease, but from asphyxia, the result of foul air; this happened only where a new trench was dug near an old one. It was very difficult to obtain men for this service, and no wonder.

One of the largest lazarettos was close by the gate of this cemetery; indeed, all the bodies had to pass between two of the buildings, and through the open windows the patients could look out upon the endless procession. I suppose that they were too ill to heed it, but to the poor *sertanejo* who saw his friend brought here, the hospital must have been almost identified with the cemetery. I was told that ninety per cent of the patients died, and it was a matter of convenience to have the burial-place so near.

At this time the hospitals were of little value, for they could not contain the thirty thousand sick, and the wards were so overcrowded that the patients received less care than they would have had in their own huts. It seems probable to me that, in a place so thoroughly infected, slight cases may have been aggravated by fresh poison, until the mortality was greatly increased. Be this as it may, the death-rate was very high here, and the disease assumed its worst forms.

As in many other epidemics the mortality was greatest among strong, vigorous men; children often escaped. I was told of one merchant who had twenty-four workmen in his employ; of these, seventeen died during November and December. Another man had nine clerks in his office, of whom he lost six within two weeks. Whole households were swept away. In many of the richer families, the ladies were driven to the menial services, because their servants had died, and it was impossible to obtain new ones. Vaccination was not always a complete preventive, but it invariably served to check the violence of the disease, so that the patient generally recovered. It was reported—with what truth I do not know—that men had been known to have the small-pox twice within a few months; in this case the second attack was very slight.

When the small-pox scourge was at its height, a strange and terrible disease appeared at Fortaleza; by some this was supposed to be a new epidemic, and there were fearful whispers of black plague. It is probable, however, that this was an aggravated form of small-pox; it was characterized by the appearance of black spots on the body, and I believe that the cases were invariably fatal, even before the pustules appeared. About the end of December, the wife of the provincial president was attacked with this "black small-pox" and died within two days.

Amid all this suffering the people celebrated the Christmas festival, with music and feasting and rejoicing. Of the two thousand men and women who knelt in the church, probably many were infected, but no one seemed to fear the contact of a neighbor. Before the service, some who were dying were brought in hammocks to the church-door, to be confessed.

I believe that the priests of Fortaleza did their duty well, all through the pestilence. There were, indeed, no funeral services and few ante-mortem confessions; the death-harvest was too great. But I often saw the younger priests visiting the worst infected camps, not with attendants and gorgeous trappings, but alone, doing their work as the old missionaries did, in the face of danger.

At Pacatuba I found the state of affairs even worse than at Fortaleza. More than half the inhabitants were stricken, and the daily death-rate was frightful. Here, crawling about the railroad station and begging, were diseased children; here, at the house where I stopped, the servants were convalescent patients. I visited many huts in succession, and in each there were from one to five sick.

From this point, almost to Baturité, I rode along the line of the new railroad, where thousands of workmen were employed. Here the change was as agreeable as it was great. The workmen and their families were domiciled in good barracks, and the sick were rigidly isolated; sanitary rules were enforced to some extent. Vaccination had been introduced, and no well man was permitted to be idle. Under these circumstances, I found a steady improvement as I advanced, until I felt that I had left the pestilence and its horrors behind me. Then indeed the ride became a delightful one. Along the hill-sides there had been a few showers, and the trees, which had been bare for eighteen months, began to put out a few timid buds. At Baturité there was running water, for the springs had held out even through two years of drought; here the hill-sides, in many places, were fresh and green, with bright plantations and tangled forests; it was an oasis in the wilderness.

.   .   .

In December of this year the daily deathrate at Baturité was one in three thousand; and most of these cases were among the new arrivals. In Fortaleza, at the same time, the rate went as high as one in ninety, and at Pacatuba it was one in thirty.

❦

48. The Social Classes in Rio de Janeiro during the Last Decade of the Empire*

Professor Sérgio Buarque de Holanda has characterized the period 1850-1888 as one in which the urban bourgeois replaced the agrarian patriarch who had dominated Brazil for over three centuries. Statistics seem to document his thesis. By 1888 the population numbered about fourteen million, and of these less than one-twentieth were slaves—a startling contrast with the figures of 1822. Plantation owners, including their families, amounted to only slightly more than one-quarter of a million. Between the two extremes of slave and slaveholder, a large middle sector, located primarily in or near the urban centers, had appeared and was rapidly growing stronger. The once sleepy coastal cities were taking on a new appearance with the arrival of immigrants, the increase in foreign trade, the rise in the number of university graduates, the establishment of new industries, and so forth. On those invigorated cities, the political, economic, and social life of the nation began to focus. Visiting the largest and most important city, Rio de Janeiro, in 1879, Herbert Smith

....

* From Herbert H. Smith, *Brazil, the Amazons and the Coast* (London: Sampson, Low, 1880), pp. 460-461, 463-466, 468-469.

took a close look at a society, which he found composed of four principal classes.

Here, as everywhere else, it takes all sorts of people to make up a community. Only, in Brazil, the proportion of really good families, refined, educated ones, is very much smaller than in the United States: too small as yet, to exercise much influence over the country. When you meet with these families you find a social life differing very little from that to which we are accustomed at home; pure manners, intelligent conversation, and a hearty respect for every true lady. The ladies themselves are quick-witted, lively, brilliant; one of them would flash all over a northern drawing-room, to the utter extinction of dull conversation.

But the mass of Rio society is much lower; it is a bad imitation of the Parisian. I think, indeed, that there is a deal of unconscious truth in the boastful title which the people have given to their city—"Paris in America." French fashions, French literature, French philosophy, French morals, are spread broadcast through the educated circles. . . .

Ladies go about with their husbands and fathers, and are always treated with politeness; they are witty and lively, but often superficial. The time is past when women were shut up like nuns, behind latticed windows, invisible to the street; when they were only shown at balls and on state occasions. But true social freedom is hardly more accorded to them than it was a hundred years ago.

. . .

So far, we have been considering only that portion of the population which would be distinguished as the "society" of Rio; people who, by birth, or education, or wealth, are able to retain a certain standing, which separates them from the mass of their countrymen. Classes are strongly marked in Brazil. Below this "society" stratum, we may distinguish three others, pretty sharply defined: the mechanics and small shop-keepers, the laborers and peasants, and the slaves.

In the United States we have nothing precisely parallel to

the second Brazilian class. . . . In Brazil, the importance of the second class is very much underrated, simply because official statistics do not recognize it as a class at all. In it we may include peddlers, shop-keepers in the smallest way, low eating-house keepers, and finally, every mechanic who does any honest work; for mind you, in Brazil a mechanic is no more admitted into society than a boot-black would be at home. These men are mostly Portuguese immigrants; sometimes white or half-breed Brazilians. They work hard to keep themselves above the common laborers, whom they look down on; they never aspire to the magnificence of the privileged class, the educated ones, who look down on them, or rather ignore them, except as they must make use of their services. With this lower stratum, education never extends beyond writing and accounts, but even that is enough to secure the respect of the *sans culottes*, who, very often, cannot even read. Then there is the added dignity of proprietorship; the owner of a street-corner pagoda, who sells coffee and lottery tickets at his windows, is a superior being to the porter or boatman, or even to the cartman, who may get his morning lunch there.

Rather a negative element is the stratum next below this —the free laborers. In this class I may include, not only the porters and cartmen and marketmen of Rio and the other cities, but all the peasantry of Brazil . . . stationary people, who work only when they must, and never accumulate property. . . .

In Rio, this class includes Portuguese and free Negroes; the latter, probably, the more intelligent and honest. There are boatmen and cartmen, porters waiting for a job at every streetcorner, hawkers of fish and fruit and poultry; thousands who have no regular employment, but pick up their living by doing "odd jobs." Our boot-blacks, and news-boys, and street Arabs, generally, might belong to this class; the "longshoremen" are a grade above it. . . .

So we come to the fourth and lowest class in Brazil—the slaves. The class that originated in barbarism and selfishness —the class which Brazil, for very shame, is trying to get rid of, but whose influence will curse the children with the sins of their fathers for dreary years. . . .

I came to Brazil, with an honest desire to study this question of slavery in a spirit of fairness, without running to emotional extremes. Now, after four years, I am convinced that all other evils with which the country is cursed, taken together, will not compare with this one. . . .

In mere animal matters, of food and clothing, no doubt many of the Negroes are better off than they were in Africa; no doubt, also, they have learned some lessons of peace and civility; even a groping outline of Christianity. But it would be hard to prove that the plantation slave, dependent, like a child, on his master, and utterly unused to thinking for himself, is better, mentally, than the savage who has his faculties sharpened by continual battling with the savage nature around him.

. . .

The treatment of slaves in Brazil depends, of course, on the master; largely, too, on the district. In the provinces north of the São Francisco, I am bound to say that they are treated with great kindness; on the Amazons, they would be, from necessity, if not from choice, for every ill-used slave would run off to the woods, as many have done. . . . But around Rio and Bahia, where the vast majority of the slaves are now owned, they are masters who treat their servants with a severity that is nothing short of barbarism. . . .

Yet Brazil should have a certain credit above other slaveholding countries, present and past; for she alone has voluntarily set herself to getting rid of her shame. Other nations have done it by revolutions, or because they were forced to by a stronger power, or because the system died out of itself. But Brazil, among all, has had the nerve to cut away the sore flesh with her own hand; to cut it away while it was yet strong, while it seemed her best vitality. . . .

49. The Law Abolishing Slavery*

Patience with the slow emancipation brought about by the Law of the Free Womb wore thin. Public opinion began to clamor for immediate liberation. After its establishment in 1880, the Brazilian Anti-Slavery Society directed that public opinion effectively. The first result of its campaign was the Saraiva-Cotegipe Law of 1885, which declared free all slaves at the age of sixty. Still that was not enough. Total extinction of the unpopular institution was demanded. It came on May 13, 1888, when Princess-Regent Isabel rushed to the Chamber of Deputies to sign at once the "Golden Law" abolishing slavery. The majority wildly cheered the act. Only the plantation owners stood back, disappointed and frustrated, and refused to approve it. Their chagrin deprived the monarchy of one of its strongest and most traditional supporters.

The Princess Imperial Regent, in the name of His Majesty the Emperor Dom Pedro II, makes known to all subjects of the Empire that the General Assembly has decreed, and she has approved, the following Law:—

Art. 1. From the date of this Law slavery is declared abolished in Brazil.

2. All contrary provisions are revoked.

She orders, therefore, all the authorities to whom belong the knowledge and execution of the said Law to execute it, and cause it to be fully and exactly executed and observed.

The Secretary of State for the Departments of Agricul-

....

* From *British and Foreign State Papers*, 1887-1888, LXXIX (London: Harrison and Sons, n.d.), 259.

ture, Commerce, and Public Works, and *ad interim* for Foreign Affairs, Bachelor Rodrigo Augusto da Silva, of the Council of His Majesty the Emperor, will cause it to be printed, published, and circulated.

Given in the Palace of Rio de Janeiro, May 13, 1888, the 67th year of Independence and of the Empire.

PRINCESS IMPERIAL REGENT.

RODRIGO AUGUSTO DA SILVA.

III

REPUBLICAN
PERIOD

50. The Proclamation Ending the Empire*

Alienation first of the Church and then of the landed aristocracy deprived the monarchy of two of its strongest supporters. The army grew dissatisfied and restive. The officers had become imbued with the positivist, republican doctrines taught by Benjamin Constant Botelho de Magalhães in the military academy. The republicans took advantage of the situation and sought to use the army to put into effect their goals stated in the Republican Manifesto. The fate of the empire was doomed when the principal military leader, Marshal Deodoro da Fonseca, at the last minute switched his allegiance and proclaimed himself in favor of a republic. Under his leadership, on November 15, 1889, the army surrounded the royal palace, occupied the important governmental buildings, and silenced Rio de Janeiro. The military officers and the chiefs of the Republican Party thereupon arbitrarily declared the end of the empire.

Fellow citizens: The people, the army, and the navy, in perfect harmony of sentiment with our fellow citizens resident in the provinces, have just decreed the dethronement of the

....

* From *Papers Relating to the Foreign Relations of the United States* . . . 1889 (Washington, D.C.: Government Printing Office, 1890), pp. 61-62.

Imperial dynasty, and consequently the extinction of the representative monarchical system of government.

As an immediate result of this national revolution, of a character wholly patriotic, a provisional government has just been instituted, whose principal mission is to guaranty by public order the liberty and the rights of citizens.

To compose this Government until the sovereign nation by means of competent organs shall proceed to the choice of a definitive Government, the undersigned citizens have been chosen by the chief of the executive power.

Fellow citizens: The provisional government, simply a temporary agent of the national sovereignty, is the government of peace, of liberty, of fraternity, and of order.

In the use of the extraordinary attributions and faculties with which it is invested for the defense of the integrity of the nation and for the security of public order, the provisional government, by all the means in their reach, promise and guaranty to all the inhabitants of Brazil, native or foreign, security of life and property, respect for all rights, individual and political, except as to the latter the limitations required by the safety of the country and defense of the Government proclaimed by the people, by the army, and by the navy.

Fellow citizens: The functions of ordinary justice, as well as of civil and military administration, will continue to be exercised by the officials hitherto employed in relation to all acts, in the fullness of their effects; in relation to persons, the advantages and rights acquired by each functionary will be respected; but the life-term of the senate is hereby abolished, and also the council of state. The chamber of deputies is dissolved.

Fellow citizens: The provisional government recognizes and will respect all national obligations contracted during the previous regimen, treaties subsisting with foreign powers, the public debt, external and internal, existing contracts, and further obligations legally contracted.

MARSHAL MANOEL DEODORO DA FONSECA,
Chief of the Provisional Government.

ARISTIDES DA SILVEIRA LOBO, *Minister of the
Interior.*

RUY BARBOSA, *Minister of Finance and pro tem.
of Justice.*

Lieutenant-Colonel BENJAMIN CONSTANT,
Botelho Magalhães, Minister of War.

EDWARD WANDENKOLK, *Chief of Squadron,
Minister of Marine.*

QUINTINO BOCAYUVA, *Minister of Foreign Affairs
and pro tem. of Agriculture, Commerce, and Public
Works.*

❀

51. The Abdication of Pedro II*

*The swiftness of the coup d'état cut Pedro II off from any
popular support he enjoyed. Accepting the rapid change, the
old emperor issued his abdication and, like his father before
him, sailed into European exile. The historian and diplomat
Manoel de Oliveira Lima pronounced a funeral judgment on
the empire with these words: "If my own country can boast
of her history during the last century [the 19th], if she can
relate it to other countries with some pride, she owes it above
all to the liberal influence of imperial institutions."*

In view of the representation which was delivered to me today at 3 o'clock in the afternoon, I resolve, yielding to the
power of circumstances, to depart with all my family for Eu-

....
* From *Papers Relating to the Foreign Relations of the United
States* . . . 1889 (Washington, D.C.: Government Printing Office,
1890), p. 64.

rope tomorrow, leaving this country, beloved by us all, and for which I have exerted myself to give constant proofs of deeply seated love, and dedication for almost half a century, during which I filled the position of chief of the state. In departing, therefore I with all the persons of my family, shall always retain the most tender remembrances of Brazil in offering ardent prayer for its greatness and prosperity.

D. PEDRO DE ALCANTARA.
Rio de Janeiro, November 16, 1889.

❊

52. The Decree Establishing the Republic*

With the empire abolished, the military and civilian leaders of the coup d'état proceeded to establish a federal, republican form of government. The first decree of Deodoro da Fonseca created a provisional government until a constitution could be written.

The provisional government of the United States of Brazil decrees:

Art. 1. The form of government of the Brazilian nation proclaimed and decreed is a federative republic.

Art. 2. The provinces of Brazil, joined together in the

....

* From *Papers Relating to the Foreign Relations of the United States* . . . 1889 (Washington, D.C.: Government Printing Office, 1890), p. 62.

bonds of federation, constitute the United States of Brazil.

Art. 3. Each one of these States, in the exercise of its legitimate sovereignty, will decree in due time its definitive constitution, electing legislative assemblies and local governments.

Art. 4. Until elections are held in a regular way for members to constitute a constitutional congress, and for legislative assemblies in each of the States, the Brazilian nation will be governed by the provisional government of the Republic; and the new States by the governors that may be proclaimed, or in default of these, by governors delegated by the provisional government.

Art. 5. The respective governments of the federated States will adopt with urgency all necessary providences in order that order be maintained and public security preserved, and that the rights and liberty of citizens, whether Brazilians or foreigners, be guarantied.

Art. 6. Wherever public order may be disturbed, in any of the States, and wherever the local government shall not possess the means of repressing disorders and securing peace and tranquillity, the provisional government will enforce, by means of the public force, the free exercise of the rights of citizens and the unconstrained action of the constituted authorities.

Art. 7. The federative Brazilian Republic being the form of government proclaimed, the provisional government does not recognize, nor will it recognize, any local government contrary to a republican form, awaiting, as in duty bound, the final sentence of popular suffrage, as expressed by the free vote of the nation.

Art. 8. The regular army and navy, and public forces of the three arms of which there are garrisons or detachments in the different provinces, will continue subordinated to and exclusively dependent on the provisional government of the Republic, the local government being, however, empowered to decree the organization of a civil guard for the policing of the territory contained in their respective States.

Art. 9. All civil and military departments hitherto subject to the control of the central government of the Brazilian nation will remain under the direct control of the provisional government of the Republic.

Art. 10. The territory embraced within the municipality neuter will remain for the time being under the immediate jurisdiction and control of the provisional government of the Republic, and the city of Rio de Janiero will continue to be the seat of the federal power.

Art. 11. The secretaries of state in the different departments or bureaus of the actual provisional government will be encharged with the execution of this decree in the part relative to each.

MARSHAL MANOEL DEODORO DA FONSECA,
Chief of the Provisional Government.
Rio de Janeiro, November 15, 1889.

❀

53. The Decree Separating Church and State*

In classic positivist tradition, the new leaders of Brazil separated church from state in a decree dated January 7, 1890. Still resentful of the government's treatment of the bishops in the 1870's, the Church agreed to the separation. The hierarchy believed that a free church in a free society promised more for the Roman Catholic Church than the continuation of the former relationship.

....

* From *Papers Relating to the Foreign Relations of the United States . . . 1890* (Washington, D.C.: Government Printing Office, 1891), pp. 20-21.

Marshal Manoel Deodoro da Fonseca, chief of the Provisional Government, constituted by the army and navy, in the name of the nation, decrees:

Article I. It is prohibited to the federal authority, as well as to that of the states, to grant any laws, regulations, or administrative acts, by establishing any religion, or prohibiting it; or create any difference among the inhabitants of the country, whether in the service paid for by the budget or not, through reason of philosophical or religious belief or opinions.

Art. II. All religious sects have an equal right to exercise their forms of worship according to their faith, and shall not be molested in their private or public forms of worship.

Art. III. The liberty herein instituted embraces not only individuals in their individual acts, but also churches, associations, and institutes, in which they may be associated; every one shall enjoy the perfect right to constitute societies and to live collectively according to their creed and belief without any interference of the public authority.

Art. IV. The state church is abolished with all its institutions, rights, and prerogatives.

Art V. All churches and religious sects are allowed the juridical right of personality, to acquire property and administer it subject to the limits imposed by the laws of mortmain, with the right to the domain and administration of their property as well as their houses of worship.

Art. VI. The Federal Government will continue to provide for the livings of the present incumbents of the Catholic faith and will grant the usual subsidy to the seminaries for one year; each state will have the right to maintain the future ministers of that or of any other faith without countervening the provisions of the preceding articles.

Art. VII. Revokes all provisions to the contrary.

[Signed by Manoel Deodoro da Fonseca and by all the seven ministers.]
January 7, 1890.

54. The Constitution of 1891*

On December 3, 1889, the provisional government appointed a special committee of five jurists to prepare the bases for a new constitution. In their deliberations, they drew heavily on the Constitution of the United States and also found a useful model in the Constitution of Argentina. The committee presented its proposed constitution to the government for examination, and Minister Rui Barbosa made extensive revisions to it. One of his chief contributions was to give the document a strong presidential flavor. The modified constitution was submitted on November 15, 1890, to the Constituent Congress, which by and large accepted the recommendations of the government. The new constitution promulgated on February 24, 1891, was presidential, federal, democratic, and republican in character. Excerpts from it are given below.

TITLE I.—Of the Federal Organization.
Preliminary Provisions.

Art. 1. The Brazilian nation adopts as a form of Government under the representative system the Federal Republic proclaimed on the 15th November, 1889, and constitutes itself, by the perpetual and indissoluble union of its former provinces, into the United States of Brazil.

Art. 2. Each of the former provinces will form a State, and the former neutral municipality will constitute the Federal District, and continue to be the capital of the Union, until the provisions of the following Article shall have been carried out.

....

* From *British and Foreign State Papers, 1890-1891* (London: Harrison and Sons, 1897), pp. 487, 489, 491-499, 502.

Art. 3. A zone of 14,400 square kilom. on the central plateau of the Republic, which will be marked out in due course in order to found therein the Federal capital, is reserved for the Union.

§. When the transfer of the capital has been effected, the present Federal District shall become a State.

. . .

Art. 6. The Federal Government cannot intervene in matters exclusively affecting the States, except for the purpose of—

1. Repelling foreign invasion, or the invasion of one State by another;

2. Maintaining the Federal Republican form of Government;

3. Re-establishing order and tranquillity in the States at the request of their respective Governments;

4. Insuring the execution of the Federal laws and sentences.

. . .

Section 1.—*Of the Legislative Power.*
Chapter 1.—*General Provisions.*

Art. 16. The legislative power is exercised by the National Congress, with the sanction of the President of the Republic.

§1. The National Congress is composed of two branches, the Chamber of Deputies and the Senate.

. . .

Chapter 2.—*Of the Chamber of Deputies.*

Art. 28. The Chamber of Deputies is composed of the representatives of the people elected by the States and by the Federal district, by means of direct suffrage, the representation of the minority being guaranteed.

§1. The number of Deputies will be fixed by law in a proportion of not more than one Deputy for every 70,000 inhabitants, but there must not be less than four Deputies to a State.

§2. For this purpose the Federal Government will order a census of the population of the Republic to be taken at once, which census will be revised every ten years.

Art. 29. It is the province of the Chamber of Deputies to take the initiative in proposing the adjournment of the Session, all Laws respecting taxes, Laws fixing the number of the land and sea forces, and in discussing Bills presented by the Executive Power; as also to declare whether there are sufficient grounds, or not, for impeaching the President of the Republic under the provisions of Article 53, and the Ministers of State in the case of crimes connected with those of the President.

Chapter 3.—*Of the Senate.*

Art. 30. The Senate is composed of citizens eligible in accordance with the terms of Article 26 and who are over thirty-five years of age, to the number of three Senators for each State and three for the Federal district, to be elected in the same way as the Deputies.

Art. 31. The mandate of Senator will last for nine years, one-third of the Senate being renewed triennially.

. . .

§. A Senator elected to fill up a vacancy will exercise his mandate during the unexpired term of office of the Senator whom he replaced.

Art. 32. The Vice-President of the Republic will be President of the Senate, where he will only have a casting vote, and when absent or incapacitated from performing his duties he will be replaced by the Vice-President of the said Chamber.

Art. 33. It is the exclusive province of the Senate to try the President of the Republic and such other Federal functionaries as the Constitution expressly mentions, under the conditions and according to the forms prescribed by the same.

§1. When the Senate sits as a Court of Law it will be presided over by the President of the Supreme Federal Tribunal.

§2. It can only pronounce a sentence of condemnation in accordance with a vote of two-thirds of the members present.

§3. It cannot inflict any penalties beyond the loss of office and ineligibility to fill another, without prejudice to the action of the ordinary Courts of Justice against the accused.

Chapter 4.—*Of the Powers of Congress.*

Art. 34. It is the exclusive province of the National Congress—

1. To estimate the Federal receipts and to fix the amount of Federal expenditure each year, and to examine the accounts of the receipts and expenditure of each financial year.

2. To authorize the Executive Power to contract loans and undertake other operations of credit.

3. To legislate in regard to the Public Debt, and to establish means for its payment.

4. To regulate the collection and distribution of Federal revenues.

5. To regulate foreign trade and also that of the States among themselves and with the Federal district, and to establish customhouses at the outports and to create or suppress bonded warehouses.

6. To legislate respecting the navigation of rivers which flow through more than one State, or extend into foreign territories.

7. To settle the weight, value, inscription, type, and denomination of coins.

8. To establish banks of issue, legislate in regard to the emission of notes, and impose taxes thereon.

9. To determine the standard of weights and measures.

10. To decide in the last resort in cases respecting the boundaries of the States among themselves, those of the Federal district and those of the national territory with neighbouring nations.

11. To authorize the Government to declare war if recourse be not had to arbitration, or if the same should fail, and also to make peace.

12. To decide in the last resort as to Treaties and Conventions with foreign countries.

13. To change the capital of the Union.

14. To grant subsidies to the States under the circumstances mentioned in Article 5.

15. To legislate in regard to the Federal Postal and Telegraph Service.

16. To take the measures necessary for the safety of the frontiers.

17. To fix annually the number of the land and sea forces.

18. To legislate on the organization of the army and navy.

19. To grant or refuse to foreign forces the right of passage through the national territory for the purpose of military operations.

20. To mobilize and employ the National Guard, or citizen militia, in the cases provided for by the Constitution.

21. To declare one or more places in the national territory to be in a state of siege in an emergency of foreign aggression, or internal disorder, and to approve, or suspend, the state of siege which may have been declared by the Executive Power, or its responsible agents, during the recess of Congress.

22. To determine the conditions and procedure of election to Federal offices throughout the country.

23. To legislate in regard to the civil, commercial, or criminal law of the Republic, and to the procedure of the Federal judiciary.

24. To establish uniform laws in regard to naturalization.

25. To create and suppress Federal public offices and to settle the duties and salaries attaching to the same.

26. To organize the Federal judiciary in accordance with the provisions of Article 55 and the following ones of section 3.

27. To grant an amnesty.

28. To commute, or remit, penalties imposed on Federal officers for breaches of duty.

29. To legislate in regard to lands or mines belonging to the Union.

30. To legislate in regard to the municipal organization of

the Federal district, as also in regard to the police, higher education, and the other services which have been reserved in the Federal capital to the Government of the Union.

31. To subject to special legislation those places in the territory of the Republic which are needed for the establishment of arsenals, or other establishments and institutions for Federal use.

32. To regulate cases of extradition between the States.

33. To decree the necessary Laws and Resolutions for the exercise of the powers which belong to the Union.

34. To decree the organic Laws necessary for the entire execution of the Constitution.

35. To prorogue and adjourn its sessions.

Art. 35. It is also the duty, but not the exclusive duty, of Congress—

1. To watch over the keeping of the Constitution and the Laws, and to provide for necessities of a Federal character.

2. To encourage the development of literature, arts, and sciences, as well as of immigration, agriculture, industry, and trade in the country, without granting privileges which might interfere with the action of the local Governments.

3. To establish institutions for higher, and secondary, education in the States.

4. To provide for superior and secondary education in the Federal district.

. . .

Section 2.—*Of the Executive Power.*
Chapter 1.—*Of the President and Vice-President.*

Art. 41. The President of the Republic of the United States of Brazil exercises the Executive Power as the Elective Chief of the nation.

§1. The Vice-President, who is elected simultaneously with the President, will replace the latter if incapacitated, and succeed him in the event of his death or removal.

§2. Should the Vice-President be incapacitated or die, the President or Vice-President of the Senate, the Presidents of the Chamber of Deputies and of the Supreme Federal Tribunal, will be successively called to the Presidency.

§3. The following are indispensable conditions for election to the Presidency or Vice-Presidency of the Republic:—

(1.) To be a native-born Brazilian.

(2.) To be in the enjoyment of political rights.

(3.) To be not less than thirty-five years of age.

Art. 42. In the event of the Presidency or Vice-Presidency being vacant, from whatever cause, before two years of the Presidential term have elapsed, a new election must take place.

Art. 43. The President will hold his office for four years, and cannot be re-elected for the Presidential period immediately following.

§1. A Vice-President who holds the office of President during the last year of the Presidential term cannot be elected President for the ensuing term.

§2. The President will necessarily cease to perform the duties of his office on the very day when his Presidential term ends, being at once succeeded by the one who has just been elected.

§3. If the latter be incapacitated or absent, he will be replaced in the manner prescribed by Article 41, §§1 and 2.

§4. The first Presidential term will end on the 15th November, 1894.

Art. 44. On assuming office the President will make the following declaration before Congress in Session, or, if the latter be not assembled, before the Supreme Federal Tribunal:—

"I promise to maintain and carry out with perfect loyalty the Federal Constitution, to promote the general welfare of the Republic, keep its laws and uphold its unity, integrity, and independence."

Art. 45. Neither the President nor Vice-President may leave the country without permission from Congress, under pain of losing their office.

Art. 46. The President and Vice-President will receive a salary to be fixed by Congress in the preceding Presidential term.

Chapter 2.—*Of the Election of the President and Vice-President.*

Art. 47. The President and Vice-President of the Republic will be elected by the direct suffrage of the nation and by an absolute majority of votes.

§1. The election will take place on the 1st day of March of the last year of the Presidential term of office, and the counting of the votes received in the several districts will be carried out at the Federal capital and at the capitals of the States. Congress will examine the votes during its first Session of the same year, irrespective of the number of members present.

§2. If none of the candidates has obtained an absolute majority of votes, Congress will select, by a majority of the votes of those present, one of those who obtained the two highest number of votes in the direct election.

In case of the votes being equally divided, the elder of the two will be considered as elected.

§3. The mode of election and of counting the votes will be regulated by ordinary law.

§4. The blood relations and connections in the first and second degrees of the President and Vice-President who are in office at the time of the election, or who may have resigned within six months, are ineligible for the office of President or Vice-President.

Chapter 3.—*Of the Attributes of the Executive Power.*

Art. 48. It is the exclusive province of the President of the Republic—

1. To sanction, promulgate, and cause to be published the Laws and Resolutions of Congress, and to issue decrees, instructions, and regulations to secure their faithful execution.

2. To freely appoint and dismiss the Ministers of State.

3. To exercise, or nominate the person who shall exercise, the supreme command of the land and sea forces of the United States of Brazil, when the same are called to arms for the internal or external defence of the Union.

4. To administer the army and navy, and distribute the

forces belonging thereto in accordance with the Federal laws and the requirements of the National Government.

5. To fill up the civil and military offices of a Federal character, with due regard to the express restrictions laid down in the Constitution.

6. To pardon and commute punishments for crimes committed within the Federal jurisdiction, excepting the cases referred to in Article 34, No. 28, and Article 52, §2.

7. To declare war and make peace in accordance with the terms of Article 34, No. 11.

8. To declare war immediately in cases of foreign invasion or attack.

9. To report to Congress every year on the situation of the country, pointing out urgent measures and reforms to be effected, in a Message he will present to the Secretary to the Senate on the opening day of the Legislative Session.

10. To convene Congress in extraordinary Session.

11. To appoint Federal Magistrates upon the recommendation of the Supreme Tribunal.

12. To appoint the members of the Supreme Federal Tribunal, as also Diplomatic Ministers, submitting such appointments to the Senate for approval. During the recess of Congress, to appoint them temporarily until the Senate shall decide.

13. To appoint the other members of the Diplomatic Body and Consular Agents.

14. To maintain relations with foreign States.

15. Either in person, or through his responsible agents, to proclaim a state of siege in any part of the country in cases of foreign attack or serious internal disturbance (Article 6, No. 3, Article 34, No. 21, and Article 80).

16. To enter into international negotiations, conclude Agreements, Conventions, and Treaties, but always subject to reference to Congress, and likewise to approve of those concluded by the States in accordance with Article 65, submitting the same, when necessary, to the authority of Congress.

Chapter 4.—*Of the Ministers of State.*

Art. 49. The President of the Republic is assisted by the Ministers of State, who are his confidential agents and countersign his acts, and each of whom will preside over one of the Departments into which the Federal Administration is divided.

Art. 50. The Ministers of State are precluded from taking over any other office or public function, nor can they be elected President or Vice-President of the Union, Deputy, or Senator.

§. A Deputy or Senator who accepts the post of Minister of State will vacate his seat, and a new election, at which he cannot be elected, must at once be held.

Art. 51. The Ministers of State may not appear at the sittings of Congress, and they will only communicate with that body in writing, or by personal interviews with Committees of the Chambers.

The Annual Reports of the Ministers will be addressed to the President of the Republic, and will be distributed to all the members of Congress.

Art. 52. The Ministers of State are not responsible to Congress or to the Tribunals for advice given to the President.

§1. They are, however, answerable in regard to their own acts for crimes defined by law.

§2. In the case of ordinary crimes and breaches of duty, they will be prosecuted and tried by the Supreme Federal Tribunal, and when accessories to crimes committed by the President of the Republic, they will be dealt with by the authority competent to try the latter.

. . .

Section 3.—*Of the Judicial Power.*

Art. 55. The Judicial Power of the Union shall be exercised by a Supreme Federal Tribunal, with its seat in the capital of the Republic, and by as many Federal Judges and Courts throughout the country as Congress may establish.

Art. 56. The Supreme Federal Tribunal will be composed

of fifteen Judges appointed in the manner laid down by Article 48, No. 12, from among citizens of noted knowledge and reputation possessing the necessary qualifications for election to the Senate.

Art. 57. The Federal Judges are appointed for life, and can only lose their offices by a judicial sentence.

. . .

TITLE II.—*Of the States.*

Art. 63. Each State will be governed by the Constitution, and by the laws it may adopt, observing the constitutional principles of the Union.

Art. 64. Mines and waste lands are the property of the States in which they are situated, the Union reserving so much land only as is necessary for frontier defences, fortifications, and Federal military works and railways.

§. National real property not required for Union purposes will belong to the State in which it may be situated.

Art. 65. The States are free—

1. To conclude among themselves Treaties and Conventions of a non-political nature (Article 48, No. 16).

2. To exercise, in general, each and every power or right which is not denied them by an express clause, or one implicitly contained in an express clause, of the Constitution.

Art. 66. The States are precluded from—

1. Refusing recognition to documents of the Union, or of other States, of a legislative, administrative, or judicial character;

2. Rejecting coin or bank notes in circulation by order of the Federal Government;

3. Waging or declaring war among themselves, or using reprisals;

4. Refusing the extradition of criminals claimed by the Judiciaries of other States, or by the Federal District, in accordance with the Union laws which regulate matters of this nature (Article 34, No. 32).

Art. 67. Saving restrictions specified in the Constitution

and in the Federal laws, the Federal District will be administered by its municipal authorities.

§. Expenditure of a local nature in the Federal capital solely concerns the municipal authorities.

TITLE III.—*Of the Municipalities.*

Art. 68. The States will organize themselves in such a way as to guarantee the autonomy of the municipalities in all that concerns their particular interests.

. . .

55. A Naval Proclamation Favoring the Monarchy*

A major threat to the existence of the republic came in 1893. In February of that year an ill-defined, ultra-federalist revolt backed by some monarchist sentiment broke out in Rio Grande do Sul. The navy, a monarchist stronghold, joined in the revolt in September and blockaded Rio de Janeiro. Although never clearly proclaiming its goals, the naval hierarchy seemed to support a return to monarchical government. Certainly such sentiments animated Admiral Saldanha da Gama when he issued the proclamation printed below. Nowhere does he speak favorably of the republic. Indeed, he proposed "to replace the Government of Brazil where it was on the 15th of November, 1889." Threatening as the com-

....

* From *Papers Relating to the Foreign Relations of the United States* . . . 1893 (Washington, D.C.: Government Printing Office, 1894), p. 84.

bined revolts were, they eventually collapsed and the republican government triumphed in its first test under fire.

To my Fellow-citizens:

Being averse, both on principle and by instinct, to all manner of revolt, I have never engaged in intrigues of any kind.

Now, however, in the painful historical crisis through which our native land and our government are passing, the situation of the country compels me to take part in the contest.

Accepting this situation, which patriotism forces upon me, I join hands—without any preliminary arrangement, in broad daylight, and with a realizing sense of the responsibility which I am assuming—with my brethren who have been valiantly fighting for a year past on the plains of Rio Grande do Sul, and for three months past in the harbor of this capital, to free Brazil from a military despotism, which is rendered still more unbearable by a combination of partisan bigotry with the most unbridled Jacobinism.

Being a naval officer and having been an opponent of militarism all my life, I am now going to fight it with the sword. Being a Brazilian, it is to my interest to make every effort to put an end to this terrible crisis which has brought our country to anarchy and into discredit, and has crushed out all its liberties.

Both logic and justice warrant us in seeking, by force of arms, to replace the Government of Brazil where it was on the 15th of November, 1889, when in an unguarded moment—a moment of national stupefaction—it was overthrown by a military insurrection, of which the present Government is but a continuation.

The respect, however, which is due to the will of the nation, freely expressed, tells us that it is proper for it to choose, on its own responsibility, the kind of institutions that it desires to adopt.

I offer my life, together with the lives of my companions in arms, as a sacrifice on the altar of my country.

The army, which is now doing battle with its proverbial

bravery, can no longer continue to defend a Government that has lost the moral support of the nation and its credit in foreign countries. Its persistence in that inglorious role, even should it be successful, would at length change it from a national force, as it is now, into a pretorian guard, like those under the later Roman Empire.

The cry for our political redemption, which was raised on our southern frontier, and which passed through Santa Catharina, Paraná, and S. Paulo until it reached this capital, has now re-echoed in the extreme north.

Brazilians, in order to hasten the victory which, sooner or later, is sure to come, you must lend the weight of your moral influence to the struggle. It is a well-known fact that the national cause in whose defense I am about to enlist already has the support of all the conservative classes of Brazilian society, of the toilers and producers, and of those, too, who are opposed to sedition, mutiny, and disorder.

The will of these classes must prevail, and they must, therefore, unmistakably make it known that they are determined to shake off the abominable yoke of slavery which the military despotism of 1889 would fain keep on their necks.

Compatriots, nations that yield up their rights can not complain of their oppressors.

Brazil, whose past history is brief but honorable, has a great future before her. She can only attain it by freeing herself from a despotism which degrades her, both in her own eyes and in those of the civilized world.

Show that we are not a conquered but a free people that is conscious of its destiny.

This is the situation.

I hope to be able to perform my duty as a Brazilian, whatever sacrifices it may cost.

Do you perform yours?

Luiz Felippe Saldanha da Gama,
Rear-Admiral in the National Navy.
Ilha das Cobras, December 7, 1893.

56. The Missions Award *

Under the able guidance of the Baron of Rio-Branco, the Luso-Brazilian policy of territorial expansion reached its fruition. During four centuries the Luso-Brazilians had expanded into the heartland of South America contrary to the provisions of the Treaty of Tordesilhas. The Treaty of Madrid in general terms recognized that expansion. Brazil then sought to solidify its position by the definitive demarcation of those frontiers. Using the principle of uti possidetis, the diplomat Rio-Branco did just that. His brilliant presentation of Brazil's claims to the Missions territory, disputed with archrival Argentina, won the award from the arbiter, President Grover Cleveland, in 1895. That diplomatic victory was the first of many. By 1908, Rio-Branco had advantageously closed the nine-thousand miles of borders separating Brazil from its neighbors. By eliminating causes for distrust, dispute, and even war, he prepared his country for a new policy of friendship and cooperation with its sister republics.

Now, therefore, be it known, that I, Grover Cleveland, President of the United States of America, upon whom the functions of arbitrator have been conferred in the premises, having duly examined and considered the arguments, documents, and evidence to be submitted by the respective parties pursuant to the provisions of said treaty, do hereby make the following decision and award:

That the boundary line between the Argentine Republic and the United States of Brazil, in that part submitted to me

....

* From N. Andrew N. Cleven, *Readings in Hispanic American History* (Boston: Ginn and Co., 1927), pp. 676-677.

for arbitration and decision, is constituted and shall be established by and upon the rivers Pepiri (also called Pepiri-guazu) and San Antonio, to wit, the rivers which Brazil has designated in the argument and documents submitted to me as constituting the boundary, and herein before denominated the Westerly system.

For convenience of identification these rivers may be further described as those recognized, designated, marked, and declared as the Pepiri and San Antonio, respectively, and as the boundary rivers, in the years 1759 and 1760, by the Spanish and Portuguese commissioners in that behalf, appointed pursuant to the treaty of limits concluded January 13, 1750, between Spain and Portugal, as is recorded in the official report of the said commissioners. The mouth of the affluent of the Uruguay last aforesaid, to wit, the Pepiri (also called Pepiri-guazu), which, with the San Antonio, is hereby determined to be the boundary in question, was reckoned and reported by the said commissioners who surveyed it in 1759 to be one and one-third leagues upstream from the Great Falls (Salto Grande) of the Uruguay, and two-thirds of a league above a smaller affluent on the same side called by the said commissioners the Ytayoa. According to the map and report of the survey made in 1887 by the Brazilian-Argentine joint commission, in pursuance of the treaty concluded September 28, 1885, between the Argentine Republic and Brazil, the distance from the Great Falls of the Uruguay to the mouth of the aforesaid Pepiri (also called Pepiri-guazu) was ascertained and shown to be four and one-half miles as the river flows. The mouth of the affluent of the Yguazu last aforesaid, to wit, the San Antonio, was reckoned and reported by the said commissioners of 1759 and 1760 to be nineteen leagues upstream from the Great Falls (Salto Grande) of the Yguazu, and twenty-three leagues from the mouth of the latter river. It was also by them reported as the second important river that empties itself on the south bank of the Yguazu above its Salto Grande, the San Francisco, about seventeen and one-fourth leagues above the Great Falls, being the first. In the report of the joint survey made in 1788 under the treaty of October 1, 1777, between

Spain and Portugal, the location of the San Antonio with reference to the mouth and the Great Falls of the Yguazu agrees with the above stated.

In testimony whereof I have hereunto set my hand and caused the seal of the United States to be affixed.

Done in triplicate at the city of Washington on the fifth day of February in the year one thousand eight hundred and ninety-five, and of the Independence of the United States the one hundred and nineteenth.

GROVER CLEVELAND.

❦

57. The Shift of Brazil's Diplomatic Axis: London to Washington*

The new foreign policy formulated by the Baron of Rio-Branco emphasized friendship with the United States. The highlights of a decade of close cooperation between the two giant republics, paralleling the years of the Baron's ministry, 1902-1912, were the mutual elevation of their legations to embassies in 1905 and the visit of Secretary of State Elihu Root to Rio de Janeiro in 1906. Such events demonstrated that Brazil's diplomatic axis was shifting from London to Washington. In one of his rare public statements of foreign policy, Rio-Branco, an habitual journalist, placed or inspired an article in the Foreign Ministry's unofficial mouthpiece, the Jornal do Commercio. *Entitled "The Pan American Conference," the article begins by discussing one of his primary preoccupations, the equality of the New World with*

....

* Translated from the *Jornal do Commercio* (Rio de Janeiro, December 11, 1905), p. 2.

the Old, and then proceeds to affirm his agreement first with the Monroe Doctrine and then with the Roosevelt Corollary. It ends with a justification for the close friendship Brazil was consciously manifesting toward the United States.

The last meeting of the Pan American Congress was in 1901 in Mexico. In these five years, great international events have been so varied and grave that in the political ideas of our continent one notes a sudden change, originating in a lively sentiment of the universality of its destiny, which inspires and aggrandizes the conscience of the American peoples.

In this important variation of principles, of which the additions made to the Monroe Doctrine by President Roosevelt already impress us, there is surely much of interest for the coming conference in Rio de Janeiro.[1]

Our age has witnessed the most illustrious congresses, and the right to deride the declarations of principles of these international conferences is justified by the repeated deceptions inflicted on the human spirit by the failure to execute those principles. . . .

It is probable, however, that the Pan American Congress will have important results. With the intense necessity which the American nations have of assuring their international existence, they are formulating a collective ideal of a continent which wants to participate with Europe on the basis of equality. It is to be hoped that the declarations of the Congress will express perfectly the intimate aspirations of the American nations. Therefore, the fact that an all-American conference is meeting ought not to lead to the conclusion that America is challenging Europe and that its collective sentiment is hostile to European progress or ideals. What America wants is equality in international law, which up to now she has enjoyed, and the sovereignty of her nations to be as respected as that of the European nations. What America refuses is any attempt to apply the so-called African princi-

....

[1] The 3rd Pan American Conference held in Rio de Janeiro in mid-1906 [ed.].

ples to any portion of this free continent. This territory cannot be touched by European greed or conquest. America only wants to be conquered peacefully by that culture which is the glory of Europe, the dignity of the human spirit. Absorbing with the surprising forces of our physical world the energies of the white race, we aspire to attract to this side of the ocean the illuminating wave of European genius. But any violent form of domination, no matter what it be, will be energetically repelled by the Americans with one vibration of sentiment which will unite all of these different countries and will manifest itself like an electrical discharge penetrating the atmosphere heedless of boundaries. We are certain that an American law different from the European law will not be proclaimed in the Conference; what there is and will be is the same law of one civilization which seeks to include all people without distinction of climate or race.

Relative to this continent the greatest service given by the Monroe Doctrine is the liberty which it assures to the development of the forces of each American nation.

Without fear of external and unjustified violences, not even provoked by savagery and corruption, each American nation can attain the maximum of its development within the protection of that doctrine, which in the history of political ideas has an amazing and singular destiny. A simple doctrinaire principle rarely is seen to transmute the course of others reputed more natural; and instead of the expansion of the strong, the elimination of the weak, the occupation of the uninhabited regions—the dominant theory since the discoveries of the sixteenth century—in America, at any rate, there has appeared a new principle of respect for the independence and sovereignty of all nations, a principle which England followed since Canning and only came to repudiate in the Transvaal War. But in South America no one needs to fear the transformation of the English policy because the Monroe Doctrine is not an abstraction. It has for its base the prodigious ascendency of the United States.

Latin America has nothing to fear from Anglo-Saxon America. The United States is a nation of English origin and principles and therefore beneficial for the civilization of other people because the sentiment of individualism is so much a part of their race that English or North American imperialism, if it should manifest itself, never would be of the same type as German or Latin imperialism which seeks to destroy and annihilate everything, contorting everything, in order to create from the incompatibilities and irreconcilables the same kind of country in all the regions of the world. Nothing, absolutely nothing, in the policies of the United States would be able to cause uneasiness to the national sensitivity of the other American countries. Just the opposite, these nations find in the preponderance of the first nation of the continent support for their causes and aspirations.

If at any time some nation showed itself unhappy with the American Republic, it was when President Roosevelt proclaimed that the Monroe Doctrine could not serve as a protection for policies of bankruptcy and international piracy.

Brazil, which is solidly in favor of this honest interpretation of Monroeism, prides itself on the spontaneous and affirmed friendship of that American nation and of its great president. There is no friendship more coveted in the world. England proclaims this friendship as unbreakable and in order not to break it submitted to the Cleveland message, considered as an ultimatum, in which the United States appealed to arbitration in the question between British Guiana and Venezuela. The German emperor, whose sagacity and power the entire world recognizes, sent his brother Prince Henry of Prussia to visit the American Republic, and requested Miss Alice Roosevelt to christen a German cruiser built in the United States. France, Russia, Japan, whatever their systems of alliances, aspire to count on the good will of the United States as a factor of capital importance. The Peace of Portsmouth was the culminating point of that marvelous prestige.

In the diplomatic history of Brazil there is no trace of any occurrence, as always happens in international life, which could be interpreted in a manner to weaken our friendship with the United States. During the Empire the three unpleasant incidents of Condy Raguet in the First Empire and of Wise and Webb in the Second were resolved with honor for Brazil, without the intervention of any other country, by the American government, which disapproved of and punished its agents. And the emperor, who had no motives to keep resentments of such incidents, went to the United States in 1876 and returned from there full of amazement and stimulation. During the Republic our approximation with North America was predetermined.

As proof of how much the good will of the United States has served us, it is sufficient only to refer to the Oyapoc dispute arbitration which was due in a great part to the certainty in Paris that Brazil would not be isolated in case of a new attempt at military occupation. Only a few months had passed since Cleveland made his ultimatum.

The quick reciprocity with which the American government raised the rank of its representation in Rio de Janeiro and the initiative it took in the selection of this capital for the meeting of the next Pan American Congress are significant demonstrations of a good and comforting friendship.

If the political reasons were not sufficient to emphasize the importance of the meeting in Rio de Janeiro, the presence in our country of the Secretary of State of the United States, Mr. Elihu Root, is sufficiently expressive to be considered as an event of great importance in our time. He is not a delegate; he is a member of the American government who will for the first time in history visit another nation. Brazil receives the honor of that distinction because the United States knows that it has won our loyalty and friendship.

Accompanying the American Secretary to Brazil will be Mr. Joaquim Nabuco, our Ambassador in Washington.

After an absence of seven long years, during which time he has ennobled the name of Brazil, that eminent statesman, of whom all Brazil is proud, could not return to his native land at a more significant or auspicious time.

Mr. Root comes from a truly amazing country. His eyes may not be dazzled by our small material progress, but his American philosophy will surely be pleased to note the new phenomena in the Brazilian nation: activity, energy, and hope.

Transformed by science and energy we want to assure our

nation a preeminent place among the American nations. Our collective duty is to realize that high ideal of a wonderful land which the emigrant races, desirous of peace and work, are making of Brazil. It is necessary that in the face of those industrial and scientific problems we are not overcome by any of those political evils which so greatly hurt the South American nations. There is nothing more ridiculous and extravagant than the manifestations of dictators, the pronouncements, the revolutions for possession of power, the military demagoguery. The foreigners who are coming to honor us will certainly be surprised at the change in our temperament. We will not delude them with a mistaken notion of Brazilian progress. We present instead the reality of our achievements.

❖

58. The Intellectuals View the New Brazil

Brazil elected its first civilian president in 1894; and by the time of the inauguration of the second one, four years later, the nation was settling down again into tranquillity. Financial reform and mounting coffee exports were bringing prosperity, so that by the turn of the century the First Republic had been strengthened and was entering its heyday. The rubber boom in the distant Amazon was changing isolated Manaus into a cosmopolitan city with electricity, streetcars, cinemas, a grandiose opera house, and an international society. Under the direction of Prefect Francisco Pereira Passos, Rio de Janeiro was being transformed into one of the world's most beautiful and—thanks to Osvaldo Cruz—most healthy cities. Coffee prosperity metamorphosed São Paulo, whose population grew from 35,000 in 1883 to 350,000 in 1907, into the bustling commercial center of the nation. *Santos was rapidly becoming one of the world's busiest ports, sending the all-important coffee exports to the distant cities of Europe and North America. While all this material change was taking place, the country was also undergoing a literary renaissance. The intellectuals at the turn of the century fixed their critical eyes on the New Brazil and analyzed it carefully. Two of the foremost novelists, Machado de Assis and Lima Barreto, took a penetrating look into Brazilian society. Other significant contributors to the new quest for national self-understanding were Euclides da Cunha and Graça Aranha. The selections below indicate some of the themes with which they dealt.*

*

EUCLIDES DA CUNHA'S REBELLION

IN THE BACKLANDS *

In 1902, one of the most significant works of the new analytical school of literature, Rebellion in the Backlands *by Euclides da Cunha, appeared. Da Cunha described the rebellion of Antônio Conselheiro, a religious mystic, in the backland town of Canudos in Bahia. To Da Cunha, the rebellion symbolized the struggle of man against nature, of civilization against barbarism. The tragedy of the backlands, he believed, was that civilization had abandoned both the area and its inhabitants to barbarism. The villain of the plot is the cities; while the victims are Antônio Conselheiro and his rustic followers. To Da Cunha, the mission to carry civiliza-*

....

* Reprinted from *Rebellion in the Backlands* by Euclides da Cunha, trans. by Samuel Putnam (Chicago: University of Chicago Press, 1957), pp. 89-91, 160-162, 405-406, 443-444. By permission of the University of Chicago Press. Copyright 1957 by The University of Chicago.

tion into the backlands was the only justification for the war. He wrote: *"This entire campaign would be a crime, a futile and barbarous one, if we were not to take advantage of the paths opened by our artillery, by following up our cannon with a constant, stubborn, and persistent campaign of education, with the object of drawing these rude and backward fellow countrymen of ours into the current of our times and of our national life. . . . Our biological evolution demands the guarantee of social evolution. We are condemned to civilization. Either we shall progress or we shall perish. So much is certain and our choice is clear."*

The sertanejo, or man of the backlands, is above all else a strong individual. He does not exhibit the debilitating rachitic tendencies of the neurasthenic mestizos of the seaboard.

His appearance, it is true, at first glance, would lead one to think that this was not the case. He does not have the flawless features, the graceful bearing, the correct build of the athlete. He is ugly, awkward, stooped. Hercules-Quasimodo reflects in his bearing the typical unprepossessing attributes of the weak. His unsteady, slightly swaying, sinuous gait conveys the impression of loose-jointedness. His normally downtrodden mien is aggravated by a dour look which gives him an air of depressing humility. On foot, when not walking, he is invariably to be found leaning against the first doorpost or wall that he encounters; while on horseback, if he reins in his mount to exchange a couple of words with an acquaintance, he braces himself on one stirrup and rests his weight against the saddle. When walking, even at a rapid pace, he does not go forward steadily in a straight line but reels swiftly, as if he were following the geometric outlines of the meandering backland trails. And if in the course of his walk he pauses for the most commonplace of reasons, to roll a *cigarro*, strike a light, or chat with a friend, he falls—"falls" is the word— into a squatting position and will remain for a long time in this unstable state of equilibrium, with the entire weight of his body suspended on his great-toes, as he sits there on his heels with a simplicity that is at once ridiculous and delightful.

He is the man who is always tired. He displays this invincible sluggishness, this muscular atony, in everything that he does: in his slowness of speech, his forced gestures, his unsteady gait, the languorous cadence of his ditties—in brief, in his constant tendency to immobility and rest.

Yet all this apparent weariness is an illusion. Nothing is more surprising than to see the sertanejo's listlessness disappear all of a sudden. In this weakened organism complete transformations are effected in a few seconds. All that is needed is some incident that demands the release of slumbering energies. The fellow is transfigured. He straightens up, becomes a new man, with new lines in his posture and bearing; his head held high now, above his massive shoulders; his gaze straightforward and unflinching. Through an instantaneous discharge of nervous energy, he at once corrects all the faults that come from the habitual relaxation of his organs; and the awkward rustic unexpectedly assumes the dominating aspect of a powerful, copper-hued Titan, an amazingly different being, capable of extraordinary feats of strength and agility.

This contrast becomes evident upon the most superficial examination. It is one that is revealed at every moment, in all the smallest details of back-country life—marked always by an impressive alternation between the extremes of impulse and prolonged periods of apathy.

It is impossible to imagine a more inelegant, ungainly horseman: no carriage, legs glued to the belly of his mount, hunched forward and swaying to the gait of the unshod, mistreated backland ponies, which are sturdy animals and remarkably swift. In this gloomy, indolent posture the lazy cowboy will ride along, over the plains, behind his slow-paced herd, almost transforming his "nag" into the lulling hammock in which he spends two-thirds of his existence. But let some giddy steer up ahead stray into the tangled scrub of the caatinga, or let one of the herd at a distance become entrammeled in the foliage, and he is at once a different being and, digging his broad-roweled spurs into the flanks of his mount, he is off like a dart and plunges at top speed into the labyrinth of jurema thickets.

Let us watch him at this barbarous *steeple chase*.

Nothing can stop him in his onward rush. Gullies, stone heaps, brush piles, thorny thickets, or riverbanks—nothing can halt his pursuit of the straying steer, for *wherever the cow goes, there the cowboy and his horse go too.* Glued to his horse's back, with his knees dug into its flanks until horse and rider appear to be one, he gives the bizarre impression of a crude sort of centaur: emerging unexpectedly into a clearing, plunging into the tall weeds, leaping ditches and swamps, taking the small hills in his stride, crashing swiftly through the prickly briar patches, and galloping at full speed over the expanse of tablelands.

His robust constitution shows itself at such a moment to best advantage. It is as if the sturdy rider were lending vigor to the frail pony, sustaining it by his improvised reins of caroá fiber, suspending it by his spurs, hurling it onward—springing quickly into the stirrups, legs drawn up, knees well forward and close to the horse's side—hot on the trail of the wayward steer; now bending agilely to avoid a bough that threatens to brush him from the saddle; now leaping off quickly like an acrobat, clinging to his horse's mane, to avert collision with a stump sighted at the last moment; then back in the saddle again at a bound—and all the time galloping, galloping, through all obstacles, balancing in his right hand, without ever losing it once, never once dropping it in the liana thickets, the long, iron-pointed, leather-headed goad which in itself, in any other hands, would constitute a serious obstacle to progress.

But once the fracas is over and the unruly steer restored to the herd, the cowboy once more lolls back in the saddle, once more an inert and unprepossessing individual, swaying to his pony's slow gait, with all the disheartening appearance of a languishing invalid.

. . .

He [the sertanejo] preached against the Republic, there is no denying that. This antagonism was an inevitable derivative of his mystic exacerbation, a variant of his religious delirium that was forced upon him. Yet he did not display the faintest trace of a political intuition; for your jagunço is quite as inapt at understanding the republican form of government as he is the constitutional monarchy. Both to him are abstractions, beyond the reach of his intelligence. He is instinctively opposed to both of them, since he is in that phase of evolution in which the only rule he can conceive is that of a priestly or a warrior chieftain.

We must insist upon this point: the war of Canudos marked an ebb, a backward flow, in our history. What we had to face here was the unlooked-for resurrection, under arms, of an old society, a dead society, galvanized into life by a madman. We were not acquainted with this society; it was not possible for us to have been acquainted with it.

. . .

Instead, we looked at it from the narrow-minded point of view of partisan politics. In the presence of these monstrous aberrations, we had a revealing fit of consternation; and, with an intrepidity that was worthy of a better cause, we proceeded to put them down with bayonets, thereby causing history to repeat itself, as we made yet another inglorious incursion into these unfortunate regions, opening up once more the grass-grown trails of the bandeiras.

In the backlands agitator, whose revolt was a phase of rebellion against the natural order of things, we beheld a serious adversary, a mighty foeman representing a regime which we had done away with, one who was capable of overthrowing our nascent institutions.

And Canudos was our Vendée.

In the last days of the settlement, when it was permitted them to enter what was left of the huts, the conquerors found a grievous disappointment awaiting them. Their hard-won victory gave them the right to sack these ruined homes, and nothing was exempt from their insatiable curiosity; but it was one of the most unremunerative bits of pillaging that history has to record. In place of rich spoils, they found mu-

tilated images and cocoanut-shell rosaries; but what most excited their covetousness was the scrawled documents, and especially the terrible verses which they discovered among the
latter. Poor bedraggled sheets of paper on which the barbarous orthography paralleled the most naïve absurdities, while
the irregular and unsightly handwriting seemed to be a pho-
tographic reproduction of the twisted way of thinking of
these people; it appeared to sum up the psychology behind
the conflict. These scraps of paper were worth everything in
the world for the reason that they were worth precisely nothing. On them the sermons of Antônio Conselheiro were written down; and, as one read them over, one realized just how
innocuous his preachings really were after all, reflecting simply the poor fellow's intellectual turmoil. Every line of them
was vibrant with the same vague and incongruous religiosity,
but there was very little of political significance to be found
in any one of them, such as might have lent itself to the
messianic tendencies revealed. If the rebel attacked the established order, it was because he believed that the promised
kingdom of bliss was near at hand. He denounced the Republic as a mortal sin on the part of the people, the supreme
heresy, heralding the ephemeral triumph of the Anti-Christ.

. . .

The new expeditions, upon reaching Queimadas, were
aware of this violent transition. Here was an absolute and
radical break between the coastal cities and the clay huts of
the interior, one that so disturbed the rhythm of our evolutionary development and which was so deplorable a stum-
bling block to national unity. They were in a strange country
now, with other customs, other scenes, a different kind of
people. Another language even, spoken with an original and
picturesque drawl. They had, precisely, the feeling of going
to war in another land. They felt that they were outside Brazil. A complete social separation expanded the geographical
distance, giving rise to the nostalgic sensation of being very
far from home. The mission which had brought them there
merely served to deepen the antagonism. There was the

enemy, out there to the east and to north, hidden away in those endless highland plains; and far, far away, beyond the plains, a terrible drama was being unfolded.

It was, surely, a paradoxical kind of fatherland whose own sons had to invade it, armed to the teeth, with martial tread, ripping out its very entrails with their Krupp cannon. And, all the while, they knew nothing whatever about it; they had never seen it before but viewed with amazement the arid earth, rugged and brutal, bristling with thorns, tumultuously littered with stone heaps and pulverized mountains, torn asunder with caverns and ravines, while all about were the parched and barren tablelands, great, rolling, steppe-like plains.

What they were being called upon to do now was what other troops had done—to stage an invasion of foreign territory. For it was all a geographic fiction. This other was the reality, plain for all to see from what had gone before. The soldiers felt this and were obsessed by the thought. Here were those unknown woodsmen sending back to them, day by day, mutilated and defeated, their comrades who, a few months previously, had gone down that same road, strong of body and proud of spirit. As a result, there was no heart left in them; they had not the courage to strike out, unconcerned with what might happen, into the depths of those mysterious and formidable backlands.

. . .

What was more, they had not to fear the formidable judgment of posterity: for History would not go as far as that. Concerned with the fearful physiognomy of peoples amid the majestic ruins of vast cities, against the supremely imposing background of cyclopic coliseums, with the glorious butchery of classic battles and the epic savagery of great invasions, History would have no time for this crude slaughter pen.

The backlands are a refuge for the criminal. Whoever goes along these trails and, by the side of the road, sees a cross standing above the grave of the assassin's victim, does not pause to investigate the crime but lifts his hat and passes on.

The punitive powers of the constituted authorities assuredly do not extend to these regions. In this case the crime was a public one. The government's chief representative in Monte Santo knew all about it, and he kept silent, thereby covering it with the mantle of culpable indifference. The offenders knew that they would go unpunished, and they were further protected by anonymity and by the tacit complicity of the only ones who were in a position to repress the crimes in question. The result was, all the accumulated rancors burst forth, as a criminal multitude, armed to the teeth and paid to kill, fell upon the wretched backlands populace.

Canudos was appropriately enough surrounded by a girdle of mountains. It was a parenthesis, a hiatus. It was a vacuum. It did not exist. Once having crossed that cordon of mountains, no one sinned any more. An astounding miracle was accomplished, and time was turned backward for a number of centuries. As one came down the slopes and caught sight of the enormous bandits' den that was huddled there, he well might imagine that some obscure and bloody drama of the Stone Age was here taking place. The setting was sufficiently suggestive. The actors, on one side and the other, Negroes, caboclos, white and yellow skinned, bore on their countenances the indelible imprint of many races—races which could be united only upon the common plane of their lower and evil instincts. A primitive animality, slowly expunged by civilization, was here being resurrected intact. The knot was being undone at last. In place of the stone hatchet and the harpoon made of bone were the sword and the rifle; but the knife was still there to recall the cutting edge of the ancient flint, and man might flourish it with nothing to fear—not even the judgment of the remote future.

But, nevertheless, for the light of a future day, let this passage stand, even though it be one marked by no brilliance, uncompromising, angry, unedifying by reason of the subject matter, brutal, violent, because it is a cry of protest, somber as the bloodstain that it reflects.

*

GRAÇA ARANHA'S CANAAN *

In Canaan, *another major novel of the analytical school, Graça Aranha verbosely dissected Brazilian society and examined it through the eyes of both foreign immigrants and natives. Highly critical of his country, he observed that the nations of the New World suffered from all the evils afflicting the Old World. He also concluded that the only true Brazilian was the mulatto.*

"You gentlemen speak of independence," observed the municipal judge caustically, "but I don't see it. Brazil is, and has always been, a colony. Our regime is not a free one. We are a protectorate."

"And who protects us?" interrupted Brederodes, gesticulating with his monocle.

"Wait a minute, man. Listen. Tell me: where is our financial independence? What is the real money that dominates us? Where is our gold? What is the use of our miserable paper currency if it isn't to buy English pounds? Where is our public property? What little we have is mortgaged. The customs revenues are in the hands of the English. We have no ships. We have no railroads, either; they are all in the hands of the foreigners. Is it, or is it not, a colonial regime disguised with the name of a free nation . . . Listen. You don't believe me. I would like to be able to preserve our moral and intellectual patrimony, our language, but rather than continue this poverty, this turpitude at which we have arrived, it is better for one of Rothschild's bookkeepers to manage our financial affairs and for a German colonel to set things in order."

. . . .

* From *Canaan* by Graça Aranha (Boston: The Four Seas Company, 1920), pp. 196-198, 290-292, 294-301, copyright, 1920, by the Four Seas Company. By permission of Bruce Humphries.

"You are a cynic . . ." shouted Brederodes, livid, his lips trembling.

There was a brief silence. The lawyer was enjoying the dispute. Itapecuru feared a fight, but Paul Maciel smiled with superiority.

"Call me what you wish; what you can't do is to deny the evidence of facts. A colony we are and we shall be . . ." he persisted coolly.

Brederodes reddened, and in an uncontrollable rage, retorted daringly:

"It will be a colony so long as there are yellow dogs like you!"

"Now then, man, don't get sassy," said Maciel, quietly, and taking up the trend of his speech, he continued: "If in reality we are not within the sphere of action of a great nation, it is because we take advantage of the disputes between the great powers. The United States have cast their shadow on this continent, I know it, but some fine day, tired of preventing others from taking possession of our country, they will eat us up, as they did with Cuba."

"They say that Germany has her plans. They say . . . But my colleague knows that in such matters it is better not to say anything unless you feel perfectly sure of your remarks," pompously commented Dr. Itapecuru. And his egregious cowardice introduced a conciliatory element into the discussion.

"I can assert, without fear of being contradicted that we are coveted by the ambitious Germans. The very kaiser pays out of his own pocket missionaries and professors in Rio Grande and Santa Catharina."

. . .

"A country without justice is not a country to live in; it is nothing but a conglomeration of barbarians . . ." affirmed Maciel, following his bent of talking in general terms.

"In Brazil there is no law," he continued, "and no one can feel safe. The trial is conducted in such a way that the accused has no chance. Listen, if a man tries to seize another man's property, he finds in our judicial system, in the way of conducting trials, all possible help to carry out his nefarious intention. And if that man be a magnate, nobody can bother him. No; not even I."

"Justice is but an illusion the world over," said Milkau.

"But in Brazil conditions are much worse than elsewhere, because it is not a case of rare eclipses of justice."

Milkau listened thoughtfully to the magistrate, who went on impelled by a desire to confess the faults of his country.

"This that we call a nation is nothing, I say. We did have here once a semblance of liberty and justice, but today all that has ended. This poor Brazil is but a corpse which is rapidly decomposing . . . The *urubus*[1] are coming . . ."

"Where from?"

"From everywhere; from Europe, from the United States . . . It is a conquest . . ."

"I don't believe that," asserted Milkau.

"They will come. How could we live on in our present condition? Where is the moral foundation that shall support us abroad when here, at home, we are struggling in the greatest disorder and despair? What is happening to the country is that it is undergoing a character crisis. It hasn't one single fundamental virtue . . ."

"That is the character of the race," explained Milkau.

"Yes, my friend. Here the race is not distinguished by any prominent conservative virtue; there does not exist a common moral fund. I may add that there are no two Brazilians alike, and that, therefore, it would be futile to attempt to form an idea of the collective virtues and defects by judging merely by one of us. Which is our social virtue? Not even courage, the most rudimentary and instinctive of them all, is with us cultivated sanely and constantly, in a superior way. In this country, bravery is nothing more than a nervous impulse. Look at our wars! What cowardice is written in their history! . . . There was a time when our piety and our kindness were loudly proclaimed. Collectively, as a nation, we are bad, hysterically, uselessly bad . . . !"

....

[1] A common Brazilian black vulture [ed.].

He fell silent as if oppressed by his sad recollections. Milkau, feeling sorry for the tortures of his Brazilian soul, looked sympathetically at Maciel.

"See what happens to patriotism here," continued Maciel after a brief interval. "In Brazil the great mass of people has no such feeling. Here there is a cosmopolitanism which is not the expression of a comprehensive and generous philosophy but is merely a symptom of moral inertia, an indication of the untimely loss of a feeling—patriotism—which would very well harmonize with the backward state of our culture. You must notice that our patriots are all men of hatred and of blood, that is to say, they are savages."

"There is no doubt," assented Milkau, deeply interested in Maciel's frank analysis, "that there is a vast disparity between the different strata of the population. This lack of homogeneity is probably the cause of that instability . . ."

The judge reflected awhile, then leaning over the table, he looked at Milkau and spoke to him in a more decisive and vibrant tone.

"You are right. The Brazilian people, as a whole, offer an aspect at once of decrepitude and childishness. The decadence of our people presents a deplorable mixture of the savagery of the new-born races with the degeneracy of the races that are becoming exhausted. There is general confusion. The currents of immorality flow through our people without meeting obstacles in any of our institutions. Such a nation as ours is ready to receive the worst evil that can befall in the world: arbitrary and despotic governments. If society is a creation of suggestion, what can you expect of the feelings, the ideals of the uncultured masses when their imagination is being bewildered by the spectacle of the most brazen degradation in the governing classes? What reaction will not be caused in dull intellects by the scorn of those leaders for an ideal, for superior things, and their love for position and graft? And it isn't the government only. It is all of them: the subservient judiciary, ready to plunder private property, the public servants, the military, the clergy, all of them are sliding down a dangerous incline . . ."

. . .

"Very well," he [Maciel] said brightening up suddenly, "but here we have a real storm . . .

"It is natural. It could not be otherwise. From what I have observed and meditated, I am firmly convinced that it is due to the original formation of the country. From the very first, there were conquerors and vanquished under the form of masters and slaves. For two centuries the latter attempted to overpower the former. All the revolutions of Brazilian history signify a struggle between classes; the ruled against the ruling. The Brazilian nation was for many years neither more nor less than a nominal expression for a conglomeration of separate races and castes. And that state of affairs would continue, were it not that the powerful and imperious sensuality of the conquerors destroyed the barriers which separated them from the other races and formed that intermediate race of half-castes and mulattoes which is the link, the national tie, and which, increasing every day, has gradually gained possession of their oppressors' strongholds. . . . And when the army ceased to be the appanage of the white man and was dominated by the half-castes, the revolution was nothing more than the revenge of the oppressed who founded institutions which, due to their gravitational force, were destined to abide for some time in harmony with the psychological forces that created them. That shock was absolutely necessary to bring about what other means had not been able to accomplish for centuries: the formation of a nationality . . .

"It was necessary that out of our conflicting races there should emerge a half-caste type which, adapting itself to its surroundings and possessing the average qualities of the other peoples, should vanquish and eliminate them all. . . . Those who tend to govern us more acceptably, and with greater success than any others, belong to the same mulatto type. In fact, Brazil belongs to them . . ."

Paul Maciel paused for a moment and then, looking at his long, white hands, continued as he smiled ironically:

"There is no doubt about it . . . If I had a few drops of

African blood, I would certainly not be here grumbling . . .
I would be perfectly satisfied with the country . . . Why
was I not born a mulatto?"

❧

---

59 . The Convention of Taubaté*

---

*During the First Republic, coffee ruled Brazil economically,
and the coffee planters ruled it politically. Both the economic and political centers of the nation shifted from the
old sugar regions of Pernambuco to the new coffee regions of
São Paulo. The United States Minister in Rio de Janeiro
reported, "Never before has the country and especially everyone connected with the Government been so much under
the influence of the coffee planters as at present and any
measure which is seriously desired by that element is sure of
immediate passage by Congress." Everything went smoothly
for the coffee planters and the national economy until the
early years of the twentieth century, when overproduction
threatened the coffee prosperity. To counter that threat, representatives of the three major coffee-producing states signed
an agreement at Taubaté in March of 1906, to which the
federal government gave its cooperation, to guarantee a fair
price for coffee. That convention was significant because it
inaugurated the scheme of coffee valorization, the purchase
of excess coffee and its removal from the market in order to
maintain its world price.*

....

* From *Papers Relating to the Foreign Relations of the United
States* . . . 1906 (Washington, D.C.: Government Printing Office,
1907), pp. 109-111.

The President of the United States of Brazil.

I make known that the National Congress has decreed and I have sanctioned the following resolution:

Article 1. The convention which took place on the 26th of February of the present year between the presidents of the States of São Paulo, Rio de Janeiro, and Minas Geraes, with the modifications of the agreement signed by the same presidents on July 4 of the same year, is hereby approved. The clause referring to the *caixa do emissão de ouro e conversão* (gold issue and conversion department) is excluded from this approval, as its creation is dependent on a resolution of the National Congress.

Art. 2. All dispositions to the contrary are hereby revoked.

Rio de Janeiro, August 6, 1906, 18th of the Republic.

FRANCISCO DE PAULA RODRIGUES ALVES.
LEOPOLDO DE BULHÕES.

———

Convention between the States of Rio de Janeiro, Minas Geraes, and São Paulo, with the object of valorizing coffee, regulating its trade, and promoting its increased consumption, and the creation of a caixa de conversão (note issue and conversion department) for the fixing of the value of the currency.

Article 1. During the term that may be convenient, and which may be reduced or extended by mutual accord, the contracting States bind themselves to maintain in the Brazilian markets the minimum prices of 55 to 65 gold francs, or the equivalent in currency, per bag of 60 kilos of coffee, American type No. 7, during the first year; this price may later be raised to the maximum of 70 francs, according to the conveniences of the markets.

For the higher qualities, according to the American classification, the prices indicated will be augmented proportionally during the same periods.

Art. 2. The contracting governments will endeavor to prevent by adequate measures the exportation to foreign countries of coffee inferior to type No. 7, while favoring as far as may be possible the development of their consumption within this country.

Art. 3. The contracting States oblige themselves to organize and maintain a regular and permanent service of coffee propaganda with the object of increasing the consumption, by the development of the actual markets, by the opening and conquest of new ones, and by defensive measures against fraud and falsification.

Art. 4. The contracting governments, whenever it may be judged opportune, will establish national types, promoting the creation of exchanges of syndical chambers for the coffee trade; in accordance with these types will then be fixed the prices referred to in article 1.

Art. 5. Means will be placed at the disposal of producers for improving the quality of their product by mechanical treatment.

Art. 6. The contracting governments bind themselves to create a surtax of three francs (subject to augmentation or diminution) per bag of coffee exported by any of their States, and also to maintain the laws which impede by sufficiently high taxes the increase of the areas of land planted with coffee within their territories during the period of two years.

Art. 7. The products of the surtax, referred to in the preceding article, will be collected by the union, and is destined to the payment of interest and amortization of the capital necessary for the execution of this convention, the surpluses being applied to defray the expenses demanded by the services of the said convention, and the collection of the surtax will begin after the realization of the dispositions contained in article 8.

Art. 8. For the execution of this convention the State of S. Paulo is from this date authorized to promote in this country or abroad, with the guarantee of the surtax of three francs referred to in article 6, and with the conjoint responsibility of the three States the necessary credit operations up to the amount of 15 millions sterling, which will be applied as a gold reserve for the department for the emission and conversion of gold notes, which may be created by Congress for the fixing of the value of the currency.

1. The product of the emission against this reserve will be applied, in terms of this convention, to the regularization of the coffee trade and its valorization, without prejudice to other endowments created by law.

2. In case there should be need of the indorsement or guarantee of the Union for these credit operations, the dispositions of Clause X of article 2 of law 1452 of December 30, 1905, will be observed.

3. The State of São Paulo, before closing the credit operations indicated above, will submit the terms and conditions to the knowledge and approval of the Union and of the contracting States.

Art. 9. The organization and direction of all the services of this convention will be intrusted to a commission of three members nominated by each of the States and a president chosen by the three States, who will only have a casting vote.

1. Each director will have a substitute to replace him when absent, the nomination of these substitutes being also made by the respective States.

Art. 10. The commission referred to in the preceding article will organize all the departments and nominate all the functionaries necessary for the execution of this convention, and it may intrust, in part, its execution to some national association or company under its immediate control, in accordance with the respective regulations.

Art. 11. The domicile of the commission will be the city of São Paulo.

Art. 12. For the execution of the objects of this convention the commission will organize the necessary regulations which will be submitted to the approval of the contracting States, which will be considered to approve them if they do not state their objections within fifteen days.

Art. 13. The responsibilities and advantages of this convention will be divided among the contracting States in proportion to the quota of surtax paid on the coffee from each of them.

Art. 14. The contracting States recognize and accept the President of the Republic, as arbiter in any questions that may arise between them in the execution of this convention.

Art. 15. The present convention will come into force from the date of its approval by the President of the Republic, in terms of No. 16 of article 48 of the Constitution.

Town Hall of Taubaté, February 26, 1906.

[Signatures]—NILO PEÇANHA; FRANCISCO A. SALLES; JORGE TIBIRIÇA.

❂

----

60. Rui Barbosa on the Issue of Militarism*

Unlike Spanish America, which inherited militarism as a consequence of the protracted wars of independence, Brazil at first had no problems with its small and unambitious military. It was the prolonged war with Paraguay that fastened militarism as an institution on Brazil; thereafter, the military leaders played a more aggressive role in national life. The military rule from 1889–1894 was the nation's first experience with non-civilian government, and tradition was strong enough to return a civilian to the Palace of Catête in 1894. However, the threat of interference from the military, which considered itself heir to the imperial poder moderador, that is, the power to regulate the political life of the country, hung heavily in the air. In the presidential campaign of 1910, a marshal, Hermes da Fonseca, ran. Opposing him was

....

* Translated from Virginia Côrtes de Lacerda (ed.), *Rui Barbosa, Escritos e Discursos Seletos* (Rio de Janeiro: Editôra José Aguilar, 1960), pp. 306-308, 332-334, 344.

Rui Barbosa, a vociferous champion of civil government and an implacable foe of militarism. In his campaign speeches, such as the ones from which these selections are taken, he preached that "militarism is the common scourge of . . . all national rights" and urged men of all political faiths to unite behind him in a concerted effort to defeat militarism. His was a quixotic campaign. The marshal won the election, and the military began to play an ever more dominant role.

The Republic was the undeniable solution. But the dilettantism with which public sentiment received it threatened its existence from the beginning with incalculable dangers. An organism without reactions, our democracy naturally delivered itself to the instruments of force. The nation continued to sleep in its habits of a former day, when a system of government less accessible to the rule of ambitions had succeeded in conciliating with a relative tranquility.

Under a more delicate and complex constitution, popular lack of resistance was the open door to inordinate factionalism. As long as the nation did not take hold of itself, we were destined to be, in crisis after crisis, the humble and unprotected victim of the reappearances of our native vice. From 1889 to 1909 there was not one national movement: all were military movements. Who, on November 3, 1891, dissolved Congress? [1] Who, on November 23, deposed the first president? Who, immediately thereafter, in one State after another controlled and ran the governments and local justice? In 1892, who composed the exposed April conspiracy and who crushed it with an arbitrary blow of unconstitutional retirements, exonerations, and exiles? Who rebelled in 1893 and 1894 against the constituted government? Who, in 1897, crowned the expedition of Canudos with an assassination attempt on President Prudente de Morais? In 1901 who took President Campos Sales by surprise and induced him to

....

[1] In this and the questions which follow, Rui Barbosa refers to a number of instances when the military intervened in the government. [ed.].

imprison an admiral? Who, in 1904, during the Rodrigues Alves administration, went out into the streets of the capital with gun in hand and with a banner of insurrection unfurled against the Chief of State? Who, this year, during the administration of Afonso Pena, carried to the Palace of Catête the rumors of a candidate supported by the will of the armed forces?

These are the spasms of a periodical illness which at more or less brief intervals break national apathy. These seizures occur intermittently in each presidency so that none escapes his share of a violent crisis. And a circumstance at first glance contradictory, but on closer examination related to the character of the illness, is the fact that the military presidents are the ones most disturbed by the militaristic explosions. During the first [military presidency], the government itself caused the disturbance by a coup d'état the Marshal directed against Congress. During the second, the disturbance came from the armed forces in the form of a nearly victorious revolt against the government of a general. This helps to point out that military institutions and militaristic vices, far from blending together, oppose and destroy each other just as the organic injuries destroy the organs they afflict. Before offending civil laws, militarism attacks the core of military laws. It begins by affronting them in their essence, the subordination of armed force to civil order, in order to undermine them later in their express canons, where each one of those outrages has a severe penalty which should be applied against it.

Between military institutions and militarism there is, in substance, an abyss of radical contradiction. Militarism, government of the nation by the sword, ruins the military institutions, the legal subordination of the sword to the nation. The military institutions juridically organize force. Militarism disorganizes it. Militarism is to the army what fanaticism is to religion, what charlatanry is to science, what industrialism is to industry, what mercantilism is to commerce, what Caesarism is to royalty, what demagogy is to democracy, what absolutism is to order, what egoism is to the ego. [The military institutions] are order; [militarism] is anarchy. They, morality; it, corruption. They, national defense; it, the dismantling, the erosion, the crumbling of that defense, more expensive in the budgets but reduced in its real effectiveness to a sham.

In its present manifestation, ladies and gentlemen, our republican illness assumed a dissembling form which permits the partisans of the candidacy of the marshal the duplicity of publicly denying a militaristic tendency, which is confessed, sustained, flaunted, first in secret and with mystery, then with intrepidity and with threats from lip to lip, ear to ear, group to group. Previous presidents had suffered the attack under the form of conspiracies or of uprisings. The last one received the crafty, explosive artefact wrapped in the guise of a ministerial candidate [for president]. Against the candidacy of a civilian minister, put forth, as one would suppose, by the Chief of State, was raised, sustained with a scowl of force, the candidacy of the military minister. This head of Medusa, the political-military men imagined, ought to frighten the president and cause him to abandon hastily the candidacy of [David] Campista. Given to this allurement, the adversaries of this [candidacy of Campista] would not refuse, in exchange for their apparent victory over the presidential will, the role of the responsible party for the candidacy which they had dictated under a dilemma, the other of whose alternatives was "rebellion in the streets."

This idea [of the candidacy of Marshal Hermes da Fonseca] had been held for a long time. João Pinheiro had notice of it in February of 1908. During the excursion of the Minister of War [Hermes da Fonseca] to Berlin, there circulated timorous news of it. Later, in preparation for it there was discussion of a military manifesto to be written here but to be made public anonymously in the military districts of the North. Thus, with the Campista candidacy upset because of the retreat from the situation in Minas Gerais, the fatal thought to run [Hermes da Fonseca] had been matured through long days of incubation.

The civilian politicians knew it. More than once I heard from those political leaders, the most prominent ones today in the military campaign, expressions of horror at the possibility of "calamity" and others which emphasized "a regression of fifteen years in republican experience."

But the military politicians did not count in vain on the selfishness, cowardice, and ambition of the civilian politicians. Weakness, emotion, and personal calculation did their work. Hence, the current of opinion which expresses the rights of the country to the choice of the Chief of State formed against the nomination of the civilian minister, and in the name of those same rights leads today, gaily decked in bunting, to the nomination of the Minister of War. Well, is it not clear that those in opposition to the candidacy of Campista wanted nothing else? The monster was the candidate of Catête [Presidential Palace]. To the candidate of the barracks there would be no objection. The national candidate was found. It remained only to consecrate him with national approval, national satisfaction, and the national anthem. Let the press, oratory, and banquets do their work now and the miracle will be brought about. Now there you have it: the sword wrapped in the Constitution.

. . .

"They will have to swallow it." We will have to swallow it for good or for bad is the consecrated phrase, the last argument of that attack on the nation. We have not accustomed [this nation] to fight. Its political traditions are weak. Its republican habits are neglected. Its democracy is composed of humiliations, deceptions, and abdications. Now, in our time, militarism invaded it, corrupted it, mutilated it. The disease has left the organism in a sad condition. In such a state the conspirators count on our regression to a military epoch. Republicans who in the last days of Floriano [Peixoto] had prevented the declaration of dictatorship with a decided *non possumus* today enlist in its service. Once this is accomplished, Brazil will plunge forever into the servitude of the armed forces, continuous or remittent, periodic or uninterrupted, manifest or disguised, but eternal, organic, incurable.

From all this results a situation on which our entire future depends. In order to solve it and to avoid catastrophe it will be necessary to excite the nation, all of it, the moral forces of the country, the cooperation of all shades of opinion, moderate or radical, liberal or conservative, unbelieving or believing, all of Brazil, exactly as when a foreign enemy menaces the fatherland. Because, like the foreign enemy, militarism is the common scourge of all opinions, all interests, all national rights: the extortion of liberty, the obliteration of intelligence, the prohibition of civic pride, the destruction of credit, the negation of constitutional government, the empire of master without law, responsibility, culture, redress, or hope.

What greater program could there be than one of preventing that collapse of our system of government? Before organizing the nation into parties, it is urgent to save it. We will recapture its strength in civic order, and, in the open field of that victory, which we will have won, with dedication, competence, energy, we will then opportunely undertake an examination of the necessary reforms. Even the most impatient will not have to wait long if the nation is with us in the battle on March 1st. If that battle be lost, as it will be if we do not carry the struggle to the level of the general public, God knows how long the supporters of the party system will have to cherish their hopes. But now, in the imminence of the fight, while the invasion beats against the walls of the city and the insistent shouts of enemy bravura shock us, to defend fundamental conclusions about the organization of parties and the elaboration of political creeds could only be done by rebelling against common sense.

This matter of party platforms at this moment is beginning to take on characteristics of a morbid epidemic or a ridiculous *marotte*. Back in the period of historical republicanism one understands the zeal for a platform. I do not wish bad luck to those professions of individual or collective faith. Then I believed in them more than I now believe in them. Like others, I paid tribute to superstition because there is no spirit or age that does not have its weakness. But what really sounds to me like a carnival jest is the distribution of platforms of the civilian and military candidates carried out by the enthusiasts of the May Convention.

My platform according to them, only can be revisionism.

The platform of the Marshal is the Constitution. There is talk of another which is in the making, but that one is accessory to this other one, the principal idea, the maximum program, the supreme core: to maintain the Constitution, to defend it, to exalt it, to guard it. Now, this poor Constitution, the besmirched lady of so many slights, is going to meet, at last, with her knight-errant.

I will leave for another time the task of outlining my platform, the question of my duties toward revisionism. Everything cannot fit into one speech. For today, to conclude, I will stick to the question of the Constitution between the two candidates.

It is extraordinary how God writes the law in crooked lines. The government of the first marshal tried to place over the Constitution his own dictatorship by dissolving Congress. The government of the second marshal sought to consolidate its dictatorship over that Constitution by the postponement of Congress. The government of the third marshal would come, by acclamation of Congress, to save the Constitution from dictatorships.

In the singular discernment of this choice, what above all things makes me marvel is the penetrating judgment of those who in the midst of brute and black rock pretend to see a vein of fine gold. The annals of human perspicacity contain no greater miracle of intuition. Just what chance do the geniuses who put forth a military candidate give to the Constitution squeezed as it will be between the blade and the scabbard?

A political platform is a profession of faith in action. The faith that is professed, when the lips do not lie, is what is in the heart, beliefs, and ideas. But the ideas, beliefs, and the heart of man manifest themselves in his life. His acts are the mirror of his conscience, the reflection of his sentiments, the language of his convictions. Now, cast your glance over that career of arms, easy, accelerated, tranquil; follow its phases one by one; count one by one the incidents. You will not point out to me one instance, one moment, one trace where it was anything more than the career of a soldier: obedience, discipline, command; military aptitudes, qualities, preoccupations, and interests. Those preoccupations and interests, those qualities and aptitudes are the ones that make a man of one, not the ones that create a man of law, a man of government, a statesman.

. . .

In all my life never did I see take shape such a grave situation in the sight of my moral eyes, so antagonistic to the articles of my old creed, as this one devoid even of the guarantee of a responsible sword and of the least military prestige such as Deodoro da Fonseca or Floriano Peixoto possessed when they surrendered to the anarchy of ambition. We see it approaching aided and abetted by the weakness, intrigue, vulgarity, and consciencelessness of the civilian government and partisan factions.

It was because of the sudden alarm of this imminent danger that the August Convention met. In it all other considerations, all other preoccupations, all other apprehensions were put aside in order to propose, as the exclusive objective of this movement, as the specific function of the candidate who represents it, a reaction against the rebirth of militarism. The nation, in its most civilized elements, has a more than justified fear of that contingency impending upon us thanks to the criminal complicity of the Nilo Peçanha administration, the oligarchies of the North, and a majority in the National Congress ready to submit to military authoritarianism. Before this great danger all other questions disappear. There is only one problem on the horizon. It exclusively dominates the entire perspective of the future. Here we see the incomparable proportions of this movement which has no parallel in the history of Brazil.

❊

---

61. The Economic and Financial Conditions of the Old Republic*

Brazil's financial and economic structures always have been fragile. The early 1890's were particularly notable for financial irresponsibility and speculation. At the end of the century, Minister of Finance Joaquim Murtinho sought to rectify the deteriorating situation by reestablishing national credit, balancing the budget, and strengthening the currency. His salutary efforts encouraged succeeding governments to follow a sounder fiscal policy. Under the Hermes da Fonseca administration old and bad habits once again were resorted to, with the consequent return to an unhealthy financial situation always made more precarious by reliance on monoculture, in this case, coffee. In a public speech at the National Library on September 5, 1914, Amaro Cavalcanti summed up the financial and economic conditions in the following words, many of which are applicable to the contemporary scene as well.

Undeniably Brazil is now considered one of the most advanced nations of the American Continent and, as such, an integral part of the rest of the cultured nations of the world.

But if, because of this, we can aspire to some position in the world, we must, on the other hand, confess with sadness that our reputation in the economic realm, national or international, is one of great inferiority.

Regardless of the happy fate which bestows on us a land

....
* Translated from the *Annaes da Bibliotheca Nacional*, XXXVIII (Rio de Janeiro: Oficinas Gráphicas da Bibliotheca Nacional, 1920), 12-14, 23-25.

second to none in favorable conditions and natural wealth, we still continue in an increasing dependence on other nations for nearly everything for the material development of the country and even for the necessities of everyday life.

This fact, more than any other, is what ought to merit the constant attention of our governing classes. I do not hesitate to add that it is time to put an end, at least in part, to the petty politics which have absorbed the greatest attention of our governments and leaders of public life, in order to occupy ourselves seriously and of preference with the development of the common wealth without which no nation will be able to enjoy prestige among the others. It is important to recognize at once that the first problem of salutary politics and administration consists precisely in working without hesitation or intermittences to obtain sufficient revenue and solidity of public credit which only exist when based on the growing vigor of the economic forces of the country.

That is sufficient allusion in this respect. No people will be able to be great, respected, and happy in their relations, either internally or externally, without the essential condition of possessing their own riches at least sufficient to cover the normal needs of the State and of the diverse classes of society. The people, where this does not occur, thereby show themselves incapable of well-being and progress in the eyes of the civilized world; they will be treated with slight consideration by the other peoples, all of whom daily redouble their efforts to increase their wealth and consequently their greatness.

. . .

In the realm of economics we live today exactly as in the colonial period, importing from abroad practically everything we consume regardless of the fact that we could very well produce it, or part of it, right here given the abundance which Nature put at our disposition in the different zones of the country for the exploitation of various industries.

In the realm of finances, it would be even more unpleasant to have to recognize that the competency of our best statesmen and financiers, that is those whom we have had worthy of the name, did not succeed, with certain exceptions, in going beyond these two remedies for the solution of our difficulties: either increasing the public debt or emitting paper money.

. . .

The first republican government, which is to say the Provisional Government, at once embarked upon a plan to carry out the measures deemed most adequate for the development of national wealth and the guarantee of gold finances.

Known to all was our lack of sufficient capital for the creation and encouragement of various industries for which there was no lack of natural resources in every corner of the country; it was understood that the most useful course for the occasion would be to adopt these two measures: on the one hand, to facilitate the circulation and acquisition of money, even of a simple fiduciary character, by increasing bank emissions in this Capital and in other parts of the country; on the other hand, to generously distribute concessions and privileges of every kind, including the donation of unused lands, to whomever might want to establish or exploit any industry on it. The number of governmental acts granting such concessions and privileges was enormous.

A very large number of them, it is certain, did not become a practical reality; but, even so, a considerable number of others became companies or commercial societies and industries which, without delay, began to inundate the market with their stocks and debentures issued by the thousands.

Also dating from this time or a little earlier was the increasing amount of aleatory business in shares on the local stock market. But, then there began to appear innumerable stocks, the vast majority of which represented nothing in real value but whose quotation always remained high because of the increasing emissions of the banks where they were received as collateral security for the money there printed. It was not long before the reality of the situation showed itself nakedly and cruelly as the inevitable result of that uninhibited game given the deserving name of stock speculation [*ensilhamento*]. The discredit of all negotiable stocks and bonds, with no distinction between good and bad, true and false, was complete; there began the ruin of companies and businesses, perchance serious and worthy, because of their involvement with the fictitious organizations, simply gambling houses.

Once more it was demonstrated that the good intentions and best purposes, such as the Provisional Government had, were not sufficient to guarantee the good effect of the measures adopted.

The scope of that economic-financial disaster, which occurred during the first days of the Republic, became, it cannot be denied, the precursor and the cause, at least in part, of many other evils of the same kind which later appeared; it not only destroyed what we had recently tried to create or to undertake but also a good portion of our established economy which had existed for many years before.

. . .

We are now in mid-August of 1914.

Without darkening the colors, the picture is this: commerce and industry, without movement, are menaced by complete paralysis; factories and plants are laying off their workers; the first-rate banks, businesses, and the commercial houses are failing or asking for a moratorium; the Public Treasury is empty, without money even to pay governmental employees or the workers in state industries; the suppliers of the armed forces and other services of the nation are at the doors of the Treasury demanding payment, already long overdue, in order to avoid their own collapse; public credit is void both inside and outside the country; public revenue is declining everyday; national production is everywhere abating; misery is beginning to invade the various classes of the population; and, in the presence of such a cruel crisis, the entreaty of all is directed to the public authorities who increase the emission of paper money as the only salvation still remaining.

. . .

One thing which we do not wish to dispense with is the freedom of pointing out why it is that with nearly a century of national independence we have not succeeded in possessing the sure and sufficient elements to solve the problems of our financial life.

The cause of this great misfortune, according to our judgment, ought to be sought in that ever-identical conduct of our leaders and directors, whether in the Empire or in the republic, who give preference, as a general rule, to party interests and to the consequent spoils and enjoyments instead of attending to the real benefits for the people and the nation.

. . .

We must not forget for a single instant that while we have to extend our hand asking the outsider to pay for our ordinary necessities, whether the individual or the people do it, we cannot consider ourselves really and effectively independent. The creditor, the foreign creditor, is always a superior, more or less demanding, more or less severe.

Finally, the last word, which is very similar to the first, is this: if our governmental leaders, our able parliamentarians, our political leaders would dedicate to the material interests of the nation the time, discussion, and energy which they ceaselessly lavish on the generally sterile interests of politics, our Brazil certainly would now be great, rich, and happy as Nature intended when she gave it all the elements for greatness and prosperity.

❀

62. The Emergence of Brazilian Civilization*

In 1843 the German traveler and naturalist, Karl Friedrich Phillip von Martius, observed that the key to understanding Brazil could be found in a study of the fusion of the three races: European, African, and American Indian. This idea was neglected until the 1920's, when a young sociologist-historian, Gilberto Freyre, began to formulate along similar lines his own theses of Brazilian development. One of his most important ideas was that his country was not solely the product of Europe, as national scholars to that time expounded, but rather was shaped by a combination of European, African, and Amerindian cultures, which blended into a uniquely Brazilian civilization. The publication of this and other similar ideas in his The Masters and the Slaves *in 1933 marked the declaration of Brazil's intellectual and cultural independence, a turning away from the blind copying of European thought to introspection and to respect for national values.*

The experiment in ethnic and cultural bi-continentalism begun in Portugal centuries ago took a new dimension in Brazil: three races and cultures are fused under conditions that, broadly speaking, are socially democratic, though as yet productive of only a very imperfect social democracy defective both in its economic basis and in its political forms of

....

* From Gilberto Freyre, *New World in the Tropics* (New York: Knopf, 1959), pp. 117-118, 120-121, 143-144, and Gilberto Freyre, *The Masters and the Slaves* (New York: Knopf, 1946), pp. 87-88, 311. Reprinted by permission of the publisher.

expression. All imperfections admitted, however, Brazil stands today as a community from whose experiment in miscegenation other communities may profit. Probably in no other complex modern community are problems of race relations being solved in a more democratic or Christian way than in Portuguese America. And Brazil's experiment does not indicate that miscegenation leads to degeneration.

. . .

The native [Indian] woman must be regarded not merely as the physical basis of the Brazilian family, upon whom, drawing strength from her and multiplying itself, rested the energy of a limited number of European settlers; she must also be considered a worthwhile cultural element, at least so far as material culture goes, in the formation of Brazilian society. Thanks to her, Brazilian life was enriched, as we shall see further on, with a number of foods that are still in use today, with drugs and household remedies, with traditions that are bound up with the development of the child, with a set of kitchen utensils, and with processes having to do with tropical hygiene—including the frequent or at least daily bath, which must greatly have scandalized the sixteenth-century European, who was so filthy in his own personal habits.

She gave us also the hammock, which still rocks the Brazilian to sleep or serves him as a voluptuous couch. She brought coconut oil for women's hair and a group of domesticated animals tamed by her hand.

From the *cunhã*, or Tupí-Guaraní woman, has come the best of our indigenous culture. Personal neatness. Bodily hygiene. Corn. The cashew. *Mingau*, or porridge. The Brazilian of today, a lover of the bath and always with a comb and mirror in his pocket, his hair gleaming with lotion or coconut oil, is reflecting the influence of his remote grandmothers.

But before dwelling at length upon the contribution of the cunhã to the special development of Brazil, let us endeavor to determine that of the Indian male. It was most impressive, but only with regard to the task of invading and conquering the backlands, where he served as guide, canoeist, warrior, hunter, and fisherman. He was of great assistance to the mameluco turned *bandeirante*, the two of them surpassing the Portuguese in mobility, daring, and warlike ardor. His capacity for activity and for labor failed him, however, when it came to the dreary grind of the cane fields, where only the African's extraordinary reserves of cheerfulness and animal robustness enabled him to endure so well this life of toil. But the Indian, as friend or slave of the Portuguese, made up for his uselessness where steady and continuous exertion was involved by his brilliance and heroism as a soldier, not only in connection with the invasion of the backlands, but in defending the colony against the Spaniards, against enemy bands of Portuguese, and against corsairs.

. . .

From the standpoint of man's relationship to nature, the Negro's adaptation to the climate and other physical conditions of Brazil seems to have been perfect. From the social standpoint, he was culturally better prepared than the nomadic Amerindian to adjust himself to the status of slave—plantation and domestic slave—in Portuguese America. His adaptation to American conditions was as happy as that of the sugar cane plant, his symbiotic companion in the task of changing the Brazilian landscape from an area of virgin forest to one dominated by plantation colonization and one-crop agriculture.

Some of the millions of Negroes imported to Brazilian plantations were obtained from areas in the advanced Negro culture. This explains why some African slaves in Brazil—men of Mohammedan faith and intellectual training—were culturally superior to some of their European, white, Catholic masters. More than one foreigner who visited Brazil in the nineteenth century was surprised to find the leading French bookseller of the Empire's capital had among his customers Mohammedan Negroes of Bahia; through him these remarkable Negroes, some of them ostensibly Christian but actually Mohammedan, imported expensive copies of their sacred books for secret study. Some of them maintained schools, and the Mohammedan Negroes in Bahia had mutual-aid societies through which a number of slaves were liberated.

. . .

Brazil not only took from Africa the topsoil of a black people that was to fertilize its cane fields and coffee groves, assuage its parched lands, and round out the wealth afforded by its patches of *massapé*; there were to come to it also, from the same source: "mistresses of the house" for its colonists who were without white women; technicians for its mines; ironworkers; Negroes versed in cattle-raising and the pasturing of herds; cloth and soap merchants; schoolmasters, priests, and praying Mohammedans. The proximity of Bahia and Pernambuco to the African coast tended to give to the relations between Brazil and the Dark Continent an especially intimate character.

. . .

This fact—that Amerindians and Africans, as well as Europeans, and their mixed descendants have made an active contribution to the development of Brazil—seems to explain why Portuguese America has now a civilization with such vivid characteristics of its own, and why one of these characteristics is what has been described by some authors as Brazilian ethnic democracy. Many characteristics of modern Brazilian civilization originate in the fact that the Negro, because of the comparatively liberal treatment given to him in Brazil, has been able to express himself as a Brazilian and has not been forced to behave as an ethnic and cultural intruder. He behaves as a Brazilian of African origin and not as a "Brazilian Negro"—differing thereby from the "American Negro" of the United States. And of course the same thing has been true in an even more vivid way of the Amerindian; just as the same thing is becoming true of the Japanese, as well as of the German, the Italian, and the Polish immigrant. Some of these are becoming, in the second generation, prominent in Brazilian political life, not as German-Brazilians, or Italian-Brazilians, or Polish-Brazilians, but as Brazilians; and they are also taking their place in Brazilian art and in Brazilian literature (written, of course, in Portuguese), which has been enriched with words from other languages without losing its Portuguese structure. The new literature of Brazil is beginning to attract as much attention from Europeans and North Americans as the modern architecture, the music, and the cuisine of the Brazilians.

❃

63. Getúlio Vargas on the Philosophy and Objectives of the Estado Novo*

The Revolution of 1930, a manifestation of the dissatisfaction of the nation with the political domination of São Paulo, brought to power the dynamic gaucho of Rio Grande do Sul, Getúlio Vargas. With the cooperation of Francisco Campos, he promulgated a new constitution in 1937, which initiated the Estado Novo, meaning New State. The program and goals of the Estado Novo, in their simplest terms, were political order and economic progress for the nation. The philosophy of the Estado Novo can be broken down into four basic ideas. 1) Decadent political democracy needs to be replaced by economic democracy. 2) In accordance with the new emphasis on economic democracy, the corporative state structure provides the best model for the political-economic organization of the nation. 3) To eliminate regional and political strife all power should be centralized in a national government which does not recognize political parties. 4) The mass group of citizens as an entity is superior to

* Translated from Getúlio Vargas, A Nova Política do Brasil (Rio de Janeiro: José Olympio, 1938 & 1940), V: 188-189, 196, 259-260, 300, VI: 153-155, 183-184, 264, VII: 319. Printed by permission of the publisher.

the individual. Such a philosophy was never formalized. It appeared bit by bit during the first four years of the Estado Novo in speeches and pronouncements of Vargas such as those printed below.

The new government is above all else the adaptation of the political system to the realities of Brazil. It integrates all the forces of the collective into a framework of order, social cohesion, and governmental authority. It assures the historical fundamentals of the nation, its essential elements for existence, and its claims to progress menaced, compromised, and sacrificed by the old order which was not only incapable of defending them but permitted and even stimulated factious disturbances, armed regionalism irreconcilable with national unity, and the formation of parties of an aggressive character, refractory by nature to the democratic processes, of the kind that aimed at territorial dismemberment and the subversion of society.

. . .

Conserving the traditional lines of organic federation and what existed substantially in that system, as the autonomy of the states, the democratic form, and the representative process, the Statute of November 10 [1] created, nonetheless, a new legal structure. Among the profound changes brought about by the new regime are: the limitation of direct, universal suffrage, applicable only to specific questions of pertinence to all citizens thus making representation more valid; the municipality as the nuclear base of the political system; the substitution of the principle of the independence of powers by the supremacy of the Executive; the strengthening of the power of the Union; the effective and efficient participation of the economy, through its own organizations, in the constructive and integrating work of the government.

The new system consecrates a government of authority by instituting as law the legislative decree, by giving to the Pres-

....
[1] The Constitution of the Estado Novo, 1937.

ident of the Republic powers to expedite law-decrees when congress is not in session, by attributing to him the prerogative of dissolving it in special cases, and by taking from the Judiciary the privilege of supreme interpretation of the constitutionality or unconstitutionality of the laws which involve public interests of great importance. These new powers, placed under the guard of the government, always overcome private interests.

Profoundly nationalistic, the regime insures and consolidates national unity and formally restricts the autonomy of the states by suppressing regional symbols, extending intervention, establishing the supremacy of federal over local laws in the case of concurrent legislation by attributing to the central government the power to requisition at any time the state militias, etc.

The professions are represented in their own and independent chamber with consultative functions in all the projects concerning the national economy, and eventually it will have legislative functions.[2]

. . .

The movement of November 10th was, without doubt, brought about by the national will. We had need of order and security in order to carry on; conspiring against that was the critical state of political decomposition to which we had arrived. Slowly our public life had been transformed into an arena of sterile struggles where plots, clashing interests of the oligarchy, personal competitions, and differences in personal interests were decided. Men of character without ambition to govern drew away from it nauseated, leaving the field open to political professionals and to demagogic and audacious adventurers. It was thus that communism succeeded in infiltrating and came to be at one time a national danger. Defeated in its violent attempt to seize power, it continued, nevertheless, its work of undermining authority by utilizing as its weapons the other evils that make the situation of the nation so unstable and chaotic: the weakness of political par-

....
[2] Interview, March, 1938.

ties, regional jealousies, and dictatorial flights of fancy. Those three evils are in the final analysis simply the result of a single general cause, well formed and known: the sterility and depletion of the sources from which the agents of stimulation and renovation of public life ought to come. The political parties had abdicated their social function. They lived at the cost of electoral exploitation and they proliferated with a predominately local character attached to the fetishism of old political formulas, foreign to the modern contingencies throughout the world and to the national realities. Foresight of the danger in which we found ourselves and which was felt by all caused us decisively to favor the political unification of the nation which is precisely why the regime was established on November 10th. The Estado Novo embodies, therefore, the will and ideas which oppose and work against all the factors tending to weaken and dissolve the fatherland—extremes, sabotage, and compromise. It is ready to fight against those evils. It will mobilize all the best that we possess in order to make our nation strong, dignified, and happy.[3]

* * *

Now more than at any other time, it becomes necessary to follow a well established and cautious course. In order to dignify the efforts of the pioneers of our nationality, it is necessary for us to persist in the direction which they pointed out: to avoid harsh clashes, to impede the fragmentation of the country, to unhesitatingly place the fatherland above regional preoccupations by giving it increased power without compromising the future with ideological adventures or doctrinaire exaggerations.

I always subordinate my actions as a public figure to these postulates judging it badly advised to precipitate events and to provoke extreme situations.

As Chief of Government, I systematically seek to hear those who are informed, to appreciate the word of the technicians, to study and to boldly face the reality of facts. It was

....
[3] Interview, April, 1938.

thus that, feeling the profound sentiment of the Brazilian people, I did all possible in order to save them from the dangers of extremism, both—from the right as well as from the left—contrary to our sentiments of understanding and Christian tolerance.

I can affirm to you with certainty that the hours of greatest apprehension now have passed.

The implacable confirmation of the facts demonstrated that Brazil, that is, the alert conscience of the Nation, perfecting and adapting the state organization to the imperatives of its historical formation, denounces exotic ideologies and prefers the political rhythm of the Continent.

Through the spirit of good sense and through the persistent intention of conciliating the peace of the people with national dignity, we have given an appreciable example to the world. Thus we proceed respecting the rights of others and demanding in return that they respect ours and trying to assure internally to all and to each a greater share of well-being and tranquility within the just equilibrium between the duties and prerogatives of the citizen.[4]

. . .

Certain rivalries which perchance exist are not historically legitimate. They are the fruits of the vicious political processes of the old regime. The presidency of the Republic, even in the recent past, constituted a kind of privilege of the largest and most powerful states and served as a source of discord every four years. The motives of attrition disappeared with the corrections which the new regime applied to Brazilian federalism. The federal government, which is the nation itself, no longer recognizes either large or small states. Above all else, what exists is Brazil, devoid of regionalism which ambition for power had fed for many years. National unity is the most sensible reflex today of the Nation.[5]

. . .

....

[4] Speech, July, 1938.
[5] Interview, July, 1939.

Truly we have instituted an essentially democratic regime because it does not base its representation on a system of indications and artificialities but rather on the direct collaboration of the people through their economic forces and their organizations of production and labor. Only thus can our present political structure make known the effective representation of Brazil. The regime of November 10, which fully corresponds to the general aspirations of the country and is, I repeat, profoundly Brazilian because it is founded upon historical facts of our nationality and shuns the mystifications of the former regime and for that becomes more democratic in its essence, integrated, as it is, with the present realities. The truly democratic Estado Novo must have the conditions and the characteristics of a strong government which does not permit the survival of the spirit of disunion and the regional expressions, now overcome, which lived in the shadow of concessions and compromise of the central government. The authority of the government, thus strengthened, will not permit the growth or existence of extremism of any variety which encourages violence.[6]

· · ·

The program to be carried out by the Estado Novo includes the complete readjustment of all sectors of Brazilian life from the economic substructure to the intellectual and moral formation of the new generations. And as it could not be otherwise, it includes the rearmament, already begun, of the army and navy, so that with complete efficiency they can carry out their objectives, guaranteeing the peaceful development of the country and the fulfillment of treaties with other civilized nations.[7]

· · ·

If you would ask me what is the program of the Estado Novo, I would tell you that its program is to crisscross the nation with railroads, highways, and airlines; to increase pro-

....

[6] Speech, May, 1940.
[7] Speech, March, 1938.

duction; to provide for the laborer and to encourage agricultural credit; to expand exports; to prepare the armed forces so that they are always ready to face any eventuality; to organize public opinion so that there is, body and soul, one Brazilian thought.[8]

. . .

By examining the government's activities, anyone can verify with his own eyes that the basic problems of Brazilian life, without regional distinctions or political preferences, were resolutely attacked: the increase and expansion of industrial and agrarian nuclei; the creation of new sources of wealth and the improvement of the processes of exportation and control; the readjustment of the circulation and distribution of the utilities seeking to increase internal markets; the measures taken to raise the standard of living of the masses; financial support to the producing classes; economic assistance to the worker by means of social security institutions, a just salary, a good home, and the guarantee of his rights; the increase in the number of centers of technical, physical, and intellectual training; care for public hygiene and rural sanitation by making possible the remunerative utilization of large areas of soil abandoned or sacrificed because of climatic disturbances; the systematic repudiation of extremist ideologies and their convinced or salaried followers; the combating of all agents of dissolution or weakening of the national energies by the reinforcement of Brazilian traditions and sentiments and the prohibition from functioning in this country of any organization with anti-national activities or linked to foreign political interests; finally the preparation of internal and external defense by the rearmament of our brave armed forces and the simultaneous education of the new generations inculcating in them the spirit and love of the fatherland, faith in its destinies and the desire to make it strong and respected.[9]

....

[8] Speech, July, 1938.
[9] Speech, Jan., 1939.

❀

64. The Constitution of 1946*

With the Allied victory in 1945, Brazilians focused their attention anew on internal politics, with a consequent agitation for long-delayed presidential elections. President Vargas promised such elections, but when his political maneuvers indicated some reservations in his intentions, the army stepped in to guarantee the electoral process. General Eurico Dutra, Vargas' own choice, won. Vargas himself was elected to a seat in the Senate. Meanwhile, the new Constitution of 1946 had been promulgated. The fifth constitution and the fourth of the republican era, it bypassed the documents of 1934 and 1937 to return to the traditions of the constitutions of 1824 and 1891. It balanced the union in favor of the federal government which possessed strong powers, including the all-important power to intervene in the affairs of the states. In part, the new constitution reads as follows.

Title I—*Concerning the Federal Organization*
Chapter I—*Preliminary Provisions*

Article 1. The United States of Brazil maintain, under the representative system, the Federation and the Republic.

All power emanates from the people and shall be exercised in its name.

§1. The Union includes, in addition to the States, the federal district and the territories.

§2. The federal district is the capital of the Union.

· · ·

....
* Reprinted from *The Constitutions of the Americas*, edited by R. H. Fitzgibbon (Chicago: University of Chicago Press, 1948), pp. 60-63, 68, 70-74, 76-79, 99-100. By permission of The University of Chicago Press. Copyright 1948 by The University of Chicago.

Art. 4. Brazil shall resort to war only in case of non-applicability or failure of resort to arbitration or pacific means of solution of the conflict, regulated by any international organ of security in which it may participate; and in no case shall it embark on a war of conquest, directly or indirectly by itself or in alliance with another State.

Art. 5. The Union shall have power:

1st. To maintain relations with foreign States and to negotiate treaties and conventions with them.

2nd. To declare war and to make peace.

3rd. To decree, extend, and suspend a state of siege.

4th. To organize the armed forces, the security of the frontiers, and external defense.

5th. To permit foreign forces to pass through national territory, or, for reasons of war, to remain therein temporarily.

6th. To authorize the production of and supervise the trade in war material.

7th. To superintend, in all the national territory, the services of maritime, air, and frontier policing.

8th. To coin and issue money and to establish banks of emission.

9th. To supervise the operations of credit, capitalization, and insurance establishments.

10th. To establish a national plan of transport.

11th. To maintain the postal service and the national air mail.

12th. To develop, directly or by means of authorization or concession, the services of telegraphs, radio communication, radio broadcasting, interstate and international telephones, air navigation, and railways linking seaports and national frontiers or crossing the boundaries of a state.

13th. To organize permanent defense against the effects of drought, rural endemic diseases, and floods.

14th. To grant amnesty.

15th. To legislate upon:

I. Civil, commercial, penal, procedural, electoral, aeronautical, and labor law.

II. General norms of law with respect to finance; insurance and social security; defense and protection of health; and the penitentiary system.

III. Production and consumption.

IV. The pattern and bases of national education.

V. Public registries and commercial boards.

VI. The organization, instruction, judging and guarantees of the military police, and general conditions of their utilization by the federal Government in cases of mobilization or of war.

VII. Expropriation.

VIII. Civil and military requisitions in time of war.

IX. The system of ports and of coastwise navigation.

X. Interstate traffic.

XI. Foreign and interstate commerce; institutions of credit, exchange and transfer of values outside of the country.

XII. Subsoil wealth, mining, metallurgy, waters, electric energy, forests, hunting and fishing.

XIII. The monetary system and that of measures; title and guarantee of metals.

XIV. Naturalization, the entry, extradition, and expulsion of foreigners.

XV. Emigration and immigration.

XVI. Conditions of capacity for the exercise of technical, scientific, and liberal professions.

XVII. Use of the national symbols.

XVIII. Incorporation of forest dwellers into the national community.

Art. 7. The federal Government shall not intervene in the States, except:

1st. To maintain the national integrity.

2nd. To repel foreign invasion or that of one State into another.

3rd. To put an end to civil war.

4th. To guarantee the free exercise of any of the state powers.

5th. To assure the execution of a judicial order or decision.

6th. To reorganize the finances of any State which, without reasons of *force majeure*, may suspend, for more than two consecutive years, the service on its funded external debt.

7th. To assure the observance of the following principles:

I. A representative republican form.

II. Independence and harmony of the branches.

III. Temporality of the elective functions, the duration of the latter being limited to that of the corresponding federal functions.

IV. Prohibition of the re-election of governors and prefects for the period immediately following.

V. Municipal autonomy.

VI. The rendering of administrative accounts.

VII. Guarantees of the Judiciary.

. . .

Art. 11. The law or decree of intervention shall fix its scope, its duration, and the conditions under which it must be executed.

Art. 12. The President of the Republic shall have power to make the intervention effective and, if necessary, to appoint the interventor.

Art. 14. The reasons that may have determined the intervention, having ceased, the State authorities removed in consequence of it shall return to the exercise of their offices.

. . .

Chapter II—*Concerning the Legislative Power*
SECTION I—*Preliminary Provisions*

Art. 37. The legislative power is exercised by the national Congress, which is composed of the Chamber of Deputies and the federal Senate.

Art. 38. The election for Deputies and Senators shall be held simultaneously in all of the country.

Sole Paragraph. Conditions of eligibility for the national Congress are:

1st. To be a Brazilian (Article 129, Numbers I and II).

2nd. To be in the exercise of political rights.

3rd. To be more than twenty-one years of age for the

Chamber of Deputies, and more than thirty-five years of age for the federal Senate.

. . .

SECTION II—*Concerning the Chamber of Deputies*

Art. 56. The Chamber of Deputies is composed of representatives of the people, elected, according to the system of proportional representation, by the States, by the federal district, and by the territories.

Art. 57. Each legislature shall last four years.

Art. 58. The number of Deputies shall be fixed by law, in a proportion not to exceed one for each 150,000 inhabitants, up to twenty deputies, and, beyond this limit, one for each 150,000 inhabitants.

§1. Each territory shall have one Deputy, and seven Deputies shall be the minimum number for each State and for the federal district.

§2. The representation already fixed may not be reduced.

Art. 59. The Chamber of Deputies shall have exclusive power:

1st. To declare founded or unfounded, by vote of an absolute majority of its members, accusations against the President of the Republic under the terms of Article 88, and against the Ministers of State in crimes connected with those of the President of the Republic.

2nd. To take the initiative in demanding accounts from the President of the Republic, by means of the designation of a special committee, when they are presented to the national Congress within sixty days after the opening of the legislative session.

SECTION III—*Concerning the Federal Senate*

Art. 60. The federal Senate is composed of representatives of the States and of the federal district, elected according to the majority principle.

§1. Each State, and likewise the federal district, shall elect three Senators.

§2. The mandate of a Senator shall be eight years.

§3. The representation of each State and of the federal

district shall be renewed every four years, alternately, one-third and two-thirds at a time.

§4. The alternate elected with a Senator shall replace or succeed him under the terms of Article 52.

Art. 61. The Vice-President of the Republic shall exercise the functions of president of the federal Senate, where he shall have only a deciding vote.

Art. 62. The federal Senate shall have exclusive power:

1st. To judge the President of the Republic in crimes for which he is responsible, and the Ministers of State, in crimes of the same nature connected with those of the President.

2nd. To prosecute and judge the Ministers of the federal Supreme Tribunal and the Attorney General of the Republic in crimes for which they are responsible.

§1. The president of the federal Supreme Tribunal shall function as president of the Senate in the cases [specified] in this article.

§2. The federal Senate shall pronounce condemnatory sentence only by the vote of two-thirds of its members.

§3. The federal Senate may not impose any penalties other than loss of office with disqualification, for five years, from the exercise of any other public function, without prejudice to the action of ordinary justice.

Art. 63. The federal Senate shall likewise have exclusive power:

1st. To approve, by means of a secret vote, the appointment of magistrates in the cases established by this Constitution, of the Attorney General of the Republic, of the ministers of the tribunal of accounts, of the prefect of the federal district, of the members of the national council of economy, and of the chiefs of diplomatic mission of permanent character.

2nd. To authorize external loans by the States, the federal district, and the municipalities.

Art. 64. It shall be incumbent upon the federal Senate to suspend the execution, wholly or in part, of any law or decree declared unconstitutional by final decision of the federal Supreme Tribunal.

SECTION IV—*Concerning the Attributes of the Legislative Power*

Art. 65. The national Congress shall have power, with the approval of the President of the Republic:

1st. To vote the budget.

2nd. To vote the taxes belonging to the Union and to regulate the collection and distribution of its revenues.

3rd. To make provisions concerning the federal public debt and the means of its payment.

4th. To create and abolish public offices and to fix their remunerations always by special law.

5th. To vote the law to fix the armed forces in time of peace.

6th. To authorize the opening of credit operations and the emission of fiat money.

7th. To transfer temporarily the seat of the federal Government.

8th. To resolve questions concerning boundaries of the national territory.

9th. To legislate, except as provided in the following article, regarding property of the federal domain and regarding all matters within the competence of the Union.

Art. 66. The national Congress shall have exclusive power:

1st. To give final decision respecting treaties and conventions negotiated with foreign States by the President of the Republic.

2nd. To authorize the President of the Republic to declare war and make peace.

3rd. To authorize the President of the Republic to permit foreign forces to pass through national territory, or, by reason of war, to remain therein temporarily.

4th. To approve or suspend federal intervention, when decreed by the President of the Republic.

5th. To grant amnesty.

6th. To approve the decisions of state legislative assemblies regarding incorporation, subdivision, or partitioning of the States.

7th. To authorize the President and the Vice-President of the Republic to absent themselves from the country.

8th. To judge the accounts of the President of the Republic.

9th. To fix the defrayment of expenses and the subsidy of the members of the national Congress, as well as those of the President and the Vice-President of the Republic.

10th. To move its seat temporarily.

SECTION V—*Concerning the Laws*

Art. 67. The initiative of laws, excepting the cases of exclusive power, shall belong to the President of the Republic and to any member or committee of the Chamber of Deputies or of the federal Senate.

§1. The initiative of the law fixing the armed forces and of all laws regarding financial matters shall fall to the Chamber of Deputies and to the President of the Republic.

§2. Excepting the powers of the Chamber of Deputies, of the Senate, and of the federal tribunals, in matters concerning their respective administrative services, the President of the Republic shall have exclusive power of initiative of laws which create positions in existing services, increase salaries, or modify, in the course of each legislative session, the law fixing the armed forces.

§3. Discussion of bills initiated by the President of the Republic shall begin in the Chamber of Deputies.

Art. 68. A bill adopted in one of the Chambers shall be reviewed by the other, which, approving it, shall send it for sanction and promulgation.

Sole Paragraph. The revision shall be discussed and voted upon in a single session.

Art. 69. If a bill of one Chamber is amended in the other, it shall return to the first for decision regarding the modification, and approval or disapproval.

Sole Paragraph. The bill shall be sent for sanction in the form in which it was finally voted.

Art. 70. In the case of Article 65, the Chamber where the voting of a bill is concluded shall send it to the President of the Republic who, acquiescing, shall sanction it.

§1. If the President of the Republic shall judge the bill, in whole or in part, unconstitutional or contrary to the national interests, he shall veto it, wholly or in part, within ten working days, counted from that on which he shall receive it, and he shall communicate within this same period, to the president of the federal Senate, the reasons for the vote. If the approval should be denied when the legislative session is ended, the President of the Republic shall publish the veto.

§2. The silence of the President of the Republic, after the lapse of ten days, shall imply sanction.

§3. When the veto is communicated to the president of the federal Senate, he shall convoke the two Chambers in order to inform them in joint session; a bill which shall obtain the vote of two-thirds of the representatives present shall be considered approved. In this case the bill shall be sent for promulgation to the President of the Republic.

§4. If the law should not be promulgated within forty-eight hours by the President of the Republic in the cases of Sections 2 and 3, the president of the Senate shall promulgate it; and, if he does not do this within an equal period, the vice-president of the Senate shall do it.

Art. 71. In the cases of Article 66, the elaboration of the law shall be considered closed with the final voting, and it shall be promulgated by the president of the Senate.

Art. 72. Bills which are rejected or not approved can be renewed only in the same legislative session, by means of a proposal by an absolute majority of the members of either of the Chambers.

• • •

Chapter III—*Concerning the Executive Power*
SECTION I—*Concerning the President and the Vice-President of the Republic*

Art. 78. The executive power is exercised by the President of the Republic.

Art. 79. The President shall be replaced, in case of impediment, and succeeded, in case of vacancy, by the Vice-President of the Republic.

§1. In case of impediment or vacancy [in office] of the

President and of the Vice-President of the Republic, the president of the Chamber of Deputies, the vice-president of the federal Senate, and the president of the federal Supreme Tribunal shall be successively called to the exercise of the Presidency.

§2. In case of vacancy in the offices of the President and Vice-President of the Republic, an election shall be held sixty days after the occurrence of the last vacancy. If the vacancies should occur in the second half of the presidential term, the election for both offices shall be held, thirty days after the last vacancy, by the national Congress in the form established by law. In either of the cases, those elected shall complete the term of their predecessors.

Art. 80. The conditions of eligibility for President and Vice-President of the Republic are:

1st. To be a Brazilian (Article 129, Numbers I and II [i.e., 1st and 2nd clauses]).

2nd. To be in the exercise of political rights.

3rd. To be more than thirty-five years of age.

Art. 81. The President and the Vice-President of the Republic shall be elected simultaneously, in all of the country, 120 days before the end of the presidential term.

Art. 82. The President and Vice-President of the Republic shall exercise the office for five years.

Art. 83. The President and the Vice-President of the Republic shall take office in a session of the national Congress or, if it should not be assembled, before the federal Supreme Tribunal.

Sole Paragraph. The President of the Republic, in the act of taking office, shall give this oath: "I promise to maintain, defend, and fulfill the Constitution of the Republic, observe its laws, promote the general welfare of Brazil, support the Union, its integrity, and its independence."

Art. 84. If, after the lapse of thirty days from the date fixed for taking possession of the office, the President or the Vice-President of the Republic shall not have assumed the office, except for reason of illness, the office shall be declared vacant by the superior electoral tribunal.

Art. 85. The President and the Vice-President of the Republic may not absent themselves from the country, under penalty of loss of office, without the permission of the national Congress.

Art. 86. In the last year of the legislative term preceding the election for President and Vice-President of the Republic, their subsidies shall be fixed by the national Congress.

SECTION II—*Concerning the Attributes of the President of the Republic*

Art. 87. The President of the Republic shall have exclusive power:

1st. To approve, promulgate, and order publication of laws and to issue decrees and regulations for their faithful execution.

2nd. To veto bills, under the terms of Article 70, Section 1.

3rd. To appoint and dismiss Ministers of State.

4th. To appoint and dismiss the prefect of the federal district (Article 26, Sections 1 and 2) and the members of the national council of economy (Article 205, Section 1).

5th. To bestow federal public offices in the form of law and with the exceptions stated by the Constitution.

6th. To maintain relations with foreign States.

7th. To negotiate international treaties and conventions, subject to referendum of the national Congress.

8th. To declare war, after authorization by the national Congress, but without this authorization in the case of foreign aggression, when such occurs in the interval between legislative sessions.

9th. To make peace, with the authorization and subject to referendum of the national Congress.

10th. To permit, upon authorization by the national Congress, but without this authorization in the interval between legislative sessions, foreign forces to pass through the territory of the country or, by reason of war, to remain therein temporarily.

11th. To exercise supreme command of the armed forces, administering them through the medium of the competent organs.

12th. To decree total or partial mobilization of the armed forces.

13th. To decree a state of siege under the terms of this Constitution.

14th. To decree and execute federal intervention under the terms of Articles 7 to 14.

15th. To authorize Brazilians to accept pensions, employment, or commissions from foreign governments.

16th. To send to the Chamber of Deputies, within the first two months of the legislative session, the budget proposal.

17th. To render annually to the national Congress, within sixty days after the opening of the legislative session, the accounts relative to the preceding fiscal year.

18th. To send a message to the national Congress, upon the occasion of the opening of the legislative session, giving it an account of the state of the country and requesting of it the action which he may judge necessary.

19th. To grant pardons and commute sentences, with a hearing before the organs instituted by law.

. . .

SECTION IV—*Concerning the Ministers of State*

Art. 90. The President of the Republic is assisted by the Ministers of State.

Sole Paragraph. Essential conditions for investiture in the office of Ministers of State are:

1st. To be a Brazilian (Article 129, Numbers I and II [i.e., 1st and 2nd clauses]).

2nd. To be in the exercise of political rights.

3rd. To be more than twenty-five years of age.

Art. 91. In addition to the attributions that the law may fix, the Ministers of State shall have power:

1st. To countersign the acts signed by the President of the Republic.

2nd. To issue instructions for the good execution of the laws, decrees, and regulations.

3rd. To present to the President of the Republic a report of the services carried out each year in the ministry.

4th. To appear in the Chamber of Deputies and in the federal Senate in the cases and for the purposes indicated in this Constitution.

Art. 92. The Ministers of State, in common crimes and those of their responsibility, shall be prosecuted and judged by the federal Supreme Tribunal, and in crimes connected with those of the President of the Republic, by the organs competent for the prosecution and judgment of the latter.

Art. 93. In addition to that provided in Article 54, Sole Paragraph, the acts defined in law (Article 89), when practiced or ordered by the Ministers of State, are crimes of their responsibility.

Chapter IV—*Concerning the Judicial Power*
SECTION I—*Preliminary Provisions*

Art. 94. The judicial power is exercised by the following organs:

1st. The federal Supreme Tribunal.

2nd. The federal tribunal of appeals.

3rd. Military judges and tribunals.

4th. Electoral judges and tribunals.

5th. Labor judges and tribunals.

Art. 95. Except for the restrictions expressed in this Constitution, judges shall enjoy the following guarantees:

1st. Life tenure, they being unable to lose office except by judicial sentence.

2nd. Irremovability, except when it shall occur by reason of public interest, recognized by the vote of two-thirds of the effective judges of the competent higher tribunal.

3rd. Irreducibility of remuneration, which, however, shall remain subject to general taxes.

§1. Retirement shall be compulsory at seventy years of age or for proved invalidity, and optional after thirty years of public service, counted in the form of law.

§2. Retirement, in any of these cases, shall be decreed with full remuneration.

§3. Life tenure shall not be obligatorily extended to those judges whose functions are limited to preparing cases and substituting for trial judges; it shall be assured them, however, after ten years of continuous exercise of the office.

TITLE VII—*Concerning the Armed Forces*

Art. 176. The armed forces, constituted essentially by the army, the navy, and air force, are permanent national institutions, organized on a basis of hierarchy and discipline, under the supreme authority of the President of the Republic, and within the limits of the law.

Art. 177. The armed forces are intended to defend the Fatherland and to guarantee the constitutional powers and law and order.

Art. 178. The political direction of war, and the selection of the commanders-in-chief of the forces in operation shall be incumbent on the President of the Republic.

Art. 179. The problems relative to the defense of the country shall be studied by the council of national security and by special organs of the armed forces, charged with preparing them for mobilization and military operations.

§1. The council of national security shall be directed by the President of the Republic, and shall be participated in by such Ministers of State and chiefs of staff as the law may determine, with the character of effective members. In cases of impediment, the President of the Republic shall nominate a substitute.

§2. The law shall regulate the organization, competence, and functioning of the council of national security.

Art. 180. The following shall not be permitted in the zones indispensable to the defense of the country, without the previous consent of the council of national security:

1st. Any action relating to the concession of lands, the opening of highways, or the installation of transmitting outfits.

2nd. Construction of bridges and international roads.

3rd. Establishment or development of any industries affecting the security of the country.

§1. The law shall specify the zones indispensable to the national defense, shall regulate their utilization and shall take steps to assure that Brazilian capital and workers shall predominate in the industries situated in them.

§2. The authorizations referred to in Numbers I, II, and III [i.e., 1st, 2nd, and 3rd clauses, above], may, at any time, be modified or cancelled by the council of national security.

Art. 181. All Brazilians are obligated for military service or other duties necessary to the defense of the Fatherland, under the terms and penalties of the law.

§1. Women are exempted from military service, but are subject to such duties as the law may establish.

§2. The military obligation of clergymen shall be fulfilled in the service of the armed forces or by spiritual assistance to them.

§3. No Brazilian may hold public office or occupy a position in autarchic institutions, corporations of mixed economy, or concerns holding concession for public services, after attaining the initial age fixed by law for rendering military service without producing proof of enlistment, being in the reserve, or enjoying exemption.

§4. To favor the fulfillment of military obligations, schools of military training and private groups for military training are permitted.

Art. 182. Commissions, with the advantages, insignia, and prerogatives therein inherent, are fully guaranteed not only to active officers and those of the reserve, but also to the retired officers.

§1. Military titles, posts and uniforms can be worn only by the active, the reserve, or the retired soldier.

§2. An officer of the armed forces shall lose his post and commission only by condemnatory sentence, pronounced by a judge, whose penalty restrictive of individual liberty exceeds two years; or, in the cases provided by law, if he is declared unworthy or incompatible with the rank of officer, in conformity with the decision of a military tribunal of permanent character in time of peace, or of a special tribunal in time of war, whether external or civil.

§3. The soldier who, being on active duty, shall accept a permanent public position outside his career, shall be transferred to the reserve with the rights and duties defined by law.

§4. The soldier who, being on active duty, shall accept a temporary public position, elective or not, shall be associated with the respective list [of officers] and shall have his time of service counted only for promotion by seniority, transference to the reserves, or retirement. After eight years of removal, continuous or not, he shall be transferred, in the form [provided by] law, to the reserves, without prejudice to the counting of time for retirement.

§5. While he receives remuneration from his permanent or temporary position, the soldier shall have no claim to the income from his [military] post, either on the active list, the reserves, or the retired list.

§6. The provision of Articles 192 and 193 shall be applied to soldiers.

Art. 183. The military police, instituted for internal security and the maintenance of order in the States, the territories, and the federal district, are considered, as auxiliary forces, reserves of the army.

Sole Paragraph. Their personnel shall, when mobilized in the service of the Union in time of foreign or civil war, enjoy the same benefits attributed to the personnel of the army.

❀

65. The Suicide Letter of Getúlio Vargas*

Vargas remained the dominant figure on the political scene; and as a candidate of the Brazilian Labor Party (PTB), he was swept back into office in the presidential elections of

....

* From *The New York Times*, August 25, 1954, p. 2. © 1954 by The New York Times Company. Reprinted by permission of the publisher.

1950. But circumstances were different. Vargas no longer displayed the old flair, and he found it trying to govern under a constitution which was not of his making. Congress was uncooperative and the political parties querulous. The troubled economy tended to diminish his popularity with the workers. The army watched attentively to prevent him from resorting to his old caudilho tactics. Affairs reached a climax when an assassination attempt against the critical journalist Carlos Lacerda was traced to the personal bodyguard of the president and seemed to implicate Vargas himself. Once again the armed forces asked him to step down. He gave his response on August 25, 1954, by committing suicide. He left the following farewell note to a stunned nation. Since then, there has been some speculation as to the authenticity of this letter.

Once more the forces and interests against the people are newly coordinated and raised against me. They do not accuse me, they insult me; they do not fight me, they slander me and do not give me the right of defense. They need to drown my voice and halt my actions so that I no longer continue to defend, as I always have defended, the people and principally the humble.

I follow the destiny that is imposed on me. After years of domination and looting by international economic and financial groups, I made myself chief of an unconquerable revolution. I began the work of liberation and I instituted a regime of social liberty. I had to resign. I returned to govern on the arms of the people.

A subterranean campaign of international groups joined with national groups revolting against the regime of workers' guarantees. The law of excess profits was stopped in Congress. Hatreds were unchanged against the justice of a revision of minimum salaries.

I wished to create national liberty by developing our riches through Petrobras[1] and a wave of agitation clouded its be-

....

1 The government oil development company [ed.].

ginnings. Electrobras[2] was hindered almost to despair. They do not wish the workers to be free. They do not wish the people to be independent.

I assumed the Government during an inflationary spiral that was destroying the value of work. Profits of foreign enterprises reached 500 per cent yearly. In declarations of goods that we import there existed frauds of more than $100,000,000.

I saw the coffee crisis increase the value of our principal product. We attempted to defend its price and the reply was a violent pressure upon our economy to the point of being obliged to surrender.

I have fought month to month, day to day, hour to hour, resisting a constant aggression, unceasingly bearing it all in silence, forgetting all and renouncing myself to defend the people that now fall abandoned. I cannot give you more than my blood. If the birds of prey wish the blood of anybody, they wish to continue sucking that of the Brazilian people.

I offer my life in the holocaust. I choose this means to be with you always. When they humiliate you, you will feel my soul suffering at your side. When hunger beats at your door, you will feel in your chests the energy for the fight for yourselves and your children. When they humiliate you, you feel in my grief the force for reaction.

My sacrifice will maintain you united, and my name will be your battle flag. Each drop of my blood will be an immortal call to your conscience and will maintain a holy vibration for resistance.

To hatred, I respond with pardon. And to those who think they have defeated me, I reply with my victory. I was the slave of the people and today I free myself for eternal life. But this people to which I was a slave no longer will be a slave to anyone. My sacrifice will remain forever in your soul and my blood will be the price of your ransom.

I fought against the looting of Brazil. I fought against the looting of the people. I have fought bare-breasted. The hatred, infamy, and calumny did not beat down my spirit. I

....

[2] The government hydroelectric development agency [ed.].

gave you my life. Now I offer my death. Nothing remains. Serenely I take the first step on the road to eternity and I leave life to enter history.

❈

66. A Statement of Faith in Nationalism*

Rapid change characterized Brazil under Vargas. Industrialization increased and with it a proletarian class grew in number and in strength. Vargas knew how to enlist the new working class in his support, and he assigned it its first political role. That new political element was allied to another potent political force which the astute Vargas also knew how to manipulate: nationalism. Those two forces began, after World War II, to resent and to oppose the alliance of foreign capitalists and the local oligarchy. They believed that the foreign economic interests and the native oligarchy sought to perpetuate the colonial past by strengthening the closed society and by barring the avenues to change. Many intellectuals like Nelson Werneck Sodré rallied to the cause of the working class and of nationalism as the hope for a better Brazil, as the means of destroying the colonial past. Below is printed part of Sodré's plea for nationalism as a redeeming force.

Why Nationalism? Because now foreign economic forces are the most powerful obstacle to our development and their in-

....

* Translated from Nelson Werneck Sodré, *Raizes Históricas do Nacionalismo Brasileiro* (Rio de Janeiro: Ministério da Educação e Cultura, 1960), pp. 30-35.

ternal allies decline in resistance, they no longer tutor the nation. For any country with a colonial past, with an economic structure subordinated to foreign interests, to create itself nationally is to accomplish a task in many ways identical to what the European nations accomplished at the dawn of the Modern Age with the defeat of feudalism and the advance of capitalism. What for them were feudal relations, restrictions on development, are for us all that still remain of the colonial past. Nationalism thus presents itself as liberation. From its possibilities as a liberating force arises the impassioned atmosphere which surrounds it and which causes its enemies to consider it more passion than politics. It is proper to emphasize that passion in the abstract does not exist and that Nationalism interprets a truth—truth within the historical context, and that truth is concrete.

To those who find difficulty in placing Nationalism in the economic realm, who judge false the declarations by which it is presented as a shield against various forms of real foreign aggression, perhaps it is more easily understood within its political framework where the lines are more precisely drawn. In that framework, Nationalism represents the democratic ideal, supported solely by the rising classes, which need liberty as the human body needs oxygen, which live by the enlightenment of opinion, which need to discuss and to debate publicly. More than anything, they need popular support and only that reveals the essential democratic character of the nationalist position. The opposition forces, quite to the contrary, have lost the conditions for open life and exercise varied and repeated attempts to limit freedoms, to restrict opinions, to reduce politics to the old formulas of the combinations of a few, of clandestine decisions, of summit statements with a characteristic horror of anything that smacks of the masses.

Nationalism appears, then, on the historic scene as the escape from a difficult situation whose symptoms appear in day-to-day life. It answers the present demands, concrete necessities—it was not invented, it did not come from the imagination of a few, it does not live in theory but in practice. It is a spontaneous solution, and this seems to be one of its limitations because it is difficult for it to take on organized forms in the political struggle. Organized it is invincible. The feeling of passion which accompanies it, a positive sign of its force and not a symptom of its weakness, points out the generality and profundity of its effects: it reveals that Nationalism is popular, which should not surprise anyone, seeing that everything that is national is popular.

Inaccurate are the comparisons, slyly put forward as accusations, that Nationalism is historically outdated—so is colonialism—and that it can lead to what happened recently in other countries, particularly in Germany and in Italy. It is clear that Nationalism can lead to anything, but there is no relationship whatsoever between the situation presented by a country like Brazil with an economic structure still strongly contaminated by colonialism and the nations, like those mentioned, in which the capitalist system was fully installed. Likewise, it would be simple to establish other distinctions by an easy comparison: the economic forces which aided nazism and fascism are the same which here oppose the growth of Nationalism.

Nationalism springs from the necessity of creating a new scheme of coordinating class interests, or reducing them to a minimum common denominator, for the struggle in defense of what is national in us. It is imperative to overcome the disagreement between the national bourgeoisie and the working class which adopts Nationalism as an opportune political expression. It is understood that only by minimizing, without denying or obscuring, the contradiction between the class which furnishes the labor and increases its consciousness every day and the class which needs to strengthen itself through capitalization of the national resources and their proper use, we will be able to endure as a nation which presents Nationalism as the natural solution and gives to it that force, that penetration, and that catalytic power which the simple observation sees in it.

To set up all the obstacles to the creation of a framework in which the forces interested in national development are harmonized becomes the essential task of those who oppose Nationalism, of those who see in it the direct menace to what they represent, of those who see and fear the existence of a possibility for Brazil to overcome the remnants of colonialism by making itself into a nation. The simplest process is to divide those forces by establishing as fundamental the contradiction which separates them, by aggravating the conditions of life to force to desperation those who work and to distress those who compose the varied range of the middle class. For these reasons we see the dangers of an economic and financial policy which generates the conditions of uncertainty and propitiates those of subversion and the anomalies of a country famished for capital exporting capital, of creating difficulties for the equipping of factories which use national capital, of systematizing the desperation of those who have the right of expecting equal treatment when they do not receive preferential treatment for the simple fact that they live, invest, and work here.

Then, what is old and what is new in this phase [of the growing Brazilian Revolution which began in 1930]? Old doubtless are the semi-feudal relations which impede the amplification of the internal market; old is the policy of spreading the economic setbacks among all the classes by reducing the acquisitive power of the masses; old is the orientation of relegating the State to inertia; old is the mercantilism which requires us to ship more abroad and to receive less for it; old is the rule which imprisons us in the role as a tropical producing plantation of primary materials for foreign industries; old is our subordination to foreign reasoning, no matter how valid it might be abroad; old, particularly, is the idea that Brazil can only develop with outside aid and principally with foreign capital.

And what is new? New is the social composition which includes a bourgeoisie capable of becoming a class and beginning to understand that its opportunity is now or never and that it is a middle class attentively and ideologically receptive, through the major part of its elements, to the clamor which is raised in the depths of history in the sense that we must organize ourselves for the task we have to fulfill, and a working class which acquired a political conscience and mobilizes itself for the purpose of sharing the national undertak-

ing, seeing thereby the opening of perspectives to its historical role. New are the people. Nothing more will occur without their participation. New is the national industry, which
has passed the stage of consumers' goods to producers' goods,
limited, however, by the backwardness in the acquisitive capacity of the internal market and burdened by a policy of
obstacles and doubts. Volta Redonda[1] is what is new that is
altering the Brazilian scene and Petrobras is what is new
which affirms our capacity for progress without interferences.
New, in short, is Nationalism, which corresponds to what
pushes us forward and breaks with what held us back.

Between the new and the old the choice is not difficult.
Between the past and the future, no doubt exists. We
choose the future. We do not intend "to lose the continuity
of history."

❈

67. The Resignation of President Jânio Quadros*

*As governor of São Paulo, Jânio Quadros was considered an
able and honest administrator, and when he was overwhelm-
ingly elected president in 1960, the nation looked forward to
five years of increased industrialization and democracy. To
the disappointment of many, he soon began to display erratic
tendencies. Congress refused to follow his lead, and open*

....

[1] The largest steel mill in Brazil. Plans were made for it beginning
in 1941. It began to produce in 1946. The nations of Latin
America regard steel production as a significant milestone along the
road to economic independence [ed.].

* From *The New York Times* (August 26, 1961), p. 4. © 1961
by The New York Times Company. Reprinted by permission of the
publisher.

*hostility came to characterize the relations between legisla-
ture and executive. Then, without warning and with little
explanation, the president suddenly resigned on August 25,
1961, after only eight months in office. A surprised nation
puzzled over his cryptic letter of resignation.*

On this date and by this communication I am leaving with
the Minister of Justice the reasons for the act in which I
hereby resign my post as President of the Republic.

I have been beaten by forces against me and so I leave the
Government. In the last seven months I have carried out my
duty. I have done so night and day, always working harder
and harder without any rancor against anyone. But unfortunately all my efforts were in vain to lead this nation in the
direction of its true economic and political freedom, which
was the only way to effective social progress which this generous people are so much entitled to.

I wanted Brazil for Brazilians and because [I did] I had to
face and fight corruption, lies and cowardliness, whose only
goals are to subject the general needs of the nation to some
ambitious groups and individuals from inside and also from
outside.

However, I feel crushed. Terrible forces came forward to
fight me and to defame me by all their means with the excuse that they were only trying to collaborate. Had I remained at my post I would share no longer the confidence
and peace necessary to carry on with my duties. I believe that
I would not even be able to maintain the public peace.

Here I call a halt with my thoughts turned toward the people, the students, and the workers and also to the whole Brazilian community. Here I close this page of my life and of
the national history. I have enough courage to do so.

In leaving the government I want to make an appeal and
express my gratitude.

My gratitude to those who have helped me inside and outside my administration and especially to the armed forces
whose conduct and behaviour I wish to proclaim at this very
moment.

My appeal is that order and respect should be maintained from one and all.

This is the only way we shall have the necessary dignity to inherit our Christian destiny.

I return now to my work as lawyer and teacher. Let us all work. There are many ways of serving our nation.

68. President João Goulart Explains Some Policies of His Government*

Raised to the presidency over the protest of the military was Vice-President João Goulart, Vargas' heir to the Brazilian Labor Party (PTB). "Jango," however, lacked the talents and appeal of his mentor. The government in the new capital of Brasília swayed from left to right in its pronouncements. It spoke of land and tax reforms but failed to take any constructive action. Meanwhile, the already phenomenal inflation spiraled upward, and its first and most oppressed victims were the poor. While on an official visit to the United States early in his administration, President Goulart explained some of the policies which, at least theoretically, were supposed to be motivating his government.

The Government and the people of Brazil have spared no sacrifices in order to overcome backwardness and underdevelopment. We are trying to establish a harmonious development throughout the country to correct regional imbalances

....

* From a speech of President João Goulart to the U.S. Congress, Washington, D.C., April 4, 1962, printed in *Vital Speeches* (May 1, 1962), pp. 426-427. Reprinted by permission of the publisher.

and avoid the state of destitution in certain areas and raise them to the level, for instance, of the State of São Paulo, where the per capita income is higher than that of some of the highly industrialized countries.

In the struggle for development and for our economic emancipation, we have suffered the influence of adverse factors, which we are determined to overcome. There are permanent imbalances in the system of trade relations between countries having an adverse economic development, with prejudicial reflexes on the economically weaker countries. We can eliminate or at least attenuate these imbalances through conventions and agreements based on friendly arrangements and the adoption of realistic formulas.

The monetary inflation in Brazil, of which so much has been said both in our country and abroad is not a local phenomenon; it coincided with the wartime economy, when the old economic-financial structure suffered the impact of abrupt changes in our allies' supply and demand.

. . .

The Latin American countries, with their war-born inflation, remained devoid of any plan of international cooperation for the recovery of their agriculture and the development of their industries, depending exclusively upon the export of their primary products for the restoration of their trade. The story of the growing deterioration of the terms of trade of commodities with manufactured goods is well known to all. From year to year, the same number of bags of coffee or of cocoa or of cotton buys a lesser quantity of the same type of equipment or of manufactured products. While our primary products have remained exposed to a continuing fall in prices, the index of growth of our population has increased at such levels that Brazil is expected to possess 200 million inhabitants by the end of this century. Notwithstanding such adverse factors, Brazil has been maintaining a growing rhythm in the increase of its per capita income and of the national product. This notable effort for development is due above all to the unlimited energy and sense of patriotism of the Brazilian people.

. . .

We feel . . . that our destiny is in our own hands, and we keep our eyes open to find the adequate solutions for the development of Brazil. The political awareness of the leaders in government and of the people themselves is keenly awake to the fact that the fight for development is the fight of the people. In pursuance of this purpose, we are engaged in the realization and implementation of basic reforms, among which the agrarian reform is paramount. We recognize the importance of the foreign contribution to the process of our development.

I have repeatedly said that we nourish no prejudice against foreign capital and the technical collaboration of the more advanced countries. We desire this cooperation and will assure its full freedom within the legal limits established and the inspiration of Brazilian ideals. . . .

As a country now in a phase of full expansion, Brazil offers broad possibilities to foreign private enterprise desirous to cooperate loyally for its development. In the matter of public utilities services there are certain areas of friction which should be eliminated, all the more so because through a natural phenomenon, besides creating disagreements between the granting authority and the concessionary, they are not rarely a source of misunderstanding between friendly countries.

. . .

I wish to reaffirm the identification of my country with the democratic principles which unite the peoples of the West. Brazil forms no part of any politico-military bloc, but it abides by its freely assumed international commitments. Brazil's international action responds to no other objective than that of favoring, by all the means in our power, the preservation and strengthening of peace. It is our belief that the ideological conflict between East and West cannot and must not be decided by military action, for in the event of a nuclear war, even if we managed to save our own lives, whether in victory or in defeat, our very reason for living would be obliterated.

Brazil believes that a noninimical contact between the democratic world and the socialist world can be beneficial to the knowledge and coordination of experience of all. It is our hope that these contacts will make it evident that representative democracy is the most perfect of all forms of government and the only one compatible with the protection of mankind and the preservation of human freedom.

❀

---

69. The Inaugural Speech of President Humberto Castello Branco*

Brazilian democracy suffered under the inept administration of Goulart. His indecision, lack of ability, and gracelessness alienated most of his few supporters until even labor became disgruntled with his unfulfilled promises. The military stood restively in the background and watched while chaos enveloped the country. Then, offended and angered by the insubordination which the president openly encouraged among the enlisted ranks, the officers invoked their role as the poder moderador to depose their commander-in-chief. On April 1, 1964, the revolution was complete. Goulart had fallen with no resistance. Congress, with the blessings of the armed forces, elected as president a respected military intellectual, General Humberto Castello Branco, who promised both reforms and progress.

In the special significance of this civic ceremony and while millions of our compatriots encourage us with their trust and

....

* From a Brazilian Embassy Press Release, Washington, D.C.

their hopes, I want to assure you that the oath I have just now taken before the august representatives of the Nation embodies much more than the ritual form: it contains the reiteration of the sentiments and ideals that have accompanied and inspired us since our youth. I will preserve with honor and loyalty the Constitution of Brazil, including the Institutional Act that is a part of it. I shall observe and maintain both with determination as a slave of the laws of the country and I will remain watchful to see that all obey them with exactitude and zeal. Mine will be a Government of law, of the traditions and moral and political principles that represent the soul of Brazil. It will be a Government firmly set on the future, since it is also true that a permanent striving for progress and advancement is the hallmark as well as the general trend of our social and political history. It is no exaggeration to say that in this march to the future we should engage ourselves with ardor in a crusade in which all Brazilians should be called to participate. In this journey I expect through energy, and above all through my own example, to count on the participation of all the citizens in an endeavour that will be the supreme guarantee of every man and woman in this country. My behavior shall be that of a head of State who will harbor no hesitations in the process to elect a Brazilian to whom I shall transfer my office on January 31, 1966. I will uphold with all my ability the union, integrity, and independence of our country, within and without its territorial frontiers. And by this I mean not only the admirable heritage of national unity but the harmony of all Brazilians. I shall be the President of all of them, not the head of a faction. The independence of Brazil will be the paramount principle of our international policy. All friendly nations can rely on the loyalty of the Brazilian people, who will honor treaties and covenants entered into. All democratic nations will be our allies at the same time that all those people that wish to be free through representative democracy will have the support of Brazil in their self-determination. The historical alliances which bind us to the free nations of the Americas will be preserved and strengthened. We shall respect the independence of nations throughout the world in regard to their domestic affairs and we shall demand equal respect towards our own, not brooking the least interference, however subtle or discreet. I shall do whatever lies within my means to consolidate the ideals of the civic movement of the Brazilian Nation in these memorable days of April, when it rose united and resplendent in courage and determination, to restore democracy and liberate it from the frauds and distortions which were rendering it unrecognizable. Not through a coup d'état, but through a revolution that, born in our homes, expanded in public opinion and in our institutions, and decisively supported by the armed forces, expressed the firmness of our convictions and the depth of our concepts as to life—convictions and concepts which come to us from the past and which we must transmit in ever more perfect form to future generations. It was a revolution to ensure progress without reneging the past. We have thus seen the Nation standing up to vindicate its freedom and its will, finally affirmed under constitutional provisions, through the Congress as the lawful representative of the ideals and aspirations of our people. We advocate democratic freedom through government by the majority with the collaboration and respect of the minorities. The citizens—civilians and soldiers, men and women of Brazil—in an expressive attitude, one of the most beautiful and single-minded impulses recorded in our history, arose against the debasement of the regime. Tirelessly and without discouragement, I shall work for the general well-being of Brazil. I shall spare no sacrifice in order that this well-being be extended as swiftly as is reasonably possible to all Brazilians and particularly to those who toil and suffer in the less-developed regions of the country. The take-off towards economic development through moral, educational, material and political elevation will be a central object of the Government's attention. With this end in view, the Government will not be an impediment to private enterprise, without detriment, however, to the imperatives of social justice due to the worker, who is an indispensable factor in our prosperity. I am, indeed, one of those who believe in the benefits of constant evolution, capable of reaching an ever growing number of our people, many of whom are unfortunately still unable by far to share in the conquests of civilization. We shall forge ahead in the assurance that the remedy for the evils of the extreme left does not lead in the rise of a reactionary right, but rather in the execution of reforms that become necessary. I firmly believe in the compatibility of development with the democratic processes, but I do not believe in development through inflationary orgy, delusion and scourge of the less-favored by fortune. Inflation and backwardness must be attacked now and at once; and no one can hope to destroy them without doing his part in the work and sacrifice that lie ahead, the only source whence the well-being and prosperity of all can flow. Let each and every one do his part and carry his own weight in this task of national recovery. Each laborer and each entrepreneur—the latter especially, to whom I repeat those words by Ruy Barbosa: "It is among the more cultured and well-to-do classes that regenerative agitations must have their starting point. If we give the example to the people they will follow us." Therefore, let Brazilians that are happier or better served by fortune do their duty towards the Nation and they will see that the whole of Brazil will imitate them, to the glory and concord of this privileged homeland. The votes of the representatives of the Nation in choosing the head of government at this difficult moment are assuredly the greatest honor which a citizen could receive. To me, however, they convey also a clear idea of the magnitude of the task with which I am charged, towards fulfilling the hopes of the nation. I will go further and say that the humility of my entire life is become greater in this moment: never has a man been more in need of understanding, support and assistance from all his fellow citizens. Let the Brazilians come to me and I will go with them, so that with God's help and with serene confidence we can together seek better days ahead.

❀

70. Ambassador Juracy Magalhães
Comments on the Revolution of 1964*

President Castello Branco sent an old friend of the United States, Juracy Magalhães, as ambassador to Washington. One of his first actions after arriving on June 25, 1964, was to issue a statement explaining the revolution to the American people. It is interesting to note in that statement his reference to the military's exercise of the poder moderador, *which he treated as very much an established and accepted practice despite the silence of the constitution on the subject. His appointment and his statements indicated that Brazil, after a four-year hiatus, was returning to the policy of close cooperation with the United States, a guideline of foreign policy emphasized by the Baron of Rio-Branco.*

It is my initial desire to explain to the American people that the Brazilian Revolution was born out of the indomitable will of the people not to allow themselves to become dominated by Communism or by the corruption which was undermining our National life.

The Armed Forces of my country have traditionally acted as a moderating power on the constitutional life. Never have they interfered in the political process due to a thirst for power or inspirations of a military nature. Even now they acted only after the people went into the streets to openly condemn the Communist infiltration, governmental corruption, the break of hierarchy in the Armed Forces, the destruction of authority and the incompetence of Public Administration. They only sanctioned what the people insisted

....
* From a Brazilian Embassy Press Release, Washington, D.C.

upon, and it was done without bloodshed and without greater disruption in the life of the country.

What took place was not a Military movement and General Humberto Castello Branco only accepted his election by Congress in order to comply with the appeal of the Governors that represented the political forces of the country. His civil tradition, his love for juridical order, his democratic training, his competence and his honesty will place his country on the sure road to efficient government and the complete stability of the republican institutions.

It is true that the Government instituted by the Revolution has practiced some acts in annulment of political rights with "due process of law," but it did so inspired by the best interests of the country and without any purpose of personal persecution. President Castello Branco's spirit of justice has given all of us (the older liberal politicians) tranquillity in that his actions are exercised with a minimum of loss of individual guarantees already entirely reestablished within the time previously determined for these measures which were necessary. Some injustice, practiced perchance, will be corrected in the best Brazilian tradition, as was done after the revolution of 1930.

There is no doubt, however, that the Brazilian Revolution was a great victory for the western world and it will continue to be reaffirmed increasingly as reformist and democratic. It was not made to safeguard privileges and to nourish social inequalities. Access to land and homes is already being facilitated and the agrarian, urban, banking, fiscal and administrative reforms will highlight the serenity and spirit of social justice which motivates the present Government of Brazil.

I can affirm to the American people that my country is not on the road to a dictatorship and if such a disgrace should happen to us it would never be with the help of the civil and military officials presently responsible for the destiny of Brazil.

. . .

. . . This . . . is not the hour for recrimination of small details that are not pleasant to anyone. It is the hour of assistance; of understanding; of cooperation so that Brazil, in a short time, will be one of the bulwarks in the cause of liberty in the world; economically strong and democratically organized with a great people living united under broad social justice and a juridical order.

A Chronology of Significant Dates
in Brazilian History

1494: Treaty of Tordesilhas divided the world between Spain and Portugal.

1500: Cabral discovered Brazil.

1502: King Manoel licensed Lisbon merchants to export brazil-wood from the New World.

1530: Expedition of Martim Afonso de Sousa to colonize.

1532: Founding of São Vicente and Piratininga. First sugar mills built.

1534: King granted Brazil to twelve donees.

1539-1542: Francisco de Orellana explored the Amazon.

1549: Centralized government instituted under Tomé de Sousa in Bahia. First Jesuits arrived.

1551: Creation of the Bishopric of Brazil.

1555: The French established a colony at Rio de Janeiro.

1567: Mem de Sá expelled the French and occupied Rio de Janeiro.

1580: The union of the Iberian crowns.

1616: Belém founded.

1621: Creation of the State of Maranhão.

1624-1625: The Dutch captured Bahia.

1630: The Dutch seized Recife and began their conquest of the northeast.

1637-1639: Pedro Teixeira explored the Amazon and founded Tabatinga.

1640: Portugal declared its independence from Spain.

1654: The Dutch withdrew from Brazil.

1695: Gold discovered in Minas Gerais.

1720: The governors of Brazil henceforth known as viceroys.

1724: Foundation of the Brazilian Academy of the Forgotten, first of the European-type academies of the Enlightenment.

1727: Introduction of coffee into Brazil.

1750: Treaty of Madrid marked the abandonment of the Treaty of Tordesilhas and the adoption of *uti possidetis* to settle boundaries. Pombal began to centralize the government of Brazil.

1759: Pombal expelled the Jesuits from the empire.

1761: Treaty of Pardo annulled the Treaty of Madrid.

1763: The capital transferred from Bahia to Rio de Janeiro.

1777: Treaty of San Ildefonso remarked the Portuguese-Spanish frontiers in South America.

1789: The Inconfidência exposed.

1792: Tiradentes executed.

1798: The outbreak of the Bahian conspiracy.

1808: The Braganzas arrived in Rio de Janeiro. João VI opened the ports to world trade and lifted the restrictions on manufacturing.

1810: Treaties signed with Great Britain giving that nation commercial dominance over Brazil.

1815: Brazil raised to the status of a kingdom.

1816: Luso-Brazilian troops occupied Uruguay. French artistic mission arrived in Rio.

1817: The republican revolution in Pernambuco.

1819: At Bahia, first steamship put into operation.

1820: First organized colony of non-Portuguese immigrants established.

1821: Uruguay annexed as the Cisplatine Province. João VI returned to Lisbon.

1822: Prince Pedro declared Brazil's independence and received the title of emperor.

1824: Pedro promulgated the first constitution. The United States recognized Brazil.

1825: Portugal recognized Brazil. War broke out between Argentina and Brazil over Uruguay.

1827: By treaty Great Britain consolidated its commercial predominance over Brazil.

1828: Argentina and Brazil agreed to the creation of Uruguay as an independent nation.

1831: Pedro I abdicated. A three-man regency assumed control.

1834: Additional Act instituted federalism and a one-man regency.

1835: Outbreak of the Farroupilha Revolt in Rio Grande do Sul.

1840: Interpretive Law ended the experiment with federalism. Proclamation of the majority ended the regency. Pedro II ascended the throne.

1843: The first steamboat navigated the Amazon.

1844: First law to protect and encourage national industry.

1845: Caxias put down the Farroupilha Revolt.

1850: The Queiróz Law abolished the slave trade.

1852: Beginning of the railroad era. Brazil intervened in Argentina to help overthrow Rosas.

1858: Coffee became the principal export.

1865: The alliance of Argentina, Brazil, and Uruguay against Paraguay.

1866: Opening of the Amazon to international traffic.

1870: The Triple Alliance defeated Paraguay. The Republican Party issued its manifesto.

1871: The Law of the Free Womb freed all children born to slaves.

1873: The number of Italian immigrants arriving began to surpass the number of Portuguese.

1873-1875: The Church-State conflict over the privileges of regalism.

1885: The Saraiva-Cotegipe Law freed all slaves at the age of sixty.

1888: The Golden Law abolished slavery.

1889: The emperor dethroned and the republic established.

1890: Church and State separated.

1891: A new constitution promulgated.

1893: A naval revolt threatened the republic.

1895: The Missions award favorably settled Brazil's frontier with Argentina.

1897: Destruction of Canudos and the death of the religious mystic, Antônio Conselheiro.

1900: Amapá boundary dispute with French Guiana settled favorably for Brazil.

1902: Publication of *Rebellion in the Backlands* and *Canaan*.

1903: Treaty of Petropolis ceded Acre to Brazil.

1906: The Convention of Taubaté instituted valorization of coffee. The Third Pan American Conference met in Rio de Janeiro.

1910: Indian Protection Service established.

1917: Brazil declared war on Germany.

1920: Creation of the first university to replace scattered faculties.

1922: Modern Art Week initiated a new phase of introspection in national culture.

1924-26: March of the revolutionary Prestes column through the backlands.
1930: A revolution brought Getúlio Vargas to Power.
1932: Revolution of São Paulo and civil war.
1937: Establishment of the *Estado Novo*.
1942: Brazil declared war on the Axis.
1944: An expeditionary force sent to Europe.
1945: The military deposed Vargas.
1946: A new constitution promulgated.
1950: Vargas re-elected president.
1954: Vargas committed suicide.
1960: The capital moved inland to Brasília.
1961: The election and resignation of Jânio Quadros.
1964: The military deposed João Goulart.

Suggestions for Additional
Reading in English

*

I. BACKGROUND

There are five commendable general introductions to Brazil. Charles Wagley presents a highly interpretive study in his recent *An Introduction to Brazil* (N.Y.: Columbia Univ. Press, 1963). The introspective *New World in the Tropics* by Gilberto Freyre (N.Y.: Knopf, 1959) represents the Brazilian viewpoint. A more personal and informal approach was taken by William Lytle Schurz in his informative *Brazil, the Infinite Country* (N.Y.: Dutton, 1961). Two collections of varied essays by eminent Brazilianists merit attention: Lawrence F. Hill (ed.), *Brazil* (Berkeley: Univ. of California Press, 1947) and T. Lynn Smith and Alexander Marchant (eds.), *Brazil, Portrait of Half a Continent* (N.Y.: Dryden, 1951).

There is still no adequate history of Brazil in English. The dull and expository *A History of Brazil* by João Pandiá Calógeras (Chapel Hill, N.C.: Univ. of N. Carolina Press, 1939) is sufficient for the colonial period, but Bailey W. Diffie in his *Latin-American Civilization, the Colonial Period* (Harrisburg: Stackpole, 1945) covers the era with better interpretation and style. C. R. Boxer has written masterfully on specific periods within the colonial era. *Salvador de Sá and the Struggle for Brazil and Angola, 1602-1686* (London: Athlone, 1952) depicts seventeenth-century Brazil as the principal theater of operations for one of the most remarkable Portuguese figures of that century. In *The Dutch in Brazil, 1624-1654* (Oxford: Clarendon, 1957), he handles in detail the foremost threat to Portugal's empire in America. Finally, his *The Golden Age of Brazil, 1695-1750* (Univ. of California Press, 1962) discusses the colony during the gold-rush days. The most widely known interpretation of the colonial period—the fusion and contributions of three races—appears in Gilberto Freyre's *The Masters and the Slaves* (N.Y.: Knopf, 1963).

The imperial period has been treated from several points of view. The incisive *Empire in Brazil* by C. H. Haring (Cambridge, Mass.: Harvard Univ. Press, 1958) concentrates on the political development. Bertita Harding provides a more personal approach in her readable biography of the Braganzas in Brazil, *Amazon Throne* (Indianapolis: Bobbs-Merrill, 1941). The two Pedros have been the subjects of individual biographies. Sérgio Corrêa da Costa brings Pedro I to life in *Every Inch a King* (N.Y.: Macmillan, 1953). *Dom Pedro the Magnanimous* by M. W. Williams (Chapel Hill, N. C.: Univ. of N. Carolina Press, 1937) does the same for the second emperor. The imperial period receives its most penetrating analysis in English from Gilberto Freyre. Among other things, his *The Mansions and the Shanties* (N.Y.: Knopf, 1963) traces the decline of the sugar patriarch and the rise to power of the coffee bourgeoisie.

The history of the republican era has been neglected. An important account appears in Harry Bernstein's *Modern and Contemporary Latin America* (N.Y.: Lippincott, 1952). A standard Brazilian history of the era is the recent translation of José Maria Bello's *A History of the Republic* (Palo Alto, Calif.: Stanford Univ. Press, 1966), which is brought up to date by Rollie E. Poppino. *The Unwritten Alliance, Rio-Branco and Brazilian-American Relations* (N.Y.: Columbia Univ. Press, 1966) by E. Bradford Burns is a study of the dynamic diplomatic maneuverings of the Old Republic under the skillful leadership of the Baron of Rio-Branco.

The number of monographs and scholarly articles on various phases of Brazilian history continues to grow. Two valuable sources to consult in order to locate the material in English are: R. A. Humphreys, *Latin American History, A Guide to the Literature in English* (London: Oxford Univ. Press, 1958) and the *Handbook of Latin American Studies*, published annually since 1935. Of further possible help is E. Bradford Burns, "A Working Bibliography for the Study of Brazilian History," *The Americas* (July, 1965), pp. 54-88. Studies in English of Brazilian historiography are rare; two recent articles deserve consideration. Richard H. Morse discusses the phenomenon of unity with diversity in "Some Themes of Brazilian History," *South Atlantic Quarterly* (1962), pp. 159-182. "The Historiography of Brazil, 1808-1889" by Stanley J. Stein in *The Hispanic American Historical Review* (May, 1960), is a lucid analysis of contemporary historical treatment of imperial Brazil.

The fascinating structure and development of Brazilian society have attracted considerable attention. Notable works published on this theme are: C. R. Boxer, *Race Relations in the Portuguese Colonial Empire, 1415-1825* (Oxford: Clarendon, 1963); Charles Wagley, *Amazon Town, A Study of Man in the Tropics* (N.Y.: Knopf, 1964); and edited by the same Columbia professor is *Race and Class in Rural Brazil* (Paris: UNESCO, 1952); Arthur Ramos, *The Negro in Brazil* (Washington, D.C.: Associated Publishers, 1939); Donald Pierson, *Negroes in Brazil: A Study of Race Contact at Bahia* (Chicago: Univ. of Chicago Press, 1956); and T. Lynn Smith, *Brazil, People and Institutions* (Baton Rouge, La.: Louisiana State Univ., 1963). An outdated but still useful guide to this subject is Donald Pierson's *Survey of the Literature on Brazil of Sociological Significance Published up to 1940* (Cambridge, Mass.: Harvard Univ. Press, 1945).

A few other works in English deserve mention because they treat well special aspects of Brazil's development. Fernando de Azevedo, *Brazilian Culture* (N.Y.: Macmillan, 1950) and João Cruz Costa, *A History of Ideas in Brazil* (Berkeley: Univ. of California, 1964) are excellent intellectual histories. Celso Furtado introduces the English-speaking world to the economic problems of his country in *The Economic Growth of Brazil* (Berkeley: Univ. of California, 1963), and in *Diagnosis of the Brazilian Crisis* (Berkeley: Univ. of California, 1965). The biography, *Viscount Mauá and the Empire of Brazil*, by Anyda Marchant (Berkeley: Univ. of California, 1965) relates the activities of the most important figure in the economic development of Brazil during the nineteenth century. Stanley J. Stein has written authoritatively on two important aspects of the economy: *The Brazilian Cotton Manufacture: Textile Enterprise in an Underdeveloped Area, 1850-1950* (Cambridge, Mass.: Harvard Univ. Press, 1957) and *Vassouras, A Brazilian Coffee County, 1850-1900* (Cambridge, Mass.: Harvard Univ. Press, 1957). Alan K. Manchester analyzes the English economic dominance over nineteenth-century Brazil in *British Preëminence in Brazil: Its Rise and Decline* (Chapel Hill, N.C.: Univ. of North Carolina Press, 1933). Rural problems and the necessity for reform are the subjects of seven essays concerning Brazil found in T. Lynn Smith's *Agrarian Reform in Latin America* (N.Y.: Knopf, 1965). An informative as well as entertaining account of the rapid growth of Brazil's most dynamic city appears in Richard M. Morse, *From Community to Metropolis, A Biography of São Paulo, Brazil* (Gainesville: Univ. of Florida Press, 1958). Of interest to the English-speaking public is the comparison and contrast of the development of Brazil and the United States made by Clodomir Vianna Moog, *Bandeirantes and Pioneers* (N.Y.: George Braziller, 1964). An excellent study of those adventurous explorers of the hinterlands as well as a number of important documents from the period of their greatest activity can be found in Richard M. Morse's *The Bandeirantes* (N.Y.: Knopf, 1965). For those who might wish to go on and read in Portuguese there are two excellent bibliographical guides to the abundant material available: Rubens Borba de Moraes and William Berrien, *Manual Bibliográfico de Estudos Brasileiros* (Rio: Gráfica Editôra Souza, 1949) and Rubens Borba de Moraes, *Bibliographia Brasiliana*, 2 vols. (Amsterdam: Colibris, 1958). Of value also is Nelson Werneck Sodré's unique *O que se deve ler para conhecer o Brasil* (Rio: Editôra Leitura, 1961). Of the many general surveys of Brazilian history, a new and recommended one is *História do Brasil* by Hélio Vianna (São Paulo: Melhoramentos, 1961). The outstanding analytical discussion of Brazil's past is found in the two slim volumes published by the Comissión de Historia of the Instituto Panamericano de Geografía e Historia in Mexico City: *Brasil: Período Colonial* by José Honório Rodrigues (1953) and *Brasil: Período Nacional* by Américo Jacobina Lacombe (1956). Doubtless the most interpretive of all of Brazil's historians past and present is João Capistrano de Abreu. The reader who seeks a penetrating understanding of Brazil would also do well to consult *Caminhos Antigos e Povoamento do Brasil* (Rio: Sociedade Capistrano de Abreu, 1930), *Capítulos de História Colonial* (Rio: Briguiet, 1954), and *O Descobrimento do Brasil* (Rio: Sociedade Capistrano de Abreu, 1929).

*

II. DOCUMENTARY SOURCES

This section supplements the sources already listed in the source footnotes to the text. Besides Andrew Cleven's *Readings*, already cited, there are available two other general anthologies of readings for Latin American history: A. Curtis Wilgus, *Readings in Latin American Civilization* (N.Y.: Barnes & Noble, 1946) and the superior collection of the same title by Benjamin Keen (Boston: Houghton Mifflin, 1955). They devote some space—as usual disproportionally small—to Brazil.

The chronicles and documents for the discovery of Brazil can be found in W. B. Greenlee, *The Voyage of Pedro Alvares Cabral to Brazil and India* (London: Hakluyt Society, 1938). Full documentation for the Spanish exploration of the Amazon, including the informative account of Orellana's adventures by Friar Gaspar de Carvajal, is given in José Toribio Medina, *The Discovery of the Amazon* (N.Y.: American Geographical Society, 1934). Several other excellent sixteenth-century chronicles have been translated into English. An early description of Brazil together with a commercial evaluation compose the subject matter of *Tidings Out of Brazil* edited by John Parker (Minneapolis: Univ. of Minnesota Press, 1957). Hans Stade's vivid memoir of his experiences among the Indians of the South appears under the title *The Captivity of Hans Stade of Hesse* (London: Hakluyt Society, 1874). *The Histories of Brazil* by Pero de Magalhães de Gândavo (N.Y.: Cortes Society, 1922) was one of the first long accounts of Brazil, part of it written probably before 1570 and other parts in the early 1570's. The description of Brazil and the Indians written by Fernão Cardim in the late sixteenth century appears on pp. 417-517 of Volume XVI of *Hakluytus Posthumus or Purchas His Pilgrims* (Glasgow: MacLehose, 1906). In "The Sixteenth-Century Jesuit Letters of Brazil," *Historical Records and Studies*, Vol. 49, E. Bradford Burns gives a description as well as a sampling of the contents of the multi-volume Jesuit letters. An early English view of Brazil appears in *The Voyages of Sir James Lancaster to Brazil and the East Indies, 1591-1603* edited by Sir William Foster (London: Hakluyt Society, 1940). The pro-Spanish and anti-Portuguese Jesuit, Samuel Fritz, left his observations—principally anthropological—in *Journal of the Travels and Labours of Father Samuel Fritz in the River of the Amazons between 1686 and 1723* (London: Hakluyt Society, 1922). A few documents concerning the functioning of the municipal government of Bahia in the seventeenth century as well as an excellent essay on that important institution can be found in C. R. Boxer, *Portuguese Society in the Tropics* (Madison: Univ. of Wisconsin, 1965). Documentary material in English for the eighteenth century is exceedingly rare. C. R. Boxer recently translated an intriguing pamphlet printed in 1764 entitled

"New and Curious Relation of a Grievance Redressed or Evidences of the Right Adduced in Favour of the Black Men in a Dialogue between a Lawyer and a Miner." *Race* (Jan., 1964) published this discourse favorable to manumission under the title "Negro Slavery in Brazil." José Bonifácio presented the enlightened views of a Brazilian intellectual on the subject of slavery at the opening of the national period in *Memoir Addressed to the General, Constituent and Legislative Assembly of the Empire of Brazil, on Slavery . . . ,* translated by William Walton (London: Butterworth, 1826).

For the kingdom, empire, and thereafter, a rich storehouse of documentary material can be found in *British and Foreign State Papers* (London), published annually since 1812. It regularly contains a section on Brazil with translations of the most important documents of that year. Beginning in 1861, the annual publication printed by the United States Government Printing Office, *Foreign Relations of the United States*, does much the same thing. Carolina Nabuco has included many letters and newspaper articles pertinent for the years 1875-1910 in her *The Life of Joaquim Nabuco* (Palo Alto, Cal.: Stanford Univ. Press, 1950).

Considerable data on Brazil's diplomacy, particularly its relations with the United States, can be found in William R. Manning, *Diplomatic Correspondence of the United States Concerning the Independence of the Latin American Nations*, Vol. II (N.Y.: Oxford Univ. Press, 1925) and *Diplomatic Correspondence of the United States, Inter-American Affairs, 1831-60*, Vol. II, *Bolivia and Brazil* (Washington, D.C.: Carnegie Endowment, 1932). The Baron of Rio-Branco summed up popular views of nineteenth-century U.S.-Brazilian relations in *Brazil, the United States and the Monroe Doctrine* (Washington, D.C., 1908); he is also author of the multi-volume *Statement Submitted by the United States of Brazil to the President of the United States of America* (N.Y.: Knickerbocker, 1894), which contains many documents pertaining to the Missions dispute as well as to other international questions. Since July 1, 1939, the *United States Department of State Bulletin* has published a variety of documents dealing with various aspects of U.S.-Brazilian relations.

With the opening of Brazilian ports in 1808, another type of documentary source became increasingly prevalent: the foreign traveler who committed his observations to writing. The Humphreys bibliography lists the major ones. For the second empire, Charles G. Hamilton analyzed the contents of the travel books by Englishmen and North Americans in "English-Speaking Travelers in Brazil, 1851-1887," *The Hispanic American Historical Review*

(Nov., 1960). The importance of these travel books for a first-hand knowledge of Brazil's past cannot be overstressed.

Documentary sources are comparatively abundant for contemporary affairs. Dramatic and depressing are the adjectives which best describe Carolina Maria de Jesus' diary of life in a São Paulo *favela* (slum), *Child of the Dark* (N.Y.: Dutton, 1962). Those squalid conditions provide ample political material as exemplified in a speech by the principal representative of the depressed masses of the northeast, Francisco Julião, translated and published in *Whither Latin America* by Carlos Fuentes *et al.* (N.Y.: Monthly Review Press, 1963). The erratic Jânio Quadros has outlined Brazil's changing international role in "Brazil's New Foreign Policy," *Foreign Affairs* (Oct., 1961). The best and largest collection of documents on contemporary Brazil, principally the Goulart years, is Irving L. Horowitz's *Revolution in Brazil* (N.Y.: Dutton, 1964).

Literature of course provides a keen insight into the history and development of a nation. Fortunately, a respectable number of Brazilian works have been translated into English. Samuel Putnam outlines the literary history of Brazil as well as quotes occasionally from representative authors in *Marvelous Journey* (N.Y.: Knopf, 1948). Rio de Janeiro in the early nineteenth century furnished the background for *Memoirs of a Militia Sergeant* by Manuel Antônio de Almeida (Washington, D.C.: Pan American Union, 1959). A less romantic look at the capital is available in Aloísio Tancredo Azevedo's *A Brazilian Tenement* (N.Y.: McBride, 1926). J. M. Machado de Assis remains as Brazil's greatest and most penetrating writer. A representative number of his novels and short stories have been published in the United States. Noonday Press in 1952, 1953, and 1954 issued *Epitaph of a Small Winner, Dom Casmuro* and *Philosopher or Dog*. More recently some of his short stories have appeared in translation under the title *The Psychiatrist and Other Stories* (Berkeley: Univ. of California, 1963). The latest translation of his works is *Esau and Jacob* (Berkeley: Univ. of California, 1965), a novel set in Rio de Janeiro during the last days of the Empire and the first days of the Republic. Leading contemporary authors, such as Jorge Amado, José Lins do Rego, Graciliano Ramos, Érico Veríssimo, João Guimarães Rosa, and Rachel de Queiroz, now have editions available in English. A recent guide to Brazilian literature in English translation was published by the Ministério das Relações Exteriores do Brasil in 1962(?) under the title *Traduções de Autores Brasileiros e Livros sobre o Brasil Escritos em Idioma Estrangeiro*. Two other helpful aids are: William J. Griffin, "Brazilian Literature in English Translation," *Re-*

vista Interamericana de Bibliografía (Jan.-June, 1955), pp. 21-37; and Harvey L. Johnson, "The Brazilian Mirror: Some Brazilian Writing in English Translation," *The Americas* (April, 1965), pp. 274-294.

A NOTE ON THE TYPE

The text of this book is set in Electra, a typeface designed by W(illiam) A(ddison) Dwiggins for the Mergenthaler Linotype Company and first made available in 1935. Electra cannot be classified as either "modern" or "old style." It is not based on any historical model, and hence does not echo any particular period or style of type design. It avoids the extreme contrast between "thick" and "thin" elements that marks most modern faces, and is without eccentricities which catch the eye and interfere with reading. In general, Electra is a simple, readable typeface which attempts to give a feeling of fluidity, power, and speed.

W. A. Dwiggins (1880–1956) was born in Martinsville, Ohio, and studied art in Chicago. In 1904 he moved to Hingham, Massachusetts, where he built a solid reputation as a designer of advertisements and as a calligrapher. He began an association with the Mergenthaler Linotype Company in 1929, and over the next twenty-seven years designed a number of book types, of which Metro, Electra, and Caledonia have been used very widely. In 1930 Dwiggins became interested in marionettes, and through the years made many important contributions to the art of puppetry and the design of marionettes.

Composed, printed, and bound by
H. Wolff, Inc., New York